FIFTY YEARS OF PEASANT WARS IN LATIN AMERICA

DISLOCATIONS

General Editors: August Carbonella, *Memorial University of Newfoundland*; Don Kalb, *University of Bergen & Utrecht University*; Linda Green, *University of Arizona*

The immense dislocations and suffering caused by neoliberal globalization, the retreat of the welfare state in the last decades of the twentieth century, and the heightened military imperialism at the turn of the twenty-first century have raised urgent questions about the temporal and spatial dimensions of power. Through stimulating critical perspectives and new and cross-disciplinary frameworks that reflect recent innovations in the social and human sciences, this series provides a forum for politically engaged and theoretically imaginative responses to these important issues of late modernity.

Recent volumes:

For a full volume listing, please see the series page on our website:
https://www.berghahnbooks.com/series/dislocations

Fifty Years of Peasant Wars in Latin America

Edited by Leigh Binford, Lesley Gill, and Steve Striffler

berghahn
NEW YORK · OXFORD
www.berghahnbooks.com

First published in 2020 by
Berghahn Books
www.berghahnbooks.com

© 2020, 2023 Leigh Binford, Lesley Gill, and Steve Striffler
First paperback edition published in 2023

Library of Congress Cataloging-in-Publication Data

A C.I.P. cataloging record is available from the Library of Congress
Library of Congress Cataloging in Publication Control Number: 2019042140

British Library Cataloguing in Publication Data

A catalogue record for this book is available from the British Library

ISBN 978-1-78920-561-9 hardback
ISBN 978-1-80073-924-6 paperback
ISBN 978-1-78920-562-6 ebook

https://doi.org/10.3167/9781789205619

CONTENTS

INTRODUCTION

Fifty Years of Peasant Wars in Latin America

Lesley Gill, Leigh Binford, and Steve Striffler

In 1969, Eric Wolf published his seminal *Peasant Wars of the Twentieth Century* during the US war in Vietnam. Its publication coincided with a powerful anti-war movement and urban insurrections in the United States, anti-colonial movements in Asia and Africa, and the beginning of a revolutionary wave that washed over Latin America in the aftermath of the 1959 Cuban Revolution. *Peasant Wars of the Twentieth Century* rubbed against the grain of US anthropology, long mired in an embrace of cultural particularity and rooted in micro-studies of specific localities, by pushing the field to conceptualize peasants and their villages within broader fields of capitalist and state power. It addressed a general public at a moment of intense political and intellectual unrest.

Dispensing with the jargon-filled posturing of detached scholarship, *Peasant Wars* emerged from Wolf's passions and commitments as a young, anti-war professor at the University of Michigan, where he helped organize the first "teach-in" against the Vietnam War (Gamson 1991). Wolf was less concerned with peasant movements that flickered for a time and burned out, or that were absorbed by the state or repressed, than revolutions that qualitatively reconfigured the social order. The book was unabashed in its concern for who was most likely to engage in revolutionary activity and what kinds of alliances led to transformative social change in different historical cases. It arrived at a moment when revolution, and particularly revolution in which peasants were among the central protagonists, was more than something that had happened in the past, or in theory. A sense that revolution was possible—even likely—infused progressive intellectuals, activists, and popular struggles with both intense optimism and deep despair, as popular challenges to the established order drove states' capacities for terror. *Peasant Wars* conveyed a belief that knowledge can serve the cause of social justice and that working people can make history.

Yet the promise of revolution and of Wolf's innovative approach remained unrealized. A series of events, including the decline of (and disillusionment with) anti-colonial struggles, a Cold War counterinsurgency that decimated revolutionary actors, and the collapse of the Soviet Union, all served to diminish the hope for radical change. Revolution seemed neither possible nor desirable, and by the 1980s, a new generation of scholars turned away from structural critiques of capitalism that explored how working people were (or were not) able to forge the kinds of political alliances necessary for challenging the power of state and capital in meaningful ways. This shift was particularly apparent in anthropology, where many scholars rejected the very "metanarratives" required to understand a changing global order and embraced questions of culture and identity formation. Peasants (and the study of them), along with workers, increasingly faded from view or were understood in more cultural and less political terms. By the end of the twentieth century, the retreat from revolution, both coerced and acquiesced, had erased memories of its emancipatory possibilities.[1]

We contend that, following decades of counterinsurgency, neoliberal restructuring, displacement, the upward redistribution of wealth, and the retreat of revolution, Wolf offers a way to rethink the meaning of revolutionary social change in the twenty-first century and to reestablish continuity with the emancipatory, albeit mostly forgotten, consequences of past revolutions and the analytic projects that sought to understand and advance them. *Peasant Wars of the Twentieth Century* remains relevant for several reasons: it situates peasants and peasant politics within complex histories and interconnected fields of power; reminds us of the continuing importance of states and other centralized forms of rule at different levels; and outlines an explanatory framework that links singular, historical struggles to the caustic social, economic, and political pressures of capitalism. Wolf encourages us to make connections, to explore how social relations are organized and regulated, and to contemplate how these relations might be challenged and transformed by rural actors as they attempt to not only negotiate local relations but also advance political projects on regional and national levels.

Optimism of the Intellectuals

Richard Lee and Karen Brodkin Sacks characterized the "long 1960s decade" as "a time of infinite possibility when it seemed that global democracy might prevail if we all put our shoulders to the wheel" (1993: 181). *Peasant Wars* articulated this 1960s-era hopefulness. Wolf wrote: "Everywhere ancient monopolies of power and received wisdom are yielding to human effort to widen participation and knowledge. In such efforts—however uncertain . . . there lies the prospect for increased life, for increased humanity" (1969: 301–302). The book was a synthetic, comparative history of six successful or nominally successful revolutions—Cuba, Algeria, Russia, China, Mexico, and Vietnam—that took place from 1910 to 1975, a period whose core decades were defined by exceptional capitalist reformism and national developmentalism. Beginning with the Mexican Revolution of 1910 and ending with the Vietnamese Revolution of 1975, various forms of socialist and anticolonial nationalist movements that involved peasants pushed back economic liberalism and European imperialism.[2] This resulted in the broader recognition of the nationalist and developmentalist aspirations of formerly colonized peoples, and the recognition of the political power of peasantries, which prompted a flurry of US initiatives to press Latin American and other governments to implement agrarian reforms to stave off more revolutionary demands. This "long" period of socialist and nonsocialist national developmentalism (1910–1975) contrasts with the free-market fundamentalism and anti-welfare mania that characterized earlier nineteenth-century colonial liberalism and later post–Cold War neoliberalism (Araghi 2009: 122–130). Wolf's book spoke to the struggles of peasants and others who shaped an exceptional historical period.

Peasant Wars also tried to nudge anthropology into a greater engagement with power. It formed part of Wolf's developing analytic approach, which had been taking shape since his dissertation fieldwork in Puerto Rico, under the supervision of Julian Steward, and later in his first book, *Sons of the Shaking Earth* (1959), which explored the long history of Mexico and its different regions, including the insurgencies of Emiliano Zapata and Francisco Villa. In *Peasant Wars*, he rejected anthropological approaches that envisioned rural dwellers as inherently conservative and that remained fixated on the cultural distinctiveness of individual villages or indigenous groups. And unlike some social scientists who assessed various peasant movements in terms of vague "modernizing influences" such as teachers, radios, and road construction (e.g., Huizer 1973; Landsberger 1969),

Wolf rejected a hydra-like modernity and focused instead on how capitalism eroded the subsistence practices of peasants. He identified the "tactically mobile peasantry" (i.e., landowning "middle peasants" with secure access to land or who lived in remote frontier areas) as most likely to engage in defensive revolts and argued that middle peasants' efforts to resist the destructive force of capitalism, or, in other words, their desire to remain "traditional," made them revolutionary.

Yet even though Wolf's middle-peasant thesis made a major contribution to what was then known as "peasant studies" and is arguably the book's most enduring legacy, his concern with types of peasants sits uneasily with his broader analytic approach, which is less concerned with formulating typologies than with fluid, open-ended, historical processes and shifting configurations of power-laden social relationships. *Peasant Wars* is much more than an argument about so-called middle peasants. The book is above all an examination of how crises of power, created by the spread of North Atlantic capitalism, ripped apart the integument of rural society and opened new possibilities for scale-spanning solidarities that included some peasants, as well as other groups and organizations. It is a deep dive into thinking about who are the key actors in revolutions and what sorts of alliances provide the accelerant necessary to ignite and sustain transformative social change. In the case studies, capitalism tears rural dwellers from their social worlds; transforms them into economic actors; turns land, wealth, and labor into commodities; and forces many people to migrate in search of a livelihood. Although Wolf's analytic lens concentrates on the countryside, where most of the people in his cases lived, he is concerned with the complexity of social relations and how they are structured within and against fields of capitalist power. For example, the existence of an industrial proletariat was less important for Wolf than its relationship to village life, and one of his abiding concerns was how "rootless intellectuals" (e.g., political activists, migrants, and religious specialists) connected diverse people across uneven social landscapes. Likewise, he argues peasants are typically led by more self-consciously revolutionary groups based in urban areas. The broader point here, and one that was increasingly lost on scholars as revolutionary movements themselves declined, is the attention Wolf gives to not only how rural actors negotiate village life but also how (and with whom) they engage political worlds beyond the local level in ways that potentially advance political projects that transform the power of state and capital at regional and national levels.

In the chapter on Russia, industrial workers stage strikes, urban liberals and revolutionaries spread new ideas in rural areas, and deserting soldiers synchronize peasant uprisings with urban revolts. Similarly, in the case of Cuba, Castro's guerrillas count initially on industrial workers and an urban middle class for logistical support, because peasant recruitment is slow. In Algeria, the exposure of thousands of Algerian migrants to socialist labor unions in France gives them a model for organizing back home, where they turn to nationalism because of French settler-dominated labor unions and political parties, while reformist Islam provides the glue that binds clusters of peasants with spokespeople in the towns and cities. Finally, in Wolf's analyses of Mexico, Vietnam, and China, the role of the middle peasantry is more prominent, at least in some regions such as southern Mexico and northern Vietnam. Yet in northern Mexico, cowboys, smugglers, and middle-class merchants, clerks, and artisans are the primary supporters of the revolutionary army of Pancho Villa. The richness and diversity of the case studies overwhelms the middle-peasant argument, which is not fully laid out until the conclusion and arises perhaps from the desire of Wolf, anti-war activists, and a large swath of the US public to understand how, in Vietnam, peasants "have not only fought to a standstill the mightiest military machine in history, but caused many an American to wonder . . . why 'our' Vietnamese do not fight like 'their' Vietnamese" (Wolf 1969: ix).

Peasant Wars paid attention to how the abrasive force of global capitalism acted as a solvent of social relationships, while opening new possibilities for alliances and organizational forms to take shape. It attended to social, cultural, and political differences that defined regions historically, and it was attuned to how the combination of particular groups and circumstances could dynamite the social order. As Jane Schneider observed, Wolf was "always receptive to the possibility that new complexes might well appear . . . [and he] always expected to be surprised, to stumble on anomalies, to discover instances that do not fit into a pattern" (1995: 8, 11).

Peasant Wars was Wolf's most political book, one of a number of works written in the heat of the radical 1960s that grew out of and spoke to the debates of the time. Although in hindsight it is easy to criticize the optimism of the era and the belief that people armed with the proper knowledge will do the right thing, radical scholars were subjecting the established wisdom to withering critique, pioneering new analytic approaches, and breaking out of the intellectual prison of McCarthyism. A key feature of this period was the blurring of disciplinary boundaries and the political nature of analytic debates (Roseberry 1995: 163). Kathleen Gough (1968), for example, published "Anthropology and Imperialism" two years before *Peasant Wars*. Gough argued anthropology was a handmaiden of colonialism and took anthropologists to task for their failure to study imperialism. She also noted how dependence on imperial powers for funding and access to research sites impoverished anthropology, producing either putatively "value-free social science" or a reformist kind of social work that avoided challenges to capitalist power, and she urged anthropologists to compare capitalist and socialist forms of development among Third World peoples.

Along with the work of other scholars, *Peasant Wars* rescued Marxism from paradigms of progress that privileged the urban working class as the protagonist of revolution[3] and ignored the colonial and neocolonial experiences of people in Africa, Asia, and Latin America. Eric Hobsbawm (1959), for example, turned attention to "primitive rebels" and "social bandits." E. P. Thompson's magisterial *The Making of the English Working Class* (1963) explored how rural and artisan traditions nourished working-class consciousness and, breaking with Communist Party orthodoxy, opened new ways of thinking about class that focused on process and privileged human agency. Like Wolf, he and Hobsbawm were less fixated on the particular than on integrating working-class experience into an understanding of conflictive social processes, state formation, and social transformation. In addition, Peter Worsley's *The Trumpet Shall Sound* (1957) offered an early comparative and historical study of Melanesian revitalization movements, based on a close reading of secondary sources. It placed "cargo cults" and nationalist movements within the same analytic framework, demonstrating that the former were not backward expressions of religious atavism but responses to exploitation by and resentment of European missionaries, traders, labor recruiters, and police. *The Trumpet Shall Sound* preceded Worsley's best-known book, *The Third World* (1964), in which he examined the class structures, nationalist movements, state forms, and international alliances of postcolonial states and designated the "Third World" to refer to newly independent states and the distinct challenges they confronted in the age of the Cold War. Together, these works reenergized Marxist theory with insights about peasants, rural artisans, and anti-colonial revolts in the emergent "Third World."

Similarly, in Latin America, the economist André Gunder Frank and the writer Eduardo Galeano undercut Eurocentric developmentalist paradigms of capitalist progress. Gunder Frank, who obtained a degree in economics from the University of Chicago and studied with none other than Milton Friedman, published his influential *Development of Underdevelopment in Latin America* (1969) in which he argued capitalist development in the First World "produces" underdevelopment in the Third World. Although he overstated the case (see Cardoso and Faletto 1979) and the absence of class analysis was troubling, his dependency perspective represented an alternative to both modernization theory and the advocacy of import substitution industrialization associated with Raúl Prebisch and others working with the United Nations–sponsored Economic Commission on Latin America (ECLA). Galeano's *Open Veins of Latin America* (1971) delved into Latin America's violent colonial history and more recent subjection to US economic exploitation, tracing a long arc of imperial and neo-imperial plunder.

Most of these scholars found ways to reach beyond the academy and speak to an educated public. For Wolf, the Vietnam War represented "the overriding issue of the moment," and speaking out against it was "an obligation of citizenship" (1969: x). Unsurprisingly, Wolf elected to publish *Peasant Wars* with a trade press, which made it accessible to a general audience. Thompson wrote *The Making of the English Working Class* for his students in an adult education program. Gunder Frank reached a left-wing US readership through his publisher, Monthly Review Press, as well as the magazine *Monthly Review*, while a growing Latin American middle class found answers to their political questions in his approach. Gunder Frank supported the socialist regime of Salvador Allende (1970–1973), and from his position at the University of Chile, which he joined in 1967, he played an important role in *Chile Hoy*, a magazine directed to a nonacademic audience. As Aldo Marchesi writes, Gunder Frank's "work was part of a singular moment in the relationship between academic production and political commitment in Chile, where certain actors of academia legitimized their studies by adopting certain political stances, while political actors looked to academic work as a way of legitimating their practices" (2018: 119–120). Indeed, dependency theory was particularly important, and in many ways unique in its role of informing and shaping revolutionary actors and movements in Latin America (see Edelman and Haugerud 2005: 11–14).

These radically engaged scholars often paid a high price for their commitment to progressive political change. As Chairman of the first American Anthropological Association (AAA) Ethics Committee, Wolf became embroiled in a 1970 controversy over the collaboration of anthropologists with the US government in developing counterinsurgency strategies in Thailand. The dispute divided the association and led to Wolf's removal from the committee, although he was eventually vindicated when fellows of the association voted to reject a report of the "Mead Committee," which chose to ignore the ethical problems raised by AAA members who colluded with government counterinsurgency programs (Wakin 1992). University administrators offered little support for faculty members who criticized government policy. Kathleen Gough was told she had no future at Brandeis University following a pro-Cuban talk on the eve of the 1962 missile crisis. After relocating to the University of Oregon, she refused to grade students harshly and expose them to the draft as the Vietnam War heated up. Gough and her husband, David Aberle, left for Canada, but her advocacy of student participation in departmental affairs at Canada's Simon Fraser University led to her dismissal. Despite a stellar publication record and the respect of her colleagues, she spent the last fifteen years of her life without a university appointment (Jorgensen 1993). Intelligence agencies also had these scholars in their sights, as Peter Worsley discovered when Great Britain's national intelligence agency, MI5, denied him permission to carry out dissertation fieldwork in Africa because he was a member of the British Communist Party (Peel 2013). MI5's decision pushed Worsley to abandon anthropology for sociology and fieldwork for library research.

Third World scholars suffered the most serious consequences of Cold War repression. Gunder Frank, who spent much of his life in Latin America, fled Chile after the 1973 US-supported coup that ushered in the dictatorship of Augusto Pinochet (1973–1990). He became a persona non grata in the United States, denied visas or subjected to severe restrictions on those occasions when he was invited to lecture or give a course. Similarly, US-supported military dictatorships banned Galeano's books throughout the Southern Cone, and Galeano himself was imprisoned in Uruguay following a 1973 military coup. He eventually went into exile in Argentina, but after the 1976 military takeover there, he fled to Spain. Hundreds of other scholars and activists shared similar fates—or worse.

We can appreciate how the Cold War and the repression that accompanied it undermined the development of a critical left scholarship that was challenging the status quo and reaching a nonacademic audience.[4] Reconsidering how Wolf and other key scholars from his generation posed questions, formulated problems, and developed answers to the overriding political concerns of their time not only reconnects us to a tradition of critical scholarship but also is useful for confronting issues arising today, because many questions and concerns from the 1960s remain relatively open and unresolved.

The Agrarian Question, Capitalist Triumphalism, and Shifting Intellectual Paradigms

Between the mid-1960s and mid-1980s, heated debates about "reform or revolution" echoed from the halls of government to the Latin American countryside. These debates turned to a considerable degree on the "agrarian question," which Karl Kautsky defined in the late nineteenth century as "whether and how, capital is seizing hold of agriculture, revolutionizing it, making old forms of production and property untenable and creating the necessity for new ones" (quoted in Akram-Lodhi and Kay 2010a: 179). Would Latin American societies, which were still primarily rural, gradually reform within the parameters of a modernized capitalism, or would they follow a revolutionary path to socialist transformation? Key to the futures imagined by these questions was the fate of the peasantry—its transformation into wage laborers or persistence as petty commodity producers—and the balance of class forces in the countryside, especially alliances between peasants and other groups. The agrarian question took on particular urgency after the 1959 Cuban Revolution, which provided Latin Americans with an alternative to US-backed capitalist developmentalism. The success of the Cuban revolutionaries, shifts in Catholic Church doctrine (especially the rise of liberation theology; e.g., chap. 4), and a post-World–War II period of economic growth inspired peasants and leftist revolutionaries from Central America to the Southern Cone to demand the state provide economic justice, equality, access to social services, political inclusion, and freedom.

The eruption of the scholarly debate around Lenin and Chayanov emerged a few years after the publication of *Peasant Wars* and represented a reframing of the original discussion on the agrarian question that had strong repercussions in Latin America (the focus of this book), with its large peasant population. Although Lenin and Chayanov never actually debated, their perspectives on the peasantry exercised academics in the United States, Latin America, and elsewhere, even though the two positions were not necessarily incompatible (Lehman 1980). Lenin argued the Russian peasantry was prone to an internal process of differentiation, with most "small" peasants becoming proletarians and some "large" peasants developing into rural capitalists. "Middle peasants" might go either way (Lenin 1964), but Lenin's broader point was there is a fairly stable class divide in the countryside that defined social relations and necessarily shaped revolutionary praxis. Understanding the peasantry and developing an agrarian strategy, especially ceding to peasant demands for land confiscation, was important to Lenin, because he believed building a "worker-peasant" alliance was key to revolution in Russia. In contrast, Chayanov (1966) treated peasant production as outside capitalist processes. Against the capitalist imperative to generate profits, accumulate wealth, and reinvest in an endless drive to expand, he argued peasants eschewed capital accumulation and aimed merely to satisfy subsistence requirements, laboring more or less intensively in accord with a household's demographic circumstances, seasonal price variation, and weather patterns. The mid-twentieth-century Lenin-Chayanov controversy was inscribed within a fundamentally teleological position on the survival of the peasantry and took the nation-state as the unit of analysis. It drowned out Wolf's sensitivity to heterogeneous and contradictory social relations, regional and national variation, and historical contingency.

US and Latin American Cold War policy makers, who feared the spread of communism and "another Cuba" in the Americas, placed agrarian reform on their agendas to stave off revolution. They aimed to appease militant peasants through the creation of individual, family farms—the hoped-for pillar of a conservative social base disconnected from urban radicals and nationalist and socialist liberation movements. In addition, they combined agrarian reform with measures to support urban consumers and accommodate the urban and agricultural bourgeoisies. Following the recommendations of the Santiago-based ECLA, most Latin American governments adopted import-substitution industrialization to promote the growth of domestic industries and the development of a home market.[5] Agrarian reform and import-substitution industrialization represented a form of market-led, national developmentalism, one that aimed to prevent socialist revolutions (Araghi 2009: 134). They arose from a range of competing views about economic development, socioeconomic rights, and revolution in Latin America and represented an accommodation to militant nationalism.[6]

Although agrarian reform initially improved rural well-being in some countries, states did not provide needed complementary resources such as credit, irrigation, and extension services, forcing peasants to abandon their lands or rely on off-farm activities for income.[7] It was not long before the limits of agrarian reformism and the failure of import-substitution industrialization to address the fundamental needs of the "popular" classes generated growing discontentment (e.g., chap. 2). Armed guerrillas, leftist rebellions, and revolutionary wars in Brazil, Argentina, Bolivia, Colombia, Mexico, Nicaragua, Guatemala, El Salvador, and elsewhere indexed rising demands for more sweeping social change amid an intensifying Cold War in which regional elites and US policy makers smeared critics with the innuendo of "communist subversion." Landowning Latin American elites resented any challenge to their wealth and turned to US-trained security forces to protect their interests, while multinational corporations chafed at the limits to capital accumulation imposed by national developmentalism. Reformist and revolutionary advocates for structural change confronted opponents (e.g., militaries, police forces, death squads) who were willing to unleash relentless violence in order to foreclose any possibility of social transformation (e.g., chap. 5).

Cold War counterinsurgent violence transformed the countryside and, combined with a 1980s debt crisis, landed a one-two punch on Latin America that opened the door for neoliberalism—a more pernicious, unregulated form of capitalism. Political violence shredded the social relations that bound peasants to each other and destroyed ties between them and urban allies. It dissolved powerful collectivities, eliminated dynamic leaders, and forced people to adopt individual survival strategies such as Pentecostalism, migration, and participation in illegal narco-economies. The destruction, poverty, wartime displacement, and repression of popular movements decimated reformist and revolutionary movements from Chile to Guatemala and exposed wide swaths of the population to new vulnerabilities (e.g., Binford 2016; Gill 2016; Grandin 2004; Winn 2004). Brazil and the Dominican Republic provided early examples in the mid-1960s, but it was Chile that captured global attention and proved to be the harbinger of what lay on the horizon. Following a brutal US-backed coup d'état that ended Allende's socialist government, the military regime of Pinochet murdered, jailed, and tortured political opponents and imposed dictatorial rule for seventeen years. In consultation with a group of Chilean economists trained by Milton Freidman at the University of Chicago and known as the "Chicago Boys," Pinochet ushered in neoliberalism on a river of blood.

Neoliberalism represented a counteroffensive against national developmentalism that spread throughout Latin America during the 1980s and 1990s as debt crises provided the leverage for northern institutions such as the World Bank and the International Monetary Fund to demand free-market reforms in exchange for the loans necessary to repay international debts. Although the nature and impact of neoliberal policies varied from country to country, neoliberalism had become hegemonic throughout the hemisphere—and the world—by the beginning of the twenty-first century. It was essentially "a political project to re-establish the conditions for capital accumulation and to restore the power of economic elites" (Harvey 2005: 19) that upended the protection of society from the market by privatizing public resources and institutions, reducing import duties, eliminating subsidies, weakening labor laws, and opening the door to foreign investment, among other provisions. Wolf's materialist approach could not predict these developments, or the ensuing consequences, but it is of great utility in helping us understand them.

The impact of neoliberalism on the Latin American countryside was dramatic. Governments under the sway of what became known as the Washington Consensus reversed agrarian reform policies enacted during the national developmentalist era in countries as diverse as Chile, Mexico, and Honduras, while the deregulation of land markets allowed renewed penetration by foreign firms and accusations of "land grabbing" in some of the most fertile and productive regions of the continent (Borras and Franco 2012; Grajales 2011). Governmental concern for the home market vanished. The reduction or elimination of tariff barriers and the promotion of export-led development enabled the dumping of cheap (and still subsidized) US-produced grains such as wheat and corn into Mexico, El Salvador, Colombia, and other countries. These policies were combined with the elimination of farm subsidies and price supports. Together, they ruined hundreds of thousands of small farmers and spurred migration to urban centers and capitalist countries in the north. Unsurprisingly, food imports increased, while domestic production for the home market declined. As export-led production became the principal means of capital accumulation, small commodity producers became more deeply integrated into global commodity chains and dependent on chemical and biotechnological inputs controlled by multinational firms.

The political implications surrounding the imposition of neoliberalism were equally profound and paved the way for the economic onslaught in the late 1980s and early 1990s. Military regimes wiped out much of the Left in South America during the 1970s and 1980s, and counterinsurgency finished the job in Central America by the early 1990s. More than this, the tentative forms of civilian-democratic rule that emerged in the 1980s and 1990s were predicated on the continued implementation of neoliberalism. Elites consolidated power under democratic rule, paving the way for structural adjustment and the rapid redistribution of wealth upward. Such a project was made possible by, and contributed to, a severely debilitated Left. Opposition forces were in no position to shift political debate, let alone advance a more progressive agenda. Structural adjustment decimated labor unions, peasant organizations, and working-class power, continuing the destruction of leftist institutions while undermining the capacity of popular groups to forge solidarity—especially on regional and national scales.

To be sure, it is not as if labor unions, peasant organizations, and revolutionary actors disappeared completely from the Latin American scene, but traditional institutions of the Left were significantly compromised by the start of the 1990s, even in countries that escaped the worst of the violence. They, along with the hundreds of NGOs that emerged throughout the region during this period, were drawn into relatively local, largely defensive, struggles aimed at lessening the worst effects of neoliberalism. As larger numbers of Latin Americans found themselves politically and economically marginalized, these struggles would eventually lead to a broader challenge to the entire system in the form of the "pink tide." In the short term, however, the situation was bleak. The 1989 Caracazo in Venezuela foreshadowed the anti-neoliberal backlash that was to come. Peasant-indigenous groups were beginning to contest neoliberalism with more consistency and ferocity by the early 1990s, but the prospects for a more sustained and large-scale opposition were not promising at that time.

Amid the devastation wrought by the Cold War and the rise of neoliberalism, including the broader political decimation of peasant, worker, and leftist institutions, the scholarly study of social movements and agrarian transformation underwent a profound shift. New analytic frameworks influenced by postmodernism, subaltern studies, and notions of everyday forms of resistance celebrated "new social movements" and "voices from below" that were engaged in mostly individual forms of resistance based on cultural claims such as ethnicity (e.g., Álvarez et al. 1998; Escobar and Álvarez 1992). These perspectives, which consolidated in the 1990s, purported to have found new forms of agency within but not against capitalism. They found "resistance" in the smallest acts of nonconformity, a discovery that made resistance banal by finding it everywhere. They also sidestepped questions of rural class formation, which meant not only that scholarly attention shifted away from peasants in a general sense but also that their relationship to changing forms of state and capital tended to be downplayed.[8] By so doing, they ignored how peasants and urban slum dwellers wanted the state to address their problems.

In addition, they erased earlier emancipatory objectives, showed little interest in revolutionary social change, and abandoned any notion of popular empowerment through the capture of state power,[9] concerns that had animated Wolf and an earlier group of scholars.

As sectors of the academy took a "cultural" turn and a chasm between social history and cultural analysis opened, there were some notable exceptions. Jeffrey Gould (1990), for example, explored the development of peasant consciousness in pre-Sandinista Nicaragua and showed how rural people forged a new, collective understanding of their social world that led to the downfall of the Somoza dynasty (see also Gould and Lauria-Santiago 2008). Similarly, William Roseberry challenged the notion that peasant consciousness evolved from an "ordered past to a disordered present," as set forth by proponents of the so-called moral economy thesis (1991: 58). He insisted peasant political history was much more dynamic, contingent, and contradictory than generally assumed and that possibilities for revolutionary social change opened and closed as peasants and their allies contended with more powerful groups. Yet, despite the exceptions, the study of peasant politics faded, while the collapse of "actually existing" socialism in Eastern Europe and the Soviet Union fed capitalist triumphalism and "end of history" narratives. Though some mainstream academics considered class analysis passé, even as global wealth and power became concentrated to a degree not seen since the Gilded Age, other analysts identified the post–Cold War era as a time of narrowing intellectual diversity. It was a moment, they argued, when postmodernist approaches had conquered anthropology and other branches of the social sciences (e.g., Boyer 2003; Roseberry 1996) and previously central scholarly figures, like Eric Wolf, and their work fell out of the bibliographies of a new generation of anthropologists (Roseberry 1995).

The Return of the Oppressed

Despite Cold War terror and the spread of no-holds-barred capitalism, social movements managed to regroup in places like Bolivia, Brazil, Ecuador, Guatemala, El Salvador, Venezuela, and Mexico and demand the state play a greater role in the provision of social welfare. They waged defensive struggles against free trade deals, the privatization of public resources, declining crop prices, and the environmental degradation wrought by extractive industries such as mining and logging. In some countries, most notably Bolivia and Ecuador, rural people—often identifying and organizing as indigenous peoples—even led the overthrow of neoliberal regimes, once their sectorial protests became class struggles that involved both indigenous and nonindigenous people and targeted the neoliberal state (chap. 7; Hylton and Thomson 2007; Webber 2012, 2017). In fact, it was precisely the draconian and violent nature of neoliberalism during the 1980s and 1990s that made Latin America "revolutionary" again and propelled a "pink tide" of left-leaning governments to power. It is no coincidence that Bolivia was ground zero for "shock therapy" or that Venezuela emerged as a revolutionary epicenter against neoliberalism.

Yet, even as governments in Bolivia, Ecuador, Brazil, Venezuela, and beyond sought alternatives to neoliberalism or softened its harshest features, they could not break out of the straitjacket of export-led development and dependence on natural resources. After riding an early twenty-first-century wave of high commodity prices until 2014, pink tide governments stumbled as commodity prices declined and along with them government revenues. With declining resources and periodic missteps, it became difficult for left-leaning governments to rebuild and sustain a developmentalist state that had been dismantled under neoliberalism—especially as the Right went on the offensive and social movements fractured. Even with more sympathetic governments in power, the central problem of peasant movements in many ways remained the same—their relation to the state, how to confront it, bypass it, use it, or accommodate it, as they sought to secure subsistence and claim a dignified life for their members against the social dislocations and environmental destruction of capitalism (Vergara and Kay 2017). Unsurprisingly, new political and intellectual challenges have arisen that were barely on the horizon in the 1960s, when *Peasant Wars* appeared in print.

The world today is more urbanized than it was fifty years ago, and a higher percentage of Latin Americans live in cities than in the countryside. Agrarian capitalism, trade policies, political violence, and climate change have displaced legions of peasants to urban peripheries, where spreading poverty moved Mike Davis (2006) to talk about a "planet of slums." In the absence of state-enforced labor rights and other regulations, gangs, paramilitaries, and mafias dominate poor urban neighborhoods and represent a challenge for social movements and for academic analysts. Such is the case in large swaths of urban Colombia, Mexico, El Salvador, Guatemala, Honduras, Brazil, and Venezuela, where drug mafias and paramilitary entities control municipal governments and popular economies and regulate social life in arbitrary ways (e.g., chap. 5). The boundaries between legality and illegality have blurred. Under such conditions, one might reasonably ask, "What is the state?" Where is it located? Who speaks in its name? The answers are not always clear. The challenge for a revitalized Left is to organize urban peripheries and build connections between rural and urban constituencies.

Peasantries have not disappeared. The proportion they represent of national populations may have declined, but in absolute numbers there are more than at any time in history (Van der Ploeg 2008, cited in Edelman and Borras 2016: 1). For those who remain in the countryside, survival increasingly entails deeper involvement with commodity circuits: suppliers, purchasers, and traders, as well as reliance on flows of remittances sent by migrants residing in nearby cities and/or distant countries. Intensified participation in credit markets, commodity production, and the use of new technologies have exposed peasants to greater and more interconnected vulnerabilities, forcing them to confront potentially destabilizing uncertainties that Wolf could not have foreseen. Henry Bernstein argues that the concrete realities of life for increasing numbers of people have become too complicated for simple labels:

> The working poor of the South have to pursue their reproduction through insecure, oppressive and typically increasingly scarce wage employment and/or a range of likewise precarious small-scale and "informal economy" survival activity, including marginal farming. In effect, livelihoods are pursued through complex *combinations* of wage employment and self-employment. Additionally, many pursue their means of reproduction across different sites of the social division of labour: urban and rural, agricultural and non-agricultural, wage employment and marginal self-employment. The social locations and identities the working poor inhabit, combine and move between make for ever more fluid boundaries and defy inherited assumptions of fixed and uniform notions of "worker," "farmer," "petty trader," "urban," "rural," "employed" and "self-employed." (2009: 111)

The forces uprooting peasantries have generated streams of international migrants who shoulder enormous risks as they cross borders and struggle to forge viable livelihood strategies in new, unfamiliar, and frequently hostile settings. They must contend with increasingly draconian US immigration policies that threaten their access to jobs in the United States, destroy their families through deportation and the separation of children from their parents, and endanger the transfer of remittances to those cut off from subsistence possibilities. In addition, international migration affects rural social movements in the home countries, as local political engagement may be undermined by migrants who chase after a better life elsewhere. Yet histories of popular struggle may also shape the political engagements of migrants in new locations (Bacon 2015; Bardacke 2011; Buhle and Georgakas 1996; Fine 2006). Finally, some rural dwellers pressure states to ensure the social and economic conditions that would enable them to remain in their communities; they are, in other words, demanding "the right to stay home" (Bacon 2013).

Yet, as the forces of global capital displace peasants and force them to cross international borders to find work, new forms of transnational networks and coalitions between peasants and their allies have engaged policy debates about climate change, land rights, food sovereignty, human rights, intellectual property, agrarian reform, and the deleterious impact of neoliberal policies and trade rules (Borras et al. 2008). These movements have frequently arisen in areas where large-scale corporate farming failed to obliterate peasant agriculture. As Marc Edelman and Saturnino Borras observe, capital's incomplete penetration of the countryside has left space for peasants to organize oppositional movements and illustrates the continuing relevance of the agrarian question in the twenty-first century. Yet, according to these authors, contemporary peasant activists are more educated, well-traveled, and technologically savvy than even two decades ago (2016: 3–5), and certainly since the period considered by Wolf.

As the reconfiguration of rural livelihoods and production processes both aggravate a subsistence crisis and deepen peasant integration into commodity circuits, the contemporary agrarian question must address both the social fragmentation that arises from reconfigured peasant livelihoods *and* the persistence of peasant farmers. It attends to new spatial relations that arise from the expanding commodification of land, labor, and natural resources and the implications of a deepening market imperative for both capitalist agriculture and petty-commodity-producing peasant households.[10] And finally, it focuses on the political response of national and transnational peasant movements (Akram-Lodhi and Kay 2010b: 279).

Although Wolf could not have foreseen all the new and remade relationships of the current moment, *Peasant Wars of the Twentieth Century* remains a useful point of departure for the analysis of contemporary, rural social movements. Today, the ideologies and configurations of power that defend an ever more alarming concentration of wealth are so hostile to liberation struggles, past and present, that a first step forward is recovering the memory of a time when transformative social change seemed possible and reestablishing a link to the radical scholarship of that period. The next step is not to mimic that scholarship but rather to learn from its strengths and weaknesses. By reconsidering the legacy of *Peasant Wars*, the chapters in this volume contribute to these goals.

Synopsis of Chapters

Although revolution was very much on the table in Latin America during the 1960s when Eric Wolf was writing *Peasant Wars*, Cold War anti-communism would ultimately destroy revolutionary movements in the region (and most of the world) for the rest of the twentieth century. With the Nicaraguan Revolution serving as the tragic exception that proves the rule, there have been no successful revolutions in Latin America since the publication of *Peasant Wars* in 1969. As a result, what this volume attempts to understand—through insights gained from Wolf's analysis of *successful* peasant revolutions—is how peasants have not only continued to engage their political worlds but also why and how it has been so difficult to forge and advance political projects that challenge the state and capital on larger scales. Unlike Wolf, however, who analyzed the transformative role of peasants in national social formations of which he had only passing personal experience, most contributors to this volume have written about regions with which they have substantial firsthand knowledge.

In chapter 1, Aaron Kappeler discusses the *longue durée* of peasant and political life in Venezuela. He explains that though peasants have declined as a proportion of the overall population, they continue to play a key role in the United Socialist Party of Venezuela of the Bolivarian Revolution. Though rural areas have constituted the strongest bases of support for the ruling party, Kappeler views urban and rural areas in terms of a "continuum" with struggles at one pole igniting or galvanizing those at the other pole, in part because of the back-and-forth movement of people between urban and rural areas as economic circumstances dictate. Kappeler develops a case study of the Ezequiel Zamora National Peasant Front and the Centro Técnico Productivo Socialista Florentino, both of which support the ruling party but also compete with one another for land.

Several chapters address Wolf's theses regarding the rebellious potential of the tactically mobile middle peasantry. In chapter 2, Steve Striffler discusses the development of a middle peasantry with a modicum of tactical mobility in coastal Ecuador on the periphery of coastal banana plantations. He explains how peasants were able to work *with and through* the state to obtain land, first on the margins of Tenguel, a United Fruit plantation near Ecuador's Pacific coast, and later through wholesale invasion of the agro-export enclave. But for a host of reasons, peasants never made the transition from reform to revolution. Striffler points to the economic and political contexts within which they operated, the fact that they worked through rather than against the state, and the absence of support from outside agents. He observes that agrarian reform in recent years has lost momentum and the land has been taken over by domestic capitalists who contract with foreign multinationals. Many peasants now form part of a dependent landless class with little tactical power.

Lesley Gill's chapter 3 examines the making of a foreign-dominated, oil-export enclave in early twentieth-century Colombia. Gill explores the rise and demise of a militant, heterogeneous working class that spanned the country and the city. Following Wolf's attention to "webs of group relations," she argues the hybrid rural-urban experiences of working people undermine simple dichotomies of peasants versus proletarians, waged versus unwaged workers, urban versus rural livelihoods. The chapter demonstrates how the struggles and compromises between differently labeled working people, dominant groups, and the Colombian state gave rise to changing forms of protest and spatial forms. During much of the twentieth century, these protests rattled the chains of institutional power, before succumbing to the combined power of counterinsurgency and neoliberalism.

Leigh Binford takes up the role of the "middle peasantry" in chapter 4 on northern Morazán, El Salvador. However, he focuses on the key role that landed peasants from that marginal region played in the dissemination of liberation theology. Binford points to the role of middle peasants as early catechists who joined nascent guerrillas in the early to mid-1970s and linked northern Morazán with the urban leadership of the People's Revolutionary Army, which eventually became part of the Farabundo Martí Front for National Liberation (FMLN). However, he suggests that once open warfare broke out in 1980, poor peasants and rural workers, often with minimal ideological preparation, joined the rebels in mass, forming the base of the fighting forces and civilian support personnel. Peasant mobilization and militancy declined after the war's end in 1992 as a combination of growing distaste on the part of people for direct confrontation with the state, the decline of export agriculture (and agricultural employment), the incorporation of ex-guerrillas under the umbrella of the FMLN into national political party competition, and, especially, the destabilizing effect of two decades of neoliberal policies on small-scale agriculture weakened progressive rural social movements.

In chapter 5, Casey Walsh places the Zapatista Army of National Liberation and the current drug war in the context of a history of peasant struggle in Mexico. Walsh suggests it is possible, with the proper optic, to understand the drug war as "a moment in which the long-simmering peasant war of position has emerged once again into open hostilities." Walsh argues there exist "compelling reasons to see TCOs [transnational criminal organizations] as enacting political projects of rule based in neoliberal political culture" and thus to analyze the current conflicts, which have taken somewhere between 80,000 and 150,000 victims, as a war in which peasants manifest involvement at all levels.

In chapter 6, Clifford Welsh takes up the Brazilian case through the examination of five peasant "wars" that occurred during "the long twentieth century," beginning with the Canudos conflict in the 1890s and ending with the Landless Workers Movement (MST), founded in 1984. Welsh draws on Wolf's concepts of "mediators" and "tradition" to explain why only the MST, among the five peasant movements examined, achieved national exposure. Four of the five movements were led by deficient mediators and were fundamentally defensive in orientation. Though the MST developed leadership from within the peasantry and achieved national (and international) recognition, it "opted for a nonviolent revolutionary strategy of gradual but dramatic change."

Finally, in chapter 7, Forrest Hylton discusses past and recent social movements in Bolivia. He argues that both social history and cultural anthropology are necessary to understand the evolution of political power in Bolivia, particularly its class and race/ethnicity dimensions and the ways they have been intertwined during different periods and in different regional spaces. His is less an analysis of a specific region (or even country) than a demonstration of the advantages of a materially based, historically informed social/cultural anthropology, pursued by Wolf, Roseberry, and others over the Foucauldian culturalism that predominates among many anthropologists today.

In his "Reflection" on the contemporary significance of *Peasant Wars*, Gavin Smith points to the contemporary significance of Wolf's historical method of controlled comparison and an approach that begins with the countryside "thence to inquire about connections and alliances beyond." Smith acknowledges the current political moment is very different from the one in which Wolf wrote, yet insists contemporary leftist academics and political figures still have much to learn from him.

Acknowledgments

We would like to thank Avi Chomsky, Marc Edelman, and Gavin Smith for comments, ideas, and suggestions that improved an earlier version of this introduction. We, of course, are responsible for any remaining problems.

Lesley Gill teaches anthropology at Vanderbilt University. She is the author of *A Century of Violence in a Red City* (2016) and *The School of the Americas* (2004).

Leigh Binford is Professor Emeritus of the College of Staten Island of the City University of New York. He writes on rural social economies, international migration, and struggle in Mexico and El Salvador. He coauthored (with Scott Cook) *Obliging Need: Rural Petty Industry in Mexican Capitalism* (1990) and authored *The El Mozote Massacre: Anthropology and Human Rights* (published in an enlarged edition in 2016 as *The El Mozote Massacre: Human Rights and Global Implications*) and *Tomorrow We're All Going to the Harvest: Temporary Foreign Worker Programs and Neoliberal Political Economy* (2013).

Steve Striffler is Director of the Labor Resource Center and Professor of Anthropology at the University of Massachusetts Boston. He writes on labor and the Left in Latin America and the United States. His first book, *In the Shadows of State and Capital* (2001), examines the United Fruit Company and peasant-worker struggle in Ecuador. His second book, *Chicken: The Dangerous Transformation of America's Favorite Food* (2005), explores the history of the poultry industry and Latin American immigration into the Southern United States. His latest book is *Solidarity: Latin America and the US Left in the Era of Human Rights* (2019).

Notes

1. For more on the legacy of revolution, see Palmer and Sangster (2016).
2. Wolf divided the Vietnamese revolution into three stages: the war against the Japanese; the anti-colonial war against the French (1945–1954); and the war to reunite the country, fought against the United States and US-based South Vietnamese regimes (1960–1975). *Peasant Wars* mainly treated the anti-colonial war against the French. Although Wolf wrote in the heat of the anti–Vietnam War struggle and clearly hoped to influence public opinion (and perhaps provide opponents of the war with a broader historical perspective on peasant struggles), the US withdrawal began in 1973 and Saigon fell in April of 1975, four and six years, respectively, after the publication of *Peasant Wars*.

3. Although Wolf references Marx approvingly in *Peasant Wars* and elaborates an analysis that clearly owes a debt to Marx, his publisher, Harper & Row, blurbed a review by *The Economist* on the back cover of the 1969 paperback edition stating, "The best thing about this book is that it represents a non-Marxist attempt at class analysis."

4. See Price (2016) for an extensive discussion of the relationship between anthropology, the military, and the Central Intelligence Agency during the Cold War.

5. In Central America, five small countries collaborated to form a free-trade economic zone in the Central American Common Market, which functioned from 1960 to 1969.

6. See Young (2017) for an interesting discussion of the mid-twentieth-century Bolivian debate about hydrocarbon nationalism.

7. El Salvador eschewed reform until 1980, when, on the verge of revolution, the government enacted a three-phase land reform. The first phase was overseen by the army, which often treated land recipients—former estate workers—as rebel sympathizers. Phase II of the reform would have affected 30 percent of the valuable coffee land but was stalled by conservative politicians and eventually canceled. Phase III, called "Land to the Tiller," converted renters of small parcels into owners (Diskin 1985).

8. See Edelman (1999) for an interesting example of how Costa Rican peasants combined class politics and concerns about identity to confront the Costa Rican state over neoliberal austerity measures.

9. See Brass (1991, 2003) for a critique of these approaches.

10. See Smith (2018) for a discussion of "uneven and combined development" and the problem of scale intertwined with the agrarian question.

References

Akram-Lodhi, A. H., and Cristobal Kay. 2010a. "Surveying the Agrarian Question (Part 1): Unearthing Foundations, Exploring Diversity." *Journal of Peasant Studies* 37 (1): 177–202.

———. 2010b. "Surveying the Agrarian Question (Part 2): Current Debates and Beyond." *Journal of Peasant Studies* 37 (2): 255–284.

Álvarez, Sonia, Evelina Dagnino, and Arturo Escobar, eds. 1998. *Cultures of Politics/Politics of Culture: Revisioning Latin American Social Movements*. Boulder, CO: Westview Press.

Araghi, Farshad A. 2009. "The Invisible Hand and the Invisible Foot: Peasants, Dispossession, and Globalization." In *Peasants and Globalization: Political Economy, Rural Transformation and the Agrarian Question*, ed. A. H Akram-Lodhi and Cristobal Kay, 111–47. London: Routledge.

Bardacke, Frank. 2011. *Trampling out the Vintage: César Chávez and the Two Souls of the United Farm Workers*. London: Verso.

Bacon, David. 2013. *The Right to Stay Home: How US Policy Drives Mexican Migration*. Boston, MA: Beacon Press.

———. 2015. "The Pacific Coast Farm-Worker Rebellion." *The Nation*, 28 August. http://www.thenation.com/article/the-pacific-coast-farm-worker-rebellion.

Bernstein, Henry. 2009. *Class Dynamics of Agrarian Change: Agrarian Change & Peasant Societies*. Sterling, VA: Kumarian Press.

Binford, Leigh. 2016. *The El Mozote Massacre: Human Rights and Global Implications*. Tucson: University of Arizona Press.

Borras, Saturnino M., Jr., and Jennifer C. Franco. 2012. "Global Land Grabbing and Trajectories of Agrarian Change: A Preliminary Analysis." *Journal of Agrarian Change* 12 (1): 34–59.

Borras, Saturnino M., Jr., Marc Edelman, and Cristóbal Kay, eds. 2008. *Transnational Agrarian Movements: Confronting Globalization*. Malden, MA: Wiley Blackwell.

Boyer, Dominick. 2002. "The Medium of Foucault in Anthropology." *Minnesota Review* 58 (1): 265–272.

Brass, Tom. 1991. "Moral Economists, Subalterns, New Social Movements, and the (Re-) Emergence of a (Post-) Modernised (Middle) Peasantry." *Journal of Peasant Studies* 18 (2): 173–205.

———, ed. 2003. *Latin American Peasants*. London: Frank Cass Publishers.

Buhle, Paul, and Dan Georgakas. 1996. *The Immigrant Left in the United States*. Albany: State University of New York Press.

Cardoso, Fernando Henrique, and Enzo Falleto. 1979. *Dependency and Development in Latin America*. Berkeley: University of California Press.

Chayanov, Alexander V. 1966. *The Theory of Peasant Economy*. Homewood, IL: American Economic Association.

Davis, Mike. 2006. *Planet of Slums*. London: Verso.

Diskin, Martin. 1985. "Agrarian Reform in El Salvador: An Evaluation," Food First research report. San Francisco, CA: Institute for Food and Development Policy.

Edelman, Marc. 1999. *Peasants against Globalization*. Stanford, CA: Stanford University Press.

Edelman, Marc, and Saturnino M. Borras Jr. 2016. *Political Dynamics of Transnational Agrarian Movements: Agrarian Change and Peasant Studies*. Halifax: Fernwood Publishing.

Edelman, Marc, and Angelique Haugerud. 2005. "Introduction: The Anthropology of Development and Globalization." In *The Anthropology of Development and Globalization: From Classical Political Economy to Contemporary Neoliberalism*, ed. Marc Edelman and Angelique Haugerud, 1–74. Oxford: Blackwell.

Escobar, Arturo, and Sonia Álvarez, eds. 1992. *The Making of Social Movements in Latin America: Identity, Strategy and Democracy*. Boulder, CO: Westview Press.

Fine, Janice Ruth. 2006. *Worker Centers: Organizing Communities at the Edge of the Dream*. Ithaca, NY: Cornell University Press.

Galeano, Eduardo. 1971. *Open Veins of Latin America*. New York: Monthly Review.

Gamson, William A. 1991. "Commitment and Agency in Social Movements." *Sociological Forum* 6 (1): 27–50.

Gill, Lesley. 2016. *A Century of Violence in a Red City: Popular Struggle, Counterinsurgency, and Human Rights in Colombia*. Durham, NC: Duke University Press.

Gough, Kathleen. 1968. "Anthropology and Imperialism." *Monthly Review* 19 (1): 12–27.

Gould, Jeffrey L. 1990 *To Lead as Equals: Rural Protest and Political Consciousness in Chinandega, Nicaragua, 1912–1979*. Chapel Hill: University of North Carolina.

Gould, Jeffrey L., and Aldo Lauria-Santiago. 2008. *To Rise in Darkness: Revolution, Repression and Memory in El Salvador, 1920–1932*. Durham, NC: Duke University Press.

Grajales, Jacobo. 2011. "The Rifle and the Title: Paramilitary Violence and Land Control in Colombia." *Journal of Peasant Studies* 38 (4): 771–792.

Grandin, Greg. 2004. *The Last Colonial Massacre: Latin America in the Cold War*. Chicago: University of Chicago Press.

Gunder Frank, Andre. 1969. *Development and Underdevelopment in Latin America*. New York: Monthly Review.

Harvey, David. 2005. *A Brief History of Neoliberalism*. Oxford: Oxford University Press.

Hobsbawm, Eric. 1959. *Primitive Rebels*. Manchester: Manchester University Press.

Huizer, Gerrit. 1973. *Peasant Rebellion in Latin America*. London: Penguin.

Hylton, Forrest, and Sinclair Thomson. 2007. *Revolutionary Horizons: Past and Present in Bolivian Politics*. New York: Verso.

Jorgensen, Joseph. 1993. "Kathleen Gough's Fight against the Consequences of Class and Imperialism on Campus." *Anthropologica* 35 (2): 227–234.

Landsberger, Henry A., ed. 1969. *Latin American Peasant Movements*. Ithaca, NY: Cornell University Press.

Lee, Richard, and Karen Brodkin Sacks. 1993. "Anthropology, Imperialism and Resistance: The Works of Kathleen Gough." *Anthropologica* 35 (2): 181–193.

Lehmann, David. 1980: "Ni Lenin ni Chayanov." *Estudios Rurales Latinoamericanos* 3 (1): 5–23.

Lenin, Vladimir Illich. 1964. *The Development of Capitalism in Russia*. Moscow: Progress Publishers.

Marchesi, Aldo. 2018. *Latin America's Radical Left: Rebellion and Cold War in the Global 1960s*. Cambridge: Cambridge University Press.

Palmer, Brian, and Joan Sangster. 2016. "The Distinctive Heritage of 1917: Resuscitating Revolution's *Longue Durée*." In *Socialist Register 2017: Rethinking Revolution*, ed. Leo Panitch and Greg Albo, 1–34. London: Merlin Press.

Peel, J. D. Y. 2013. "Peter Worsley Obituary: Sociologist Who Did Much to Define the Idea of a 'Third World.'" *The Guardian*, 28 March. https://www.theguardian.com/education/2013/mar/28/peter-worsley.

Price, David. 2016. *Cold War Anthropology: The CIA, the Pentagon, and the Growth of Dual Use Anthropology*. Durham, NC: Duke University Press.

Roseberry, William. 1991. "Images of the Peasant in the Consciousness of the Venezuelan Proletariat." In *Anthropologies and Histories: Essays in Culture, History, and Political Economy*, 55–79. New Brunswick, NJ: Routledge Press.

———. 1995. "Latin American Peasant Studies in a 'Postcolonial' Era." *Journal of Latin American Anthropology* 1 (1): 150–177.

———. 1996. "The Unbearable Lightness of Anthropology." *Radical History Review* 65: 5–25.

Smith, Gavin. 2018. "Elusive Relations: Distant, Intimate and Hostile." [The 10th Eric Wolf Lecture.] *Current Anthropology* 59 (3): 247–267.

Schneider, Jane. 1995. "Introduction: The Analytic Strategies of Eric Wolf." In *Articulating Hidden Histories: Exploring the Influences of Eric Wolf*, ed. Jane Schneider and Rayna Rapp, 3–30. Berkeley: University of California Press.

Thompson, E. P. 1963. *The Making of the English Working Class*. New York: Vintage Books.

Van der Ploeg, Jan Douwe. 2008. *The New Peasantries: Struggles for Autonomy and Sustainability in an Era of Empire and Globalization*. London: Earthscan.

Vergara-Camus, Leandro, and Cristobal Kay. 2017. "Agribusiness, Peasants, Left-Wing Governments, and the State in Latin America: An Overview and Theoretical Reflections." *Journal of Agrarian Change* 17 (2): 239–257.

Wakin, Eric. 1992. *Anthropology Goes to War*. Madison: University of Wisconsin Press.

Webber, Jeffrey R. 2012. *Red October: Left Indigenous Struggles in Modern Bolivia*. Chicago: Haymarket Books.

———. 2017. *The Last Day of Oppression and the First Day of the Same: The Politics and Economics of the New Left in Latin America*. London: Pluto Press.

Winn, Peter, ed. 2004. *Victims of the Chilean Miracle: Workers and Neoliberalism in the Pinochet Era, 1973–2002*. Durham, NC: Duke University Press.

Wolf, Eric. 1959. *Sons of the Shaking Earth*. Chicago: University of Chicago Press.

———. 1969. *Peasant Wars of the Twentieth Century*. New York: Harper & Row.

Worsley, Peter. 1957. *The Trumpet Shall Sound*. London: MacGibbon & Kee.

———. 1964. *The Third World: A Vital New Force in International Affairs*. London: Weidenfield & Nicolson.

Young, Kevin. 2017. *Blood of the Earth: Resource Nationalism, Revolution, and Empire in Bolivia*. Austin: University of Texas Press.

Chapter 1

THE RIGHT HAND OF THE PARTY

The Role of Peasants in Venezuela's Bolivarian Revolution

Aaron Kappeler

~~~

El cielo encapotado anuncia tempestad,	The overcast sky announces a tempest,
y el sol tras las nubes pierde su	and the sun behind the clouds loses its
claridad	clarity
¡Oligarcas, temblad! Viva la Libertad!	Tremble, Oligarchs! Long Live Freedom!
Marchemos, liberales en recia	March, we liberals, in robust
multitude	multitude
a romper las cadenas de vil esclavitud	to break the chains of vile slavery
La espada redentora del general	The redemptive sword of General
Falcón	Falcón
confunde al enemigo de la revolución	confounds the enemies of the revolution
¡Oligarcas, temblad! Viva la Libertad!	Tremble, Oligarchs! Long Live Freedom!
Las tropas de Zamora al toque del	The troops of Zamora at the sound of
clarín	the bugle
derrotan las brigadas del godo	defeat the brigades of the wicked
malandrín	conservatives
¡Oligarcas, temblad! Viva la Libertad!	Tremble, Oligarchs! Long Live Freedom!
Aviva las candelas el viento barines	Stoke the candles, wind of Barinas
el sol de la victoria alumbra en	The sun of victory shines in
Santa Inés	Santa Inés

—"El Himno de la Federación," song of peasant
rebels in nineteenth-century Venezuela

Over the past two decades, the Bolivarian Revolution in Venezuela has garnered the attention of a variety of scholars for its challenge to the neoliberal Washington Consensus and its inspiration of popular movements across Latin America. Studies of the Bolivarian Revolution have focused on the "social missions" of the current government and its use of the revenue of the state oil company to support mass urban constituencies (Ciccariello-Maher 2013; Fernandes 2010;

Schiller 2018; Valencia 2015; Velasco 2015). Yet, far less attention has been paid to agriculture and rural areas. In this chapter, I contribute to a growing body of literature that recognizes the centrality of agrarian reform to the Bolivarian Revolution and its patterns of mass mobilization (e.g., Enriquez 2013; Enriquez and Newman 2015; Lavelle 2013; McKay et al. 2015; Page 2012).

Drawing on the writings of Eric Wolf and his contention that peasants are "transmitters of urban unrest" (1969: 292), I argue that although peasants represent a tiny portion of the total population in Venezuela, they nevertheless exercise disproportionate political influence and that the support of campesino organizations has been crucial to the hegemony of the United Socialist Party of Venezuela (PSUV) in many areas. Largely conceived in urban terms, the ranchos or slums of the major cities have been celebrated as the mass base of the Bolivarian Revolution. However, in electoral terms, the rural areas have been the strongest bases of support for the ruling party, and popular mobilization has straddled the urban-rural divide. Thus, I argue mass politics in Venezuela is better understood in terms of an urban-rural continuum in which struggles at one pole can ignite or galvanize struggles at the opposite pole.

Based on fieldwork in the state of Barinas, an epicenter of agrarian reform and the campesino movement, I present a case of agrarian rebellion in which members of the Frente Nacional Campesino Ezequiel Zamora (Ezequiel Zamora National Peasant Front) invaded a state-run, agro-industrial farm in 2014 and laid claim to portions of its uncultivated lands. Showing how this struggle was embedded in the wider fields of urban capitalist and state power, I provide an analysis based on what Wolf calls a "micro-sociology" to illustrate how a particular stratum of the peasantry was instrumental in facilitating the invasion and in turn, how this stratum enlisted the support of key urban allies. Exposing critical tensions in the Bolivarian Revolution, I argue that although "the transcendental ideological issues only appear in very prosaic guise" in this context (Wolf 1969: xi), the invasion and its subsequent resolution still reflect divergent visions of social justice and contradictions in the multiclass alliance on which the revolution is based. In the analysis, I show how the leaders of campesino organizations and state agencies pressed their respective claims and how the two sides eventually arrived at a negotiated settlement that preserved a shared field of force. Ultimately, I conclude the invasion and its resolution reflect not only divergences between the ruling party and the peasantry but also cracks in the state system, which can afford insights into the future trajectory of the Bolivarian Revolution.

The Roots of Rebellion

Commenting on the case of Mexico in the early twentieth century, Eric Wolf (1969) argued the tensions that led to the largely agrarian revolution had their origins in the colonial period and conflicts that long preceded the rule of the dictator Porfirio Díaz. Suggesting the War of Independence had failed to resolve the question of land inequality and that tenure patterns had not changed radically from Spanish to home rule, Wolf argued the seeds of the conflict were sown with the introduction of new capitalist imperatives accompanying the growth of commercial agriculture. Simultaneously dependent on the labor and desiring the land of neighboring peasant communities, large-scale commercial enterprises introduced a set of irreconcilable tensions that would eventually erupt in armed violence when elite struggles at the political center opened up a vacuum of sovereignty (see also Joseph and Nugent 1995). Likewise, the origins of rural unrest in Venezuela in the late twentieth century can be traced back to the War of Independence and the failure of the liberal revolution to erase deeply entrenched inequalities.

Led by a class of merchants and landowners whose trade with other Latin American colonies was more lucrative than the trade with Spain, the principal aim of the revolution was to create a political system based on limited suffrage that would allow for unfettered commercial relations and give creole elites a free hand to run society. A prerequisite for this type of polity was the conversion of land encumbered by social obligations and aristocratic privileges into a commodity that could be traded on the market. Along with the erasure of the power of colonial officials, the bulk of whom were drawn from peninsular elites, this process was the basis for a transition to a sovereign national state that treated property in land as the basis of citizenship. Yet the eradication of the encomienda system[1] and the transfer of power to creole elites did not mean a radical redistribution of land for the average person. Except in the case of indigenous communities, which enjoyed collective tenure rights under the Spanish crown and saw these rights abolished after the war, the introduction of private property did little to alter the extreme concentration of land or the territory's highly exploitative labor relations.

During the War of Independence, Simón Bolívar promised to abolish slavery and the debts of peons as a way to build support. But the social character of the revolution he led was highly restricted, and his successors largely replaced their Spanish enemies in the existing structural positions in society (see Wolf and Hansen 1967). The classic *latifundio-minifundio* pattern, which has typified landholding in Venezuela for most of its modern history, has its origins in the efforts of Bolívar's lieutenants to enrich themselves and confine other claimants to small plots at the edges of great estates. In some cases, the new ruling elites in Venezuela were the literal descendants of the old mercantile families of Caracas and Maracaibo, while others were military chieftains who had risen to power as a result of the war, most famously in the case of President José Antonio Páez. Irrespective of whether their status was inherited or acquired, the virtual monopoly of land held by these actors was a major source of rural discontent.

In the mid-nineteenth century, the situation in the Venezuelan countryside could be described as one of extreme social disparity in which a tiny European-descended elite—derogatorily referred to as *godos*[2]—lived off the rent and labor of the mestizo majority who survived as tenants or laborers on *latifundia* or freeholders scraping a bare existence from low quality soils. Yet, with the rise of new markets, the size and character of the Venezuelan middle classes began to change, and as they changed, so did their attitudes toward property and the postcolonial state. Before, the major source of income for mercantile elites had been the export of agricultural goods, for which reason they had little problem with an open trade policy.

However, by the mid-nineteenth century, sectors of the middle class had become involved in petty crafts and domestic manufactures that increasingly brought them into conflict with the monopolistic pattern of ownership and free trade. Seeking to meet growing demand in internal markets, and in some cases employing wage labor, these actors sought to limit commercial competition from foreign sources and to protect nascent industry. Politically, the new middle classes supported a federal system that would give greater autonomy to individual states and reduce the power of the central government in the hands of older bourgeois and aristocratic elements—a contradiction that eventually crystallized in the Liberal and Conservative parties.

Closely paralleling the US Civil War, both in terms of its period and proximate causes, the Federal War in Venezuela (1859–1863) was an internecine conflict that saw the destruction of much of the nation's agriculture and the deaths of more than 150,000 people. Following a struggle for succession in the wake of the disputed election of 1855, the Liberal Party took up arms against the ruling conservatives and fought to establish itself as the legitimate government. Flocking to the ranks of the Liberal Party in the belief that they would challenge entrenched political power and carry out popular reforms, peasants and rural subalterns formed the backbone of the insurgent armies, radicalizing the conflict.

During the war, Liberal Party forces abolished slavery and tenant debts in areas under their control and redistributed land captured from conservative elites. The war ended in a stalemate, however, and the radical measures enacted during the course of the conflict were reversed in the compromise reached at the Treaty of Coche in 1863 (Figueroa 1975). This reversal and the destruction of haciendas in the plains states of Barinas, Apure, Portuguesa, Guárico, and Cojedes, meant former slaves and tenants often had no alternative but to seek new livelihoods on the western frontier (see Roseberry 1985; Yarrington 1997). But the history of this proto-agrarian reform and the slogans of its leaders would play a central role in twentieth-century agrarian politics, and this stillborn revolution would inspire other activists to try to settle the issue of citizenship through land reform.

"Free Land and Men"

From a family of petty merchants and traders, the liberal leader Ezequiel Zamora is likely the most celebrated figure of the Federal War, and his legacy remains a touchstone for radical politics in Venezuela in the twenty-first century. Embodying the burgeoning middle classes and their hostility to the conservative oligarchy, Zamora's family was part of the European-descended yeomanry that derived the bulk of its income from agriculture and small-scale commerce. Chiefly remembered for his brilliance as a military strategist and tactician, Zamora was also known as an opponent of slavery and an advocate of agrarian reform.[3]

Referred to as *catire* because of his light hair and skin color, Zamora was a figure who might otherwise have fit in well with the former supporters of the colonial regime who returned to Venezuela after the War of Independence to reclaim their land and assets. However, Zamora chose instead to rally disenfranchised Venezuelans and organized a diverse coalition of Afro-descended slaves and mestizo peasants, who stood to benefit from the breakup of large estates, as well as urban craftspeople and traders in competition with larger commercial monopolies. Advancing a Lockean ideology that declared, "All property that is not the product of work is theft," Zamora exemplified a native radicalism, which combined belief in natural equality with redistribution of social wealth and popular election of all officials.[4] Campaigning under the slogans "Tierra y Hombres Libres" and "Horror a la Oligarquía," Zamora held that the civic virtue of the nation could be justly promoted only with the labor of its majority and that average Venezuelans were systematically denied the means of self-improvement.

Raising a popular army and marching across the country, sacking haciendas and redistributing land to Liberal Party supporters along the way, Zamora and his followers sought to break the back of the conservative oligarchy and to reorganize the territory. In addition to reorganizing the governments of several states, Zamora was the architect of the military victory at the Battle of Santa Inés, in which liberal forces defeated a larger conservative army in the state of Barinas. Despite his skills as a tactician and having earned the titles "Valiant Citizen" and "General of the Sovereign People," liberal armies could not ultimately overcome the conservatives, and Zamora was killed — allegedly by a stray bullet — at the Battle of San Carlos in 1860. To this day, speculation suggests Zamora had become an obstacle to the agenda of other liberal leaders and that members of his own party were responsible for his murder. Evidence for this theory is scant, but what is certain is that following his death, Zamora's brother-in-law Juan Crisóstomo Falcón became the president of Venezuela, and the Liberal Party gradually adopted a political-economic program that was virtually indistinguishable from that of the conservatives.

With their faith in positivism and science, the liberal elites of late nineteenth-century Venezuela treated the peasantry as the target, rather than the beneficiary, of their civilizing mission. Embracing an economic model predicated on the export of agricultural products, liberal elites sought to transform Venezuela into a modern nation-state through trade and adoption of European cultural norms. Under the rule of Antonio Guzmán Blanco — the true victor of the Federal War, and Zamora's reputed assassin — Venezuela's economy shifted to coffee exports and a policy based on the idea that exchange on global markets would transform "backward" peasants into modern farmers. Yet downturns in global coffee prices and the ensuing instability eventually led to his overthrow and a period of violence that ended in the rule of another liberal dictator, Juan Vicente Gómez.

Figure 1.1. Statue of the "General of the Sovereign People" in Plaza Zamora, Barinas, Venezuela. Photo by the author.

Peasants, Petroleum, and Populism

For much of the twentieth century, discourses of modernization predicted the inevitable decline of the Venezuelan peasantry with the rise of the petrostate and rapid urbanization. The exploitation of petroleum would set the stage for an epochal transition that would free the nation from its dependency on agriculture and pave the way for the disappearance of its "backward" rural subjects (Coronil 1997; Ewell 1984). Yet the exploitation of oil did not lessen the dependence of the nation on its lands or ensure the decline of the peasantry. In the early twentieth century, Venezuela was a society starkly divided between the urban coastal centers and the rural interior. Some parts of the interior were effectively linked to global markets through commodity trade, while other parts of the territory existed largely as they had in previous generations, that is, governed by patrimonial relations in which monopoly in access to land created social power and an ability to exploit labor (Wolf 1957). However, linkages to foreign markets could suddenly be severed by price fluctuations and peasant relations with the state were similarly sporadic.

Instead of a system of sovereign institutions exercising control over territory, as in the Weberian ideal, in Venezuela rule was based on regional strongmen linked through patronage networks. This system, balancing the interests of competing power blocs, held the demands of rural subalterns and rival claimants in check and prevented serious change. The death of the dictator Juan Vicente Gómez in 1935 and the growth of the petroleum sector, however, destabilized this delicate balance of power, leading to a political transition. In 1944, the nominally socialist party Acción Democrática (AD) came to power, beginning a three-year period of reform known as El Trienio Adeco. This government under the leadership of Romulo Gallegos sought to break up *latifundia* and transfer land to the peasantry to create agrarian cooperatives. Raising the ire of conservative elites, the AD government was overthrown in a military coup and a dictatorship that lasted more than a decade was installed.

Perhaps wary of the previous experience with military intervention, AD, when it returned to power in 1958, pursued an agrarian policy that was considerably more conservative, and "colonization" was offered as the solution to the agrarian question. As the owner of the petroleum industry, the Venezuelan state was the largest landowner in the country and therefore able to distribute land resources to marginalized segments of the population. By adopting this strategy, Venezuelan leaders could avoid conflict with *latifundistas* and improve conditions for the average peasant. In step with the strictures of the Alliance for Progress and Cold War anti-communism, colonization was a way to exploit underutilized land resources (Erasmus 1967; Powell 1971). Still, land settlements were often far from social services, and their remote locations combined with a lack of basic infrastructure made it difficult for new landowners to access urban and regional markets.

In his analysis of twentieth-century agrarian rebellions, Wolf (1969) provides several examples or cases where the imposition of the colonial order displaced the traditional tenure rights of peasants and patron-client relations with landlords, who, although they may have exacted rent or tribute from peasants, nevertheless served a key social insurance function in times of bad weather and poor harvests. The landed gentry or aristocracy could be relied on to lend money to the peasant or cultivator in difficult periods and thereby guarantee survival (cf. Scott 1976). In Venezuela, however, it was not the imposition of the colonial order but rather its displacement that led to agrarian rebellions. In Venezuela, there were few places where the dissolution of patron-client relations could suffice to explain a pattern of agrarian upheaval or rebelliousness, and in those locations where such relations existed, there appears to have been less resistance. As William Roseberry (1989) notes of the Andean region, the history of the peasantry there was shallow, with most of the population arriving in the late nineteenth century. Surplus takers in the region (most of whom were merchants) never provided subsistence guarantees, and access to land was not based on social obligations (Roseberry 1985). Despite the absence of key features of "the moral economy," the Andes were still a center of agrarian upheaval (Kappeler 2019). However, in the llanos, or plains, the situation was somewhat different.

Peasants had previously been given usufruct rights in exchange for labor on haciendas. Even the slave had been afforded access to a *conuco*, or subsistence plot. But the expansion of commercial agriculture under the impetus of domestic and foreign markets, combined with the requirement to pay taxes in cash as a condition of citizenship, meant the postcolonial regime actually increased pressure on peasants, who were no longer guaranteed access to land. Even peasants that managed to acquire private property and had little access to markets often saw those lands taken over by rapacious speculators and *latifundistas*. The response to this dislocation, manifest in the Federal War, was predictably violent. Yet it was not the colonial order that brought the forces of capitalism into the rural scene in Venezuela, but rather its dissolution, and it would be the subsequent introduction of a specific form of capitalism in the twentieth century that spurred further rebelliousness among peasants.

Whereas the primary threat to dictators in the early twentieth century had been unrest among the peasantry, these actors were to a certain extent displaced with the growing power of organized labor in the petroleum sector—actors with whom peasants actively collaborated under the leadership of AD. The peasant leagues' relationship with the ruling party generally served to lessen the militancy of these organizations and integrate leaders into the existing power structure (Powell 1971). Most of the land redistribution, not surprisingly, was to key leaders of the campesino movement, forcing less influential members to turn to non-state organizations to address their grievances.

In the aftermath of the transition from the military dictatorship to democracy, deep conflicts within the ranks of AD over the future of "the Revolution" spurred leaders of the party youth league to join in armed struggle with members of the now proscribed Communist Party. Echoing an earlier generation of agrarian rebels with their call for "land to tiller," the guerrillas of the Fuerzas Armadas de Liberación Nacional (or FALN) sought to mimic the Cuban Revolution and take state power by encircling the cities. The critical flaw in this strategy was the changing status of the imagined agent of social change—the land-poor peasant—and a superficial analogy between the Venezuelan and Cuban situations. Unlike in Cuba, with its mass of proletarian cane cutters and land-hungry campesinos, in Venezuela it was chiefly market prices for commodities, rather than the failure to obtain subsistence from land, that was the basis of the woes of the middle peasant.

The segment of the peasantry that best corresponded to Wolf's typology of peasant militancy and served as the backbone of the insurgency was the Andean peasantry, but the guerrillas had difficulty spreading outside of their mountain redoubts. Internally divided and undermined by official agrarian reform efforts, the guerrillas soon discovered they did not have a strong social base outside the Andes and that the Venezuelan military had them surrounded. During the course of the insurgency, guerrillas succeeded in spreading to the lowland areas of Barinas, and these areas would become the last holdouts to a government-led "pacification process" in the 1970s, which promised amnesty in exchange for laying down arms (see Ellner 1988). The inability of the Left to capitalize on discontent, however, was rooted in changes that long preceded the armed struggle and likely ensured the insurgency was defeated before it even began.

As in other parts of Latin America, the expansion of commercial ranching and agriculture pushed peasants in the plains onto smaller and smaller parcels of land that were insufficient for subsistence needs and that could not support expanding households. But this pressure was concomitant with the rise of the petroleum industry and a petrostate whose revenue could support a surplus labor population. In the mid-twentieth century, Venezuela experienced a mass exodus from the countryside under the twin pressures of declining prices for agricultural exports and a rising petroleum economy that drew rural people away from their traditional livelihoods. Rural migrants living in the hills were integrated into the urban fabric, giving rise to the massive slums that now encircle the major cities, but they retained a great degree of social distance from the urbanites they served. Indeed, the name "ranchos" to describe these areas indexes the residents' rural origins. The reduction in the size of the *campesinado* with the rise of the petrostate and populist redistribution policies of the 1970s signaled the end of an era and a decisive break—at least demographically—with the past.

Emphasizing the distinction between peasants who are embedded in urban networks and those whose livelihoods remain largely subordinated to nonmarket, subsistence imperatives in the countryside, Wolf argued that threats to the reproduction of the peasant household were central to grasping cycles of protest and rebellion and that the disruptive features of commercial capitalism vis-à-vis such livelihoods were the key to understanding the dynamics of peasant revolt. Wolf argued that the rural scene did not easily generate, of its own accord, the types of compulsive market relations and disruptive social forces that led to nationwide agrarian rebellions, and hence, it was capitalism, the state, and urban power that should be seen as the key forces encouraging peasant militancy. In Venezuela, a particular form of resource extraction-based capitalism led to social dislocation, unrest, and a long history of agrarian struggles that regularly call forth images of the past as their ideological fulcrum.

The nationalization of the oil industry in 1976 set the stage for a shift in Venezuela's terms of trade with other nations and an elevation of the status of the nation in the global system. Yet the nationalization of petroleum did not put an end to struggles over land or the distribution of wealth from it. In the 1980s, Venezuela underwent a severe social-economic crisis as declining oil prices and profligate spending on consumption contributed to an unsustainable debt structure. Chronic budgetary shortfalls and a lack of capital for reinvestment led successive Venezuelan governments to adopt neoliberal policies that included the abolition of credits and subsidies for small producers, as well as a halt to land redistribution. In the wake of the petro-boom and reregulation of global markets, the end of official state support for peasant agriculture resulted in a decline in political influence and the rise of new radical agrarian movements (for a general history, see Martinez-Torres and Rosset 2010).

The Right Hand of the Party

In 1998, the Movement for a Fifth Republic came to power in Venezuela after a long period of political and economic instability. Arguably starting with the Caracazo riots in 1989, sparked by austerity measures and a severe decline in oil prices, the populist movement was initiated by a young military officer named Hugo Chávez. The Revolutionary Bolivarian Movement-200, as it was known,[5] sought to take power in a civilian-military coup in 1992. The coup was defeated, and its leaders were imprisoned. But Chávez claimed he was able to use his time in prison to study the history of Venezuela and develop his "Bolivarian ideology," known as "the tree of three roots." Seeking to return to the original founding principles of the nation, the ideology drew on the writings and biographies of three Venezuelan leaders: the liberator Simón Bolívar, his teacher Simón Rodríguez, and the lesser-known Ezequiel Zamora. Having studied the life of Zamora and been entranced as a boy by the stories of Zamora's military campaigns in his local environs in Barinas, Chávez effectively translated the philosophy of Zamora—already a touchstone for Venezuelan radicalism—into the language of "socialism." One of the major constituencies he sought to court with this ideology was the rural poor and the campesino movement.

In 2000, a group of activists in the western plains founded the Frente Nacional Campesino Ezequiel Zamora. Like many other social movements in Venezuela, the organization sought to take advantage of the political space opened up by the populist leadership to press its claims for land rights. The Front had a special relationship with the ruling party based on cautious, conditional support in exchange for efforts to redress longstanding social grievances. The slogans of the organization harkened back to the agrarian rebels of the nineteenth century and used the image of Zamora, implicitly linking the government's official reform agenda with their own demands.

As Wolf argues, "Peasants may join a national movement in order to settle scores which are age old in their village or region" (1969: xi). Few such scores can be settled, however, without the support of other social groups. The persistence of stark agrarian inequality in Venezuela suggests that unless something fundamental in the balance of power shifted, peasants would be unable to mount a direct challenge to rural elites. As Wolf argues further, "A rebellion cannot start from a situation of complete impotence . . . the decisive factor in making a peasant rebellion possible lies in the relation of the peasantry to the field of power which surrounds it" (290). Peasants in Barinas lacked the leverage to challenge the authority of landed property. For this challenge to take place, their organizations had to be embedded in fields of power that threatened the legitimacy of these elites. The peasant organization found precisely this leverage in the PSUV.

For its part, the ruling party cultivated ties with agrarian social movements based on its need to win an electoral majority and to demonstrate the strength of its popular appeal. In some cases, these organizations have provided much-needed muscle and even institutional capacity in rural areas where the state bureaucracy is often weak. Mobilizing its followers for the ruling party in elections, the Front has provided much of the bureaucratic support on the ground and for the party. In some areas, the memberships of the PSUV and the Front overlap almost entirely. Using forms of direct action and popular mobilization, including occupation of government offices and legal channels to press claims, the Front has served to radicalize the political process "from below," on occasion, pushing it beyond the limits set by "the revolutionary leadership" (Kappeler 2015).

When I arrived in Barinas in 2007, the Bolivarian government of Venezuela was busy building a national coalition for social transformation and a program referred to as "endogenous development." Although officially "socialist," the ruling party was drawing support from diverse quarters and using a populist language that divided the Venezuelan population into those who were concerned with "the greater national interest" and those who supported the interests of narrow cliques. "The revolution," as they called it, was enfranchising groups that had long been ignored and received little attention from the state, including the peasantry and landless people (Kappeler 2015).

Driving outside the state capital along the José Antonio Páez Highway, which ran from east to west, one could see numerous squatter settlements and land occupations in the peri-urban region. These settlements of poorly constructed houses—referred to as ranchos like their semi-regularized, urban counterparts—displayed the red flags of the PSUV and the yellow flags of the Ezequiel Zamora National Peasant Front emblazoned with the slogan "Tierras y Hombres Libres."[6] The two organizations were recruiting in the same areas, and indeed, there seemed to be no immediate contradiction in membership in both organizations.

One such settlement also held a banner calling on the governor of the state, the brother of President Hugo Chávez, to recognize the legitimacy of their occupation and give them land titles.[7] Of course, the practice of invading and occupying land to obtain title was not confined to the peri-urban region but extended well into the countryside. A subdivision of the Ministry of Agriculture, the Instituto Nacional de Tierras (National Institute of Lands—INTi), was tasked with regularizing land tenancy and adjudicating disputes in the state in accordance with the Land and Agrarian Development Law of 2001. According to that law, any land unit that did not produce at least 80 percent of the national average for the crop(s) under cultivation was subject to seizure. One of the largest land allotments in the state of

Figure 1.2. Infrastructure for the Fondo Zamorano near the Florentino enterprise. Photo by the author.

Barinas fell under the provisions of the law and was the subject of considerable contestation as a result.

A few miles from the hometown of Chávez, the estate known as La Marqueseña had been fought over during the War for Independence, and the armies of Zamora had marched through the estate during the Federal War. In the twenty-first century, the farm was the prize in a contest fought between peasants, *latifundistas*, and the Venezuelan state. Expropriated in 2005 as part of a wave of nationalizations in the interior, the farm was transformed into a state-run, agro-industrial enterprise known as the Centro Técnico Productivo Socialista Florentino. The enterprise was designed to bolster domestic food production and use technical and industrial means to increase yields. It had a large stable workforce of several hundred who were also tasked with providing aid and support to small cultivators in the region. In fact, a portion of the acreage expropriated from the original estate was allocated to a *fondo zamorano*—one of the official agrarian cooperatives started as part of a Ministry of Agriculture program to provide land to the rural poor. But the arrangement between the enterprise and its neighbors was not as efficient and friction-free as the official rhetoric suggested.

State enterprises were portrayed in government media as highly efficient and productive units that were a major advance over small-scale peasant agriculture, and employees tended to carry themselves with a degree of superiority. Nevertheless, when oil prices started dropping in 2012, it became clear these enterprises were dependent on the petrodollars of the state and that their sophisticated production systems could not operate in conditions of sudden austerity. Venezuela did not fabricate parts for the tractors and mechanical harvesters that the enterprise relied on to cultivate its extensive acreage, and those parts could not be imported without foreign currency reserves. Likewise, the salaries of technical experts were paid with revenue from the state oil company and at a certain point—with my informants spending most of their days in the office reading, watching television, or, in the case of manual laborers, gambling—it became clear the continued operation of such units was as much an exercise in buying consent and staving off instability as anything having to do with production. Indeed, the straggly rows of corn planted by hand by enterprise employees in fallow fields showed that peasant-style agriculture still remained viable in some senses, despite the high modern pretensions of enterprise leaders.

In 2014, one of my key informants, José, a sociologist working in Florentino, told me campesinos had invaded the enterprise and laid claim to five hundred hectares of its uncultivated land. The invaders were receiving the support of the Ezequiel Zamora National Peasant Front, and José explained this was a particularly tense situation, since the Front was "the right hand of the United Socialist Party in Barinas" and elected leaders relied on the Zamora Front for popular support. Moreover, the struggle also effectively set sectors of the state against one another and forced them into conflict with longstanding allies. The lawyer for the Front had previously worked for the INTi, which many employees of Florentino regarded as a betrayal. From the standpoint of these employees, the lawyer seemed to have conflicting agendas and was now using his insider knowledge of the land reform process to subvert official policy. José and a few other employees were more circumspect about the situation, defending the lawyer by saying he "wanted to help campesinos who deserved land" and that while they could not agree with the invasion, they ultimately believed an alternative solution should be sought. In fact, the invasion was hardly surprising, as the actors and their motivations were already well known.

During the course of my fieldwork from 2007 to 2016, a variety of campesino groups had tested the enterprise, and in many ways, this invasion was simply the culmination of a long period of tension. Members of the neighboring *fondo zamorano* were long criticized by Florentino employees for their lack of productivity and alleged misconduct vis-à-vis the enterprise. Alleged infractions included ignoring the boundaries between the enterprise and the cooperative, theft of enterprise crops at night, grazing cattle on Florentino lands, and mixing herds in an effort to steal animals. Residents of the nearby *poblados* created during the first agrarian reform in the 1960s were also involved in the friction and they joined with the *zamoranos* and the Ezequiel Zamora National Peasant Front in making claims on Florentino lands. The invasion was staged from neighboring *poblados* with the plots of land and houses owned by members of the organization serving as bases of operation. In a pattern familiar throughout Latin America, the invaders entered the farm and constructed temporary ranchos on the land to substantiate their claims to the acreage. Yet, crucially, the invaders did not begin to sow crops or prepare the lands for cultivation, suggesting to some that their true objectives lay elsewhere.

Although describing themselves as campesinos "fighting for land" (*peleando por la tierra*), the composition of the group was heterogeneous and included several recently returned urbanites. The ranks of the invaders also included family members of Florentino workers, such as the brother of a close friend of mine, and it was suggested in a highly contentious enterprise meeting that some Florentino workers had actively helped the invaders. But the ironies of the occupation extended far beyond the biographies of the individuals involved. Perhaps the greatest irony of the invasion was that the very provision of the Land and Agrarian Development Law that had allowed the Bolivarian government to take over La Marqueseña and build the enterprise was now being used to classify Florentino as "underproductive" and hence eligible for redistribution.

The invasion led to a drawn-out legal process that strained the alliance between the Ezequiel Zamora Front and the PSUV. The Florentino enterprise had been created in part to benefit small and medium-sized producers by way of the technical inputs and assistance it provided, as well as commercialization contracts that could serve as an outlet for peasant harvests. In exchange for electoral support and recognition of the legitimacy of the ruling party, Zamora's members received aid. But with the invasion, the implicit terms of this contract had been violated. Yet, whereas peasant activists involved in land invasion in other parts of the state and country were the victims of kidnapping and paid assassination (*sicariato*) and thus forced to live in conditions of semi-clandestinity, the response of the National Guard under the direction of the ruling party in Barinas was measured and the invaders were evicted without serious incident.

Ultimately, in early 2016, the INTi concluded Florentino lands were not eligible for transfer under the terms of the Land and Agrarian Development Law and that the occupiers would not be granted property or use titles. But the invasion of the lands and the potential threat of a repetition of the incident were sufficient for the INTi to seek an alternative solution, and lands in another location were awarded to the invaders instead. Although some writers argue the Bolivarian government has had success in reestablishing smallholder agriculture (e.g., Enriquez and Newman 2015; Page 2012), the peasantry remains an ever-declining portion of the Venezuelan population whose independent influence is largely subsumed by urban social groups. The peasantry appears most effective when it is organized to take advantage of ties with urban actors and the state bureaucracy. The *campesinado* in Venezuela lacks sufficient strength to make itself sovereign over the land, as in the case of the twentieth century's actual "peasant wars." Instead, peasant organizations have fought "a war of position" in which the political-bureaucratic apparatus, media, and lawyers have proved most effective in gaining recognition of their claims.[8]

The condition of possibility for this type of politics was a populist government that needed the peasantry as an ally in its fight with rentier elites invested in a dependent model of development based on resource extraction and the recycling of surpluses from an import/export complex. For this reason, despite the reversal of several land occupations in the state of Barinas, José's remark that the Ezequiel Zamora National Peasant Front was "the right hand of the party" was deeply true. The PSUV continued to have to negotiate with the Front, and state bureaucrats preferred to settle the conflict with a transfer of other lands to the occupiers, rather than simply evict them and risk the loss of support and a perception that they were as "anti-peasant" as *latifundistas*.

Engrams of the Past

It is difficult to know how to better describe the influence of the nineteenth-century agrarian rebel Ezequiel Zamora on twenty-first-century Venezuelan politics than Wolf (1969: 276) does when he argues the origins of the twentieth century's peasant wars lay in "a concrete historical experience which lives on in the present and continues to determine its shape and meaning." Both the Venezuelan government and campesino movement mobilized the image of Zamora, a symbol that was "only latent in the cultural memory" and able to trigger "the engrams of events not easily erased." With the Caracazo riots of 1989 and a series of coups in the wake of neoliberal austerity in the 1990s, the Venezuelan people were witness to a "greater event" that allowed popular memory of the Federal War to be resurrected.

In a classic example of anamnesis, this image of past struggles called forth in the present to make claims on the future was based on an historical gaze that was *both* forward and backward looking. Yet, whereas Wolf argued the peasant wars of the twentieth century were the result of "the diffusion of a particular cultural system, North Atlantic capitalism," to areas where its distinctive logics had not yet fully penetrated, this revolt was no longer driven by a system that was "alien to the areas . . . engulfed in its spread" (1969: 276). Instead, this "revolt" was the product of the historical development of that system and dynamics internal to it.

The "backwardness" of the Venezuelan countryside in relation to its hyper-urban coastal regions was not a product of "lost time" but rather a result of the uneven expansion of capital. The pattern of landholding in Barinas was as much a product of the logic of rentier accumulation in the oil sector as local agriculture (Gómez 2000). This unbalanced regional growth linked to the petrostate was tied to a pattern of capital circulation and recycling of surpluses that led to a loss of competitiveness and the withering of agriculture in the face of a price structure that supported foreign imports (Purchell 2017). Although the mass of poor people living in the slums carried "the stigmata of trauma and strife" from the transition to urban life and capitalism (Wolf 1969: 276), it was neither the dislocation nor alienation associated with the sale of labor power that was the basis of agrarian militancy in Barinas, but rather the weakness of the commodity fiction, or the idea that labor was a good for sale on a market (cf. Polanyi 1944).

The invasion of the Florentino enterprise was driven not by the fact that labor was a commodity or that it might be transformed into one but rather by the fact that it was a commodity that could not be fully absorbed by the market or purchased at a reasonable rate. The rebels that invaded Florentino were a mix of urban semi-proletarians and peasant smallholders from nearby communities bound together by ties of kinship and neighborhood, and it was these enduring ties, as well as the ability of precarious urbanites to retreat to rural areas in times of high unemployment, that transferred urban social pressures back to the rural community and made the Florentino enterprise a target for the reconciliation of these contradictions.

Unlike the peasant wars of the twentieth century, the invasion was not a defensive rebellion against the encroachment of commercial plantations onto the lands of local communities (e.g., Smith 1989; Striffler 2002) (unless one wanted to think of the state enterprise as a "red hacienda" and its construction as the perpetuation of an age-old pattern of usurpation—a narrative I never heard from activists in Barinas). Instead, it was an offensive action designed to seize hold of a resource—land—that held a special value for the rural poor, who could use it not only for subsistence but also to attract state credit, tapping flows of oil wealth controlled by political elites. Urged on by an organization with the legal expertise and wherewithal for a prolonged struggle, the activists in Barinas were able to take advantage of a unique historical conjuncture that made such an invasion and its resolution possible. The invaders sought forms of protection that would grant them shelter from the untrammeled operation of the market principle—and the shelter happened to be the protection of the state and the ruling party. In the colonial contexts Wolf studied, access to land was based on social obligation. In twenty-first-century Venezuela, land was already largely unencumbered from such ties, and ironically, it was liberal revolutionaries like Bolívar and Zamora who had set this process in motion.

In the *llanos*, land did not belong to a closed corporate community (cf. Wolf 1957). Indeed, efforts to form such agrarian collectives were just as likely to be the work of the Venezuelan state as the work of peasants (see Enriquez and Newman 2015; Larrabure 2010; Page 2012). The local *patrón*, or "big man," continued to exercise his traditional authority in some areas—as in the case of employees who helped Carlos Azpúrua, the owner of La Marqueseña, defend his estate from the Guardia Nacional when the Ministry of Agriculture sought to expropriate it. However, the social insurance function provided by landed elites in other contexts was more easily provided by the Venezuelan petrostate, and rural subalterns found it more useful to forge alliances with a populist government that was at least partially receptive to their demands. Yet the instincts of this modernizing government also ran counter to the aims of the occupiers, and thus a sector of the state came into conflict with "the right hand of the party."

Given their lack of credit, technical inputs, and adequate labor power, the occupiers had no serious chance of producing meaningful surpluses with the land once they held it, but they were willing to risk invasion and to barter political support for aid, which they eventually received.[9] The productivist aims of the Bolivarian government were not likely to be met by either the invaders or the capital it had invested in Florentino in its defunct state; all the same, officials wanted to evict the occupiers and, if possible, encourage them to join cultivation schemes directed by the Ministry of Agriculture (Kappeler 2015). In a time of low oil prices, however, these productive objectives seemed as remote for the Florentino enterprise as the idea that peasants would ever be allowed to possess its lands. In spite of the tensions, the leaders of the ruling party responded in a fashion that was designed to secure political consent from a key ally and to prevent a wholesale break with the campesino movement—deferring the underlying contradiction for a later date.

Conclusion

Shifting from a mostly rural to a mostly urban continent, the demographics of Latin America have changed dramatically since the mid-twentieth century, when Wolf was writing. The social weight of the peasantry, as he termed it, has fallen equally dramatically, and with it, the leverage exercised over the wider social formation. In the 1960s and 1970s, radical agrarian movements convulsed the region, and guerrilla insurgents succeeded in threatening the stability of states and capitalist elites, even in majority-urban societies like Venezuela. Yet today the peasantry is overshadowed by the sheer size and scale of the urban social forces and their disruptive power—a power openly displayed in the Caracazo riots in Venezuela in 1989 and the defeat of the coup against the Chávez government in 2002. But this set of facts does not mean peasants have lost all influence. Apart from their role in assembling an electoral majority—a key part of the strategy of the legal Left in post–Cold War Latin America—peasants in Venezuela were now part of a larger urban-rural continuum in which the stark divide between countryside and city in terms of standards of living endured, but in which the reality of labor mobility and exchange between the spheres, meant the two were more politically connected than ever.

Peasants in Venezuela could no longer be said to inhabit "parochial worlds," and while most peasants did not "send their sons and daughters to the factory" (Wolf 1969: xi), they often did send them to the street vendors, taxi stands, restaurants, and homes of the urban rich to earn a wage that was remitted to their home communities. When such sources of extra-rural, non-farm income became destabilized, however (and in cases where this situation was exacerbated by a re-duction of state income grants and subsidies), itinerant laborers often returned home to join their family members and neighbors in mak-ing claims on land—claims that were as much about tapping flows of resource rent and state largesse whose ultimate source was oil as cultivating the land. The sturdy "middle peasant" who survives by mobilizing the labor of kin and neighbors and negotiating the market is no longer a key part of the Venezuelan population after the demo-graphic shifts of the mid-twentieth century. But the political-economic dynamics that enforced the decline of the middle peasantry are still capable of arousing social protest from this stratum and its allies. The fact that the massive population shift from country to city occurred earlier in Venezuela than in the rest of Latin America did not prevent the Left from adopting the guerrilla strategy, but it did make it dif-ficult for armed organizations to capture state power by encircling the cities from the countryside.

Unlike the mostly rural societies that experienced peasant wars after the Mexican and Cuban revolutions, including Nicaragua, Gua-temala, Peru, and El Salvador, "the sea of peasants" in which guerrillas were supposed to "swim" was already drying up in Venezuela. The fact that Venezuela was also a two-party democracy—one rightly criticized for its violent excesses but which nevertheless enjoyed a degree of popular support and was relatively effective at building coalitions (Kappeler 2017)—meant radical mobilization had to take place in new ways. The pattern of rising militancy and resurgent peas-ant activism in Latin America associated with "the lost decade" of the 1980s (see Martinez-Torres and Rosset 2010) also aligned with a serious destabilization of the petroleum economy in Venezuela and a reduction of the power associated with access to land. This shift in social weight has mirrored the shift in the dialectic of urban power and peasant struggles witnessed over the past two decades.

Describing the backlash against neoliberalization in Latin Amer-ica, James Petras has argued, "coalitions of landless farm workers, small family farmers, and peasants have been central to national struggles against neoliberal regimes and free trade policies. In some cases, rural movements have detonated larger struggles, activating urban classes, trade unions, civic groups, and human rights organiza-tions" (2005: 41; see also Petras and Veltmeyer 2001). While this is an accurate description of the backlash in many parts of Latin America, the recent experience of agrarian reform in Venezuela suggests this is not a universal story for the region. In many parts of an increasingly urbanized Latin America, peasants lack the leverage over the social formation they held in the twentieth century, and the conditions of possibility are radically different as a result.

In Venezuela, the most hyper-urban society in the region, urban unrest and splits in the social fabric succeeded in igniting popular struggles in the wake of the violent imposition of austerity. That mass urban unrest ignited in the 1980s and 1990s was also the catalyst for the delegitimation of multiple neoliberal governments and the eventual installation of a populist leadership that gave peasants space to press their claims. In this sense, peasants were effectively "transmitters of urban unrest" able to take advantage of changes at the political center to challenge the power of traditional landed elites and to capitalize on years of previous organizing. The latest decline in oil prices and the effective end of the petro-boom of the early 2000s, however, has seen an attendant conservatization of the revolutionary process and a growing divergence between peasant organizations and the ruling party.

As Eric Wolf (1969) argued, peasants were the social base of national liberation movements in the Third World in the twentieth century. But at a certain point, peasants came into conflict with the urban-based leaderships and political parties that had succeeded in mobilizing them for the seizure of power. These leaderships had objectives that went far beyond peasant aspirations for land and freedom from tax collectors, merchants, and other surplus takers, and these states eventually became antagonists of peasants. As Latin America leaves a political conjuncture that many regarded hopefully—and perhaps prematurely—as "post-neoliberal,"[10] an analysis of the role of populist governments in forging links between peasants and urban allies can serve as a bridge to new scholarly and political projects—an agenda that speaks to the enduring value of Wolf's analysis and of *Peasant Wars of the Twentieth Century* as an indispensable point of reference for the future.

Acknowledgments

I would like to acknowledge the Wenner-Gren Foundation, the School of Graduate Studies at the University of Toronto, and the Centro Técnico Productivo Socialista Florentino for support of the research on which this chapter is based.

Aaron Kappeler is Lecturer in the Anthropology of Development at the University of Edinburgh. His research focuses on the politics of land and natural resource extraction in Latin America. His most recent work deals with infrastructure and populist politics in Venezuela. He is also currently studying labor migration in the wake of Venezuela's ongoing economic crisis. Before joining the University of Edinburgh, he was Visiting Assistant Professor in Anthropology at Union College, Postdoctoral Fellow in the Institute for Advanced Study at Central European University, and Adjunct Lecturer in Anthropology at the University of Toronto.

Notes

1. The encomienda was a system of landholding in which colonial settlers were granted the right to access land and exploit indigenous labor, but not private property. See Wolf and Hansen (1967) for discussion of its impact on Latin American politics.
2. *Godo* literally means "Goth" but refers to peninsular Spaniards who settled in Latin America and sided with royalist forces during the war for independence. Over time, the term became synonymous with the caste of elites tied to the Conservative Party. It also has racialized connotations, referring to individuals of European descent, rather than individuals from the mestizo majority. In recent years, the term has been redeployed to describe members of the political opposition to Chavismo.
3. There is still some controversy today as to whether Zamora sought an indemnity for the loss of his family "property" when the Liberal Party sought to free the slaves, but in all likelihood his relationship with slavery can be described analogically as "Jeffersonian" (i.e., one of deep and sincere philosophical opposition combined with practical complicity).
4. Although Zamora is known to have associated with two French revolutionaries (Murtón de Veratro and Napoleon Abril) said to have participated in the events of 1848, the influence of socialism on his ideology is still uncertain (cf. Figueroa 1975). That agrarian rebels in Venezuela would find allies among actors who would today likely be classified as "anarchists," however, is not entirely surprising.
5. The organization was named after the two-hundred-year anniversary of the struggle for Venezuelan national independence. Its leaders also consciously imitated an oath sworn by Bolívar, in which the officers pledged under a tree in Caracas to redeem the nation and restore its sovereignty.
6. The editors of the official organ of the National Institute of Lands, *Tiempo de Zamora,* recognized the implicit masculine bias in the slogan and modified it to "Tierras y hombres y mujeres libres," or "Free land and free women and men."
7. At various times, the late President Chávez invoked the concept of "right to the city" and quoted the French Marxist Henri Lefebvre to substantiate the legitimacy of peri-urban land struggles. But in practice, these struggles have been difficult to resolve and the position of the ruling party with regard to squatter settlements has been ambiguous. It has not carried out evictions of squatter settlements on the scale of earlier governments (see Castillo d'Imperio 1990), but it has also not recognized every popular land occupation, as the case presented here shows.
8. The Ezequiel Zamora National Peasant Front has called for the Bolivarian government to arm them, but the government has refrained from creating states within a

state, a charge that was one of the chief reasons listed for the coup against Acción Democrática in the 1940s.

9. Indeed, INTi workers in Barinas told me they had seen poor urbanites use land in precisely this fashion in the early years of the agrarian reform and the Vuelta al Campo campaign. After obtaining their *carta agraria*, or title, newly relocated urbanites sold the land on the private market to individuals already engaged in agriculture and returned to their homes in the city with money to invest in improved housing. It was essentially a way to obtain an interest free loan from the state without having to pay it back.

10. For discussion, see Burdick et al. (2009); Hershberg and Rosen (2006); Macdonald and Ruckert (2009); Radcliffe (2012); Rovira Kaltwasser (2011).

References

Burdick, John, Philip Oxhorn, and Kenneth M. Roberts. 2009. *Beyond Neoliberalism in Latin America? Societies and Politics at the Crossroads*. New York: Palgrave Macmillan.

Castillo d'Imperio, Ocarina. 1990. *Los años del bulldozer*. Caracas: Universidad Central de Venezuela.

Ciccariello-Maher, George. 2013. *We Created Chávez: A People's History of the Bolivarian Revolution*. Durham, NC: Duke University Press.

Coronil, Fernando. 1997. *The Magical State: Nature, Money and Modernity in Venezuela*. Chicago: University of Chicago Press.

Ellner, Steve. 1988. *Venezuela's Movimiento al Socialismo: From Guerrilla Defeat to Electoral Politics*. Durham, NC: Duke University Press.

Enríquez, Laura. 2013. "The Paradoxes of Latin America's Pink Tide: Venezuela and Its Project of Agrarian Reform." *Journal of Peasant Studies* 40 (4): 611–638.

Enríquez, Laura, and Simeon J. Newman. 2015. "The Conflicted State and Agrarian Transformation in Pink Tide Venezuela." *Journal of Agrarian Change* 16 (4): 594–626.

Erasmus, Charles J. 1967. "Upper Limits of Peasantry Bolivia, Venezuela and Mexico Compared." *Ethnology* 6 (4): 349–380.

Ewell, Judith. 1984. *Venezuela: A Century of Change*. Stanford, CA: Stanford University Press.

Fernandes, Sujatha. 2010. *Who Can Stop the Drums? Urban Social Movements in Chávez's Venezuela*. Durham, NC: Duke University Press.

Figueroa, Brito Federico. 1975. *Tiempo de Ezequiel Zamora*. Caracas: Universidad Central de Venezuela.

Gómez, Humberto. 2000. *Barinas, Estado y Economía: Petróleo y Agricultura 1909–1995*. Barinas: Universidad Nacional Experimental de los Llanos Ezequiel Zamora.

Hershberg, Eric, and Fred Rosen. 2006. *Latin America after Neoliberalism: Turning the Tide in the 21st Century?* New York: New Press.

Joseph, Gilbert M., and Daniel Nugent, eds. 1995. *Everyday Forms of State Formation*. Durham, NC: Duke University Press.

Kappeler, Aaron. 2015. *Sowing the State: Nationalism, Sovereignty, and Agrarian Politics in Venezuela*. PhD diss., University of Toronto.

———. 2017. "From Reactionary Modernization to Endogenous Development: The Revolution in Hydroelectricity in Venezuela." *Dialectical Anthropology* 41 (3): 241–262.

———. 2019. "Coffee and Socialism in the Venezuelan Andes." *Focaal* 84: 1–17.

Larrabure, Manuel. 2010. "Praxis, Learning and New Cooperativism in Venezuela: An Initial Look at Venezuela's Socialist Production Units." *Affinities: A Journal of Radical Theory, Culture, and Action* 4 (1): 288–309.

Lavelle, Daniel. 2013. "A Twenty-First Century Socialist Agriculture: Land Reform, Food Sovereignty and Peasant-State Dynamics." *International Journal of Sociology of Agriculture and Food* 21 (1): 133–154.

Macdonald, Laura, and Arne Ruckert. 2009. *Post-neoliberalism in the Americas*. London: Palgrave Macmillan.

Martinez-Torres, Maria Elena, and Peter Rosset. 2010. "La Vía Campesina: The Birth and Evolution of a Transnational Social Movement." *Journal of Peasant Studies* 37 (1): 149–175.

McKay, Ben, Ryan Nehring, and Marygold Walsh-Dilley. 2015. "The 'State' of Food Sovereignty in Latin America: Political Projects and Alternative Pathways in Venezuela, Ecuador, and Bolivia." *Journal of Peasant Studies* 41 (6): 1175–1200.

Page, Tiffany L. 2012. "Can the State Create Campesinos? A Comparative Analysis of the Cuban and Venezuelan Re-peasantization Programmes." *Journal of Agrarian Change* 10 (2): 251–272.

Petras, James. 2005. "The Centrality of Peasant Movements in Latin America: Achievements and Limitations." *Synthesis/Regeneration* 38.

Petras, James, and Henry Veltmeyer. 2001. "Are Latin American Peasant Movements Still a Force for Change?" *Journal of Peasant Studies* 28 (2): 83–118.

Polanyi, Karl. 1944. *The Great Transformation*. Boston: Beacon Press.

Powell, John Duncan. 1971 *The Political Mobilization of the Venezuelan Peasant*. Cambridge, MA: Harvard University Press.

Purchell, Thomas. 2017. "The Political Economy of Rentier Capitalism and the Limits to Agrarian Transformation in Venezuela." *Journal of Agrarian Change* 17 (2): 296–312.

Radcliffe, Sarah A. 2012. "Development for a Postneoliberal Era? Sumak Kawsay, Living Well and the Limits to Decolonization in Ecuador." *Geoforum* 43 (2): 240–249.

Roseberry, William. 1985. *Coffee and Capitalism in the Venezuelan Andes*. Austin: University of Texas Press.

———. 1989. *Anthropologies and Histories: Essays in Culture, History, and Political Economy*. New Brunswick, NJ: Rutgers University Press.

Rovira Kaltwasser, Cristóbal. 2011. "Toward Post-neoliberalism in Latin America?" *Latin American Research Review* 46 (2): 225–234.

Schiller, Naomi. 2018. *Channeling the State: Community Media and Popular Politics in Venezuela*. Durham, NC: Duke University Press.

Scott, James. 1976. *The Moral Economy of the Peasant*. New Haven, CT: Yale University Press.

Smith, Gavin. 1989. *Livelihood and Resistance: Peasants and the Politics of Land in Peru*. Berkeley: University of California Press.

Striffler, Steve. 2002. *In the Shadow of State and Capital: The United Fruit Company, Popular Struggle, and Agrarian Restructuring in Ecuador, 1900–1995*. Durham, NC: Duke University Press.

Valencia, Cristobal. 2015. *We Are the State! Barrio Activism in Venezuela's Bolivarian Revolution*. Tucson: University of Arizona Press.

Velasco, Alejandro. 2015. *Barrio Rising: Urban Popular Politics and the Making of Modern Venezuela*. Berkeley: University of California Press.

Wolf, Eric. 1957. "Closed Corporate Peasant Communities in Mesoamerica and Central Java." *Southwestern Journal of Anthropology* 13 (1): 1–18.

———. 1969. *Peasant Wars of the Twentieth Century*. New York: Harper and Row.

Wolf, Eric, and Edward Hansen. 1967. "Caudillo Politics: A Structural Analysis." *Comparative Studies in Society and History* 9 (2): 168–179.

Yarrington, Doug. 1997. *A Coffee Frontier: Land, Society and Politics in Duaca, Venezuela, 1830–1936*. Pittsburgh, PA: University of Pittsburgh Press.

— Chapter 2 —

REBELLION, REVOLUTION, AND REVERSAL IN ECUADOR'S COUNTRYSIDE

Steve Striffler

In *Peasant Wars of the Twentieth Century*, Eric Wolf explains there is no easy formula for understanding how and why local peasant struggles can become national revolutions. For Wolf, the emergence of peasant uprisings and revolutions are ultimately tied to "the relation of the peasantry to the field of power which surrounds it." And this field is necessarily complex and contingent (1969: 290). This is precisely why the "tactically mobile peasantry," comprised of the "middle" and "free" peasantry, looms so large in Wolf's account. It is the only rural actor with adequate "leverage" over the landed class to give it sufficient freedom to become politically rebellious. For the landowning middle peasantry, "possession of their own resources provides their holders with the minimal tactical freedom required to challenge their overlord." Similarly, the "free" peasant lives in relatively isolated frontier regions and is therefore only marginally controlled by outside powers. It has room to maneuver (291). In both cases, having some degree of economic, cultural, and geographic autonomy from landlords and central authorities is key.

Not only is the tactically mobile peasantry relatively well positioned in the broader field of power, but it is also "the most vulnerable to economic changes wrought by commercialism, while his social relations remain encased within the traditional design." Put a slightly different way, even though this peasantry has a degree of independence from local power holders, its existence is quite precarious and can be easily thrown off by any number of outside disruptions. When this tenuous balance is disrupted, this semi-independent peasantry will—under certain circumstances—fiercely protect its customary way of life. It has something to lose, sees its way of life threatened, and possesses the minimal means to defend it. As Wolf notes, "it is the very attempt of the middle and free peasant to remain traditional which makes him so revolutionary" (292).

And yet, there is very little romanticism in Wolf's account of local peasantries and their capacity to revolt. The tactically mobile peasantry possesses a unique combination of independence and vulnerability that can by itself lead to political unrest. But Wolf nonetheless stressed the crucial importance of "outside leadership" for generating large-scale revolution (294). The peasantry could rebel on its own against the established order, and perhaps even "reshape the social structure of the countryside closer to its heart's desires," but to capture control of the state, major centers of power, and the broader resources of society requires a wider vision and entity with the capacity of advancing such a project. Without a political party, army, or some other leading organization, it is very unlikely that local peasant uprisings will ever coalesce into national revolutions (294–300).

This chapter mines Wolf's insights about revolution to examine the history of a nation—Ecuador—whose countryside has been home to numerous rebellions but never produced a national revolution in the classic sense. What does Wolf's work on successful revolutions, as well as his insights about the middle peasantry, culture and economy, and the importance of outside leadership, say about the vast majority of rural areas in Latin America that have not experienced revolution?

The story begins and ends in the Andes but ultimately focuses on Ecuador's coast. During the late 1800s and first half of the twentieth century, or roughly the same period as large numbers of peasants were being dislocated from highland haciendas, the coastal region—first through the development of cacao plantations and then with the expansion of the banana industry—was becoming home to the most dynamic and advanced expression of agrarian capitalism in Ecuador. The emergence of what would become the largest banana industry in the world gave birth to the country's largest (and, in many ways, first) agrarian proletariat, a landless workforce that was nonetheless still "closely geared to life in the villages" (291). It also simultaneously produced a "free" peasantry that occupied lands considered marginal for banana production and existed semi-independently from both state authorities and the banana industry's landowning class. This free peasantry would eventually develop into a middle peasantry as frontier zones developed and became more deeply integrated into the nation.

Ironically, though perhaps not surprisingly, the creation of this tactically mobile peasantry on the margins of banana production happened despite the best efforts of capital. Large capitalists sought to acquire as much land as possible to both develop "factories-in-the-field" and to ensure that migrants arriving to the region did not have access to land that might allow them to survive outside the emerging plantation system. The disruptive nature of this regional land grab created a powder keg characterized by cycles of conflicts between peasants scrambling for a finca, landless workers trying to negotiate industrial agriculture, and large (often foreign) capitalists trying to transform the coast into a giant plantation. This chapter examines this political turmoil, exploring why and how it emerged, why it failed to transition from rebellion to revolution, and why a tactically mobile peasantry that was born out of conflict with capital from 1940 to 1980 was slowly decimated—and left politically impotent—by neoliberalism starting in the 1980s.

Migration and Dislocation

The poor peasant or the landless laborer who depends on a landlord for the largest part of his livelihood, or the totality of it, has no tactical power; he is completely within the power domain of his employer, without sufficient resources of his own to serve him as resources in the power struggle. (Wolf 1969: 290)

Wolf's description applies to much of the highland population in Ecuador during the late 1800s and first half of the 1900s. Most peasants had some access to land, but it was contingent on maintaining a relationship with a hacienda. Such relationships not only were unequal and exploitative but also required skillful negotiation and constant deference. Yet, once established, dependence could provide a degree of security. By attaching itself to a hacienda, a peasant family could gain access to land and (with a bit of luck and skill) the benevolence of a landlord.

By the early 1900s, however, this paternalistic security began to unravel due to a variety of factors, including efforts by highland landlords to "modernize" their enterprises. Land and livelihood became increasingly tenuous, with peasants responding in a variety of ways, from isolated attacks to more coordinated political uprisings. The most common response, however, was simply leaving, a not uncomplicated endeavor given that most highland peasants were tied to landlords through debt and lacked the resources to move.

Yet, it was also during the last two decades of the nineteenth century that Ecuador became the largest cacao producer in the world, transforming the coastal region into a compelling destination. Rural poor who managed to make the trip nevertheless found a familiarly exploitative set of social relations upon arrival. The rapid expansion of cacao production after 1880 created opportunity, but it also served to solidify and even exacerbate existing inequalities in rural areas of the coast. Cultivation expanded rapidly as established families extended the boundaries of their immense properties at the expense of both state lands and peasant holdings. Although Ecuadorian cacao production would be largely in the hands of relatively small producers after the 1970s, it was cultivated on large haciendas during the boom years at the turn of the century.

Haciendas were owned and managed by some of Ecuador's wealthiest families, who contracted with peasants to clear, plant, and then care for trees during the initial stage of cultivation. Once the trees matured, hacienda workers took over subsequent maintenance and harvesting (while contracted peasants began the process again). Even large landowners lacked the capital to create a large-scale agrarian proletariat during this period and worked to establish a dependent peasantry much like in the highlands, one that was tied to haciendas for access to land and livelihood (Chiriboga 1980).

Yet, the coast was not the highlands. The cacao boom created a dynamic, expanding economy and put peasants in a slightly better position to negotiate the terms of their livelihood. More than this, although the cacao boom led large landowners to bring previously uncultivated lands into agricultural production, cacao production remained concentrated along rivers, in large part because the development of roads, the rapid growth of regional population centers, and the massive migration from the highlands would not occur until the banana boom of the 1950s. What this meant was that in addition to signing on with a hacienda, peasants could and did occupy fairly productive lands that were outside either landlord or state control. Indeed, the line between contracted (hacienda) peasants and Wolf's free peasantry was a blurred and fluid one before the abrupt collapse of cacao production in the early 1920s. Once the boom ended, however, large landlords abandoned their workers, contracted peasants, and haciendas (often to the banks). Rural people either fled to Guayaquil or became a free peasantry out of necessity—that is, they occupied land in order to survive, at times paying nominal rents to what became bank-owned properties.

The collapse of cacao, then, briefly created a free peasantry with relatively uncontested access to land. This moment did not last long, however. By the early 1920s, partly because so much land was suddenly available after the collapse of cacao production and banana production was being threatened in Central America, several foreign fruit companies began exploring the possibility of acquiring large tracts of land and establishing banana plantations in Ecuador's coast. By the early to mid-1930s, the United Fruit Company had bought numerous properties, including what would become its main operation at Hacienda Tenguel, or what had been the largest cacao plantation in the world before the boom ended and a bank acquired the property. In this sense, United Fruit—along with other large banana companies—entered into a semi-abandoned zone covered with neglected cacao trees, dense jungle, and scattered groups of free peasants.

Like much of the coastal region, the southern coast where Hacienda Tenguel was located was only nominally integrated into the nation. There was almost no state presence in the 1930s and 1940s. United Fruit was forced to bring in everything by plane or boat, including facilities for banana production, a system of railroads that ran through the plantation, and materials for building roads, homes, a hospital, a Catholic church, the port, and even a movie theater. The company also imported people, including administrators, mechanics, agronomists, and other experts. Finding agricultural workers was difficult but aided by the fact that the collapse of the cacao economy had swelled Guayaquil with a rural poor who struggled to piece together a living in the city's growing slums. They had agricultural experience and were ready to work. Indeed, by the 1930s, many of these peasants-turned-urban-poor had been searching for some sort of stability for decades. Dislocated from highland haciendas, they had participated in the cacao boom as contracted peasants or agricultural workers, fled to Guayaquil during the collapse of the cacao economy, and now found themselves poised to ride the impending banana boom.

Rebellion from Within and Without

The banana boom would completely transform the coastal region by the end of the 1950s. It not only extended banana production onto previously uncultivated land but also expanded agriculture more generally, stimulating a massive migration from the highlands and the broader development of the region's roads, population centers, ports, and economy. The banana would quickly become Ecuador's primary export and economic engine. Extremely large, foreign-owned, haciendas like Tenguel would drive this process, even if they would never produce the majority of the country's bananas. As the epicenters of an expanding industry, they were not only the primary sites of banana production but also became regional anchors and major consumers of just about everything. They were markets in and of themselves, creating the need/opportunity for the emergence of local producers of varying sizes that supplied bananas, food, and services to these massive enterprises.

In this sense, haciendas such as Tenguel created an agrarian proletariat at the core of the plantation and a free peasantry on the margins of (what seemed to be) ever-expanding banana production. This was always a highly political process, one that United Fruit successfully negotiated during the 1940s and 1950s, even as workers posed a challenge from within and peasants continually threatened the enterprise from without. As we will see, however, by the end of the 1950s and start of the 1960s, the Panama disease threatened the enterprise, eventually leading the entire model to implode. It was during this moment—with workers laid off in mass, peasants invading land, and unrest throughout the country—that revolution appeared on the horizon throughout much of the rural coast. This chapter explores how this revolutionary impulse emerged, blossomed, and was eventually suppressed.

United Fruit would remain at the center of the process. The company was no stranger to rural unrest. The threat posed to its operations by workers in Central America had not only pushed United Fruit to explore places like Ecuador but also led the company to impose a quasi-Fordist system of labor control that offered relatively high wages and good benefits in exchange for political quiescence. Learning from past experience in Central America, United Fruit purposely hired men with families in Tenguel who lived in company housing, purchased food in company stores, attended the company church, visited the company hospital, traveled on company transportation, and participated in sports leagues and social clubs run by the company. Workers quickly got the message. Those who caused trouble not only lost a secure, well-paying, job with a range of benefits but also promptly saw their families evicted from homes and removed from the entire zone (by, yes, company police). Some "troublemakers" were even flown back to Guayaquil. For workers who had spent years, even decades, seeking some degree of security, this paternalistic model provided considerable incentive to conform to a fairly rigid work and life discipline.

United Fruit's overall control, combined with the isolated nature of the hacienda, also insured that external labor organizations were effectively barred from the zone. As one former labor leader from Guayaquil pointed out

> Sure, we had continual contact with some of the workers' leaders, but only when they came to Guayaquil. We were aware of what was going on in Tenguel because of the presence of a foreign company and the large number of workers. But it was impossible to promote our organization or our ideas among the mass of workers because we were prohibited from entering. The whole area was private property of the company. (Interview, 5 July 1996)

Wolf's outside leadership was essentially cut off during the 1940s and 1950s. United Fruit also tried to preempt internal or external efforts to organize the hacienda's more than two thousand workers by creating a company-controlled labor union. Labor unions began to form throughout Ecuador during the 1930s and then strengthened in the 1940s after the May Revolution (1944) and José María Velasco Ibarra's return to power.[1] The major national unions, along with the Socialist Party, all formed during a period that saw increased strikes and street demonstrations throughout much of the country. It was reasonable to assume a hacienda owned by a foreign multinational and employing thousands of workers might become a site of political unrest. United Fruit worked overtime to insure this did not happen.

During this same period, or roughly from the mid-1940s through the 1950s, as the company successfully managed its labor force and developed the largest banana plantation in the country, United Fruit nonetheless struggled to defend the property's boundaries from peasants. And it was not alone. The coast was defined by an ongoing battle between, on the one hand, relatively large landowners looking to expand banana production and, on the other, a free peasantry that was rapidly occupying "marginal" land. The conflict emerged and persisted in part because what started out as marginal land, and hence unobjectionable for peasants to occupy from the perspective of banana producers and state authorities at one moment, could subsequently become desirable from the perspective of an expanding banana industry. This was especially true as the Panama disease devastated existing plantations and producers sought to expand production onto disease-free lands. This meant peasant communities could live and prosper for ten, fifteen, or even twenty years on land that attracted little attention from regional authorities only to become "rebellious land invaders" in need of immediate eviction as their land became valued for banana production.

This posed a real problem for United Fruit at Tenguel because the property had fairly firm boundaries to the west, south, and north. It was only to the east, where coastal plain quickly turned into mountainous terrain unsuitable for banana production, that additional land existed. This poorer-quality land was more difficult to irrigate, but once the Panama disease began to affect the core of the hacienda in the late 1950s, the land—which represented close to one-third of the entire property—became highly valued.

In reality, the problems with neighboring peasants dated to the very origins of company's acquisition of the hacienda. In fact, almost immediately after purchasing Hacienda Tenguel in 1934, the company became embroiled in a struggle with a small group of peasants living in an area known as Mollepongo. The conflict, which lasted some twenty years, led to the formation of one of the first peasant organizations in Ecuador's southern coast—the Mollepongo Commune—and contributed to the demise of United Fruit's operations in Ecuador. The explanation as to why fewer than a dozen families were able to successfully invade more than three thousand hectares of land owned by a large, experienced, and well-connected multinational was, as Wolf suggests, rooted in the fact that this free peasantry was somewhat isolated from central authorities, including company police and state officials alike. But it was also because they became particularly skilled at negotiating what state power there was in a region that was slowly becoming integrated into the Ecuadorian nation. This is perhaps captured best by one of the leaders of the commune, José Llivichusca:

> The court said the [disputed] land belonged to [the United Fruit Company]. At this point the company thought it had won—that the conflict was over. It was just the beginning. We [the peasants] were not leaving vacant land that we had cleared and cultivated through our own efforts. We did not know what to do, so we waited, made contacts with [labor organizers]. Then we formed the Mollepongo Commune and renewed our claim with [another branch of government]. When this failed, we tried [another branch of government] (laughter). All along we controlled the land and kept on good terms with the local police. Only force could remove us from the land. (Interview, 22 April 1996)

This was to be an epic conflict started by peasants who occupied parts of Hacienda Tenguel after the collapse of cacao production but before United Fruit had purchased the property. When United Fruit arrived in the 1930s, it bought out all the peasants, some of whom then purchased shares in what was known as Hacienda Mollepongo. These shares gave them the right to possess (and through possession eventually own) parts of a property just to the east of Hacienda Tenguel. However, as the peasants freely admitted, and United Fruit documents subsequently confirmed, they not only began to plant the flatter portions near/in Hacienda Tenguel but also sold smaller sections to friends and family who promised to cultivate and populate the zone.

It was their growing numbers that motivated Hacienda Tenguel's new owner to act. In 1938, United Fruit initiated and won a court case against Victor Velez, a peasant who had bought shares in Mollepongo. The court's ruling forced Velez to legally recognize the company's dominion over the disputed property located on the frontiers of Tenguel-Mollepongo. Velez and the other Mollepongo shareholders were forced to sign rental agreements for the area they had under cultivation when the company arrived. These lands, according to the court, were located within the boundaries of Tenguel and not Mollepongo (UFC 9/5/1945, 4/40).[2]

The cultivations of the "mistaken" peasants were quite substantial. Between Torres, Barros, and Eras, they had close to seven thousand cacao trees, four thousand plantain trees, and significant quantities of cultivated pasture. This was at the time the contracts were signed. Bermeo's and Vergara's cultivations were at least as extensive and included coffee and a variety of fruits. By signing the contracts, the peasants explicitly recognized that (1) the lands in question belonged to the company and that they had no rights or claims to the area; and (2) the lands of Mollepongo and Tenguel had never overlapped. The shareholders of Mollepongo thus became tenants of Tenguel and, in so doing, affirmed United Fruit's legal ownership (UFC 4/40). Or so it seemed.

Despite signing the contracts, the peasants believed the lands were theirs by virtue of the fact that they had cleared and cultivated vacant forest. As José remembers, "We did not recognize the contracts even though we signed them. We needed time and wanted the company to leave us alone." The contracts, then, were signed in 1940 by a small and unorganized group of peasants who sought to avoid a conflict with a large company. Regardless of their legal status (shareholder, tenant, squatter), each held onto the idea that had brought them to the zone in the first place—owning their own piece of land. By 1945, this idea, combined with a strategic alliance with political activists from Guayaquil, would generate one of the first peasant organizations in the zone: the Mollepongo Commune.

The peasants' subsequent decision to form a commune—as opposed to some other form of organization—did not occur by accident. Of the nearly eight hundred popular organizations that formed during the 1930s, close to six hundred were communes (Torre 1993: chap. 2). This wave of organizing was propelled by the Law of Commune Organization in 1937. The expressed goal and motivation behind the law was to extend the state's control beyond the parish head and into smaller population centers. The myriad rural hamlets and communities that existed throughout Ecuador were instructed to appeal to the state and become communes—a geopolitical form of organization that would formally establish the existence of rural populations and legalize their relationship to the state (Barsky 1984: 31–33).

Communes were clearly an attempt on the part of the state to extend its administrative and legal reach into those rural areas that up until the 1930s had remained outside its control. However, because the state lacked the practical resources to move further into rural areas, it was forced to pass laws whose effectiveness depended on the active participation of rural groups in their own integration. The multiplicity of state ministries, agencies, commissions, and boards that were based in either Quito or Guayaquil were quite often working through the same local official. The local Teniente Político, as well as the provincial Intendente, could and did receive orders from a variety of government branches, including the president himself. These local state figures wore many hats and had considerable control in deciding which Quito-based ministry, agency, or actor would get to speak and act in rural areas (and when, how, and to what extent). Although United Fruit used its own police force to deal with plantation workers at the core of the property, the company was forced to rely on local state authorities from the small town of Balao in order to handle problems on the margins of Hacienda Tenguel.

Both the court case and the legal formation of the commune led the peasants to make contacts with labor activists from the CTE/FPTG.[3] These contacts provided important advice and legal aid, though no boots on the ground. National labor organizations did not have the resources to develop a sustained presence in rural zones during this period. Still, the information and legal resources provided by national popular organizations often proved decisive.[4] Despite all this activity, United Fruit had several reasons to be quite confident. Its ownership of the land seemed indisputable. The leaders of the commune had signed contracts recognizing the company's ownership over the disputed property. As *comuneros*, they were trying to appropriate the very same lands they were renting as tenants. From the company's (legal) perspective, the commune's formation and movement onto hacienda lands was no different than the case they had won against Victor Velez eight years earlier. Legally, it mattered little that Velez was an individual and the commune an organization.

Yet, during the next decade, as the peasants became experts in manipulating networks of power in Quito and Guayaquil, they never forgot one important fact that ultimately turned the tide in their favor. Local control could be decisive in a zone where national authorities exercised a partial and uneven authority. Legal rights and influential contacts in Quito could be made meaningless by a stubborn Teniente Político or Intendente on the local-regional level. In theory, a call from the company to the responsible ministry in Quito would result in a telegram ordering the Teniente or Intendente to carry out a particular action (i.e., eviction of squatters). Yet, this chain of command almost never worked, or at least not in the way the company envisioned. The conflict would fester for years without any action on behalf of United Fruit to remove the peasants. As it did, the peasant community grew and became more entrenched. The peasants developed extensive cultivations, houses, and a town center and even claimed (and prevented company employees from working) a portion of land that United Fruit had planted with bananas (José Llivichusca, interview, 8 November 1996).

By May 1947, inaction on the part of local police forces had become a chronic problem for the company and one that seemed to be worsening as the peasants' hold on the land grew more secure. When serious action was ordered, it was never completed. On 7 May, for example, the Ministry of Social Welfare telegraphed the Intendente from the province of Guayas, instructing him to send sufficient troops to control the intruders and take them to jail. But just when the ministry seemed determined to resolve the problem in favor of the company, it received additional reports about the peasants' increased activities. After years of handling the problem, the Ministry of Social Welfare suddenly declared the issue was now under the jurisdiction of the Ministry of Government. It was no longer a social but rather a legal problem that should be handled by the police. The Ministry of Government immediately telegraphed the Intendente, instructing him to send troops in order to rectify the problem. Claiming he had not received either telegraph (from either ministry), the Intendente insisted he had talked personally with President Velasco, who ordered him not to comply with the orders (UFC 5/47).

By the end of March 1948, the company was faced with an impossible situation. The peasants were becoming more assertive in terms of both their actions on the land and their legal-bureaucratic maneuvers. They had managed to subvert the most recent report/finding while initiating another—through the Board of Peasant Affairs—that would be authored by their own lawyer. The many faces of the Ministry of Social Welfare were hopeless; the Ministry of Government, while somewhat more sympathetic, had shown relatively little desire to become involved in the problem; the new president, whose "attitude on matters which imply responsibility . . . has been disappointing," certainly did not want to evict a group of peasants in favor of a foreign company (UFC 3/16/1948). And although the US Embassy had not fully been utilized, the threat had been made. The conflict was over, the peasants had won close to three thousand hectares of land, and the company suffered a notable defeat.[5]

The loss of land in the late 1940s had only a limited impact on United Fruit's operation. The company had no serious problems with workers, and through the late 1950s, Tenguel was the largest single producer in the country, exporting some eighty thousand stems of banana a week during its peak. By the mid-1950s, however, when the Panama disease started affecting production levels and the company sought to extend production into disease-free areas that were previously considered marginal/unsuitable, the loss of land to the Mollepongo Commune took on new meaning. More than this, Mollepongo—and the widespread formation of communes more generally—represented a dangerous precedent that provided a path forward for a rural poor whose primary goal was land acquisition. Using methods that were remarkably similar to those adopted in Mollepongo, peasants in the zone of Brasil stopped the company's efforts to expand at a moment when the long-term survival of the overall enterprise required the development of new banana groves. Mollepongo was not the end. It was the beginning.

A subsequent land invasion at Shumiral proved to be the most devastating from the perspective of United Fruit. Here was a community that was formed not by smallholders attempting to retain land they had been working for years but rather by ex-workers that United Fruit had been forced to lay off in the mid-1950s because production was down and continued expansion made difficult by neighboring peasants. In other words, when United Fruit sought to extend production to the northeast of its property, it found ex-workers had illegally occupied the land, planted crops, and developed a community called Shumiral. These workers-turned-peasants did not argue the land was somehow outside the boundaries of Tenguel or that they had some sort of legal claim to the property. This was an invasion justified through the moral-nationalist argument that they, as Ecuadorian peasants, had the right to occupy uncultivated land owned by a foreign company. As one of the more open land invasions during the period immediately preceding agrarian reform, the conflict in Shumiral—and what it foreshadowed—posed a much greater symbolic threat to the company's entire enterprise.

The invasion was a sign of things to come. In 1960, after five years of struggle, the Colonia Agrícola Shumiral would claim victory against a major multinational. Forced to sell more than 2,500 hectares for a token price, the United Fruit Company was one step closer to abandoning direct production in Ecuador. Because the invasion had been orchestrated by a small group of ex-workers and a relentless lawyer, the victory in Shumiral provided workers at the core of the hacienda with a dramatic example of the possibilities opened up by organization and unity. No one had ever imagined the company could be beaten by workers. Shumiral demonstrated otherwise.

The victory in Shumiral, which came at the precise moment when the bulk of the labor force was being laid off in Tenguel because of the impact of the Panama disease, provided both example and method. If ex-workers could defeat United Fruit and obtain marginal sections of the hacienda, what was stopping them from acquiring the core of the property as well? Most of the labor force had been laid off by 1960, were threatened with eviction, and were living in a desperate state. They were also largely on their own. Labor activists from the CTE/FPTG lent encouragement and legal aid, sectors within the state made promises, and the victory in Shumiral provided a close-to-home example. Ultimately, however, it was the workers' own history of union struggle and organization that provided the basis from which they would confront both the company and the state—now more as peasants in search of land than as workers demanding better wages and working conditions.

The full-scale invasion of Hacienda Tenguel in March 1962 could be immediately distinguished from other similar protests along a number of lines. It was the first full takeover of a major hacienda. The size, productivity, and foreign ownership of Tenguel only added to its importance. Tenguel immediately became the country's most urgent current event. Unlike strikes or isolated protests, the land invasion could not be easily resolved by the state. Increasing wages or firing a particularly oppressive supervisor was not the answer. The conflict was not about wages, the labor code, or working conditions. It was first and foremost about the land. In this sense, the invasion of Hacienda Tenguel—foreshadowed by events in Mollepongo and Shumiral—signaled the gradual shift away from labor conflicts and

the beginning of a period characterized by land struggles. Workers who had once been thoroughly dependent on their employer—
à la Wolf—were now becoming a peasantry in search of land, and
one that had little to lose. It also represented the definitive end of
enclave-style production, the beginning of agrarian reform, and the
slow emergence of contract farming in Ecuador.

Similar land conflicts would take place throughout Ecuador in the
1960s and 1970s. They were both stimulated by, and gave life to, the
movement for agrarian reform. Tenguel, first as a "communist invasion" and then as the country's first agrarian reform project, occupied a central place in the initial set of agrarian reform debates. What
did the invasion at Tenguel mean in terms of communism and agrarian reform? If workers were given land and agrarian reform implemented at Tenguel, would communism spread throughout Ecuador?
Would a successful invasion only encourage other workers to take
similar action? Did events in Tenguel signify the need for agrarian
reform on a national level? Would a national agrarian reform—by
addressing rural inequality and redistributing land—eliminate the
allure of communism and the need for land invasions? These were
the kinds of questions, and ideological boundaries, being raised in relation to events in Tenguel—a full two years before the first agrarian
reform law would be passed in 1964.

The invasion itself had been a long time coming. Mass firings
began in 1959, and the vast majority of workers were unemployed
by 1960, facing eviction, and unable to find work in the zone—in part
because they had transformed the company union into a militant
organization and were in effect blackballed by local employers. By
the second half of 1961, the company had been forced to allow the
labor union, recently transformed into a cooperative, to work part of
the hacienda. This fueled the hope that United Fruit would sell the
property to the union-turned-cooperative. State-controlled agrarian
reform was still several years away, and the idea of a worker-owned
and managed hacienda did not seem unreasonable; it also did not fall
outside the parameters of the ongoing debate over agrarian reform.
In addition, Cooperative Juan Quirumbay had developed contacts
with sympathetic state officials who were involved in negotiations
with United Fruit over the sale of Hacienda Tenguel.

From the workers' perspective, there had been no need to take
action because the state was going to resolve the entire mess. The
problem, however, was that United Fruit was actively experimenting
with a variety of arrangements that directly threatened the workers'
access to land and/or employment. Most importantly, United Fruit

sold sections of the hacienda to four or five large capitalists who provided the ex-workers with little employment and poor wages. The workers feared this represented a sign of things to come. As national capitalists, the buyers did not face the same constraints as United Fruit. They began to harass the workers and train a private police force on Tenguel's soccer field. When direct intimidation failed, they tried other tactics, including the placement of spies in the cooperative's leadership and a smear campaign. Yet, it was their final ultimatum that provoked the invasion. Two months before the invasion, local capitalists—tacitly supported by the company, sectors within the state, and armed thugs—threatened to remove the workers from the hacienda. They set the date of eviction for 30 March. That the workers invaded the hacienda just several days before their scheduled departure was hardly a coincidence.

Reform or Revolution

The takeover of Tenguel, first by groups of peasants on the margins of the property and then by workers at the core, represented the early stages of a process that was largely defined by land invasions. It would consume and transform the coastal region in the 1960s and 1970s. Most immediately, the invasions helped bring about an end to enclave production in Ecuador. With remarkable speed and uniformity, foreign-owned companies were forced out of direct production throughout the coast in the early 1960s (Larrea 1987). As a result, foreign banana companies, particularly United Fruit, began to rely more heavily on Central American bananas for supply, creating a crisis within Ecuador's industry and exposing its vulnerability as a reserve supplier. In other words, a series of factors—including the withdrawal of foreign banana companies from direct production, crisis within the industry, an early wave of land invasions, and the inevitability and undetermined nature of agrarian reform—created a climate in which the range of political and economic outcomes appeared open-ended. Anything seemed possible.

Yet, although land conflicts would define the coast during the 1960s and 1970s and produce energy, excitement, and several regional peasant organizations, they never coalesced into something that could be called a coherent movement on even a regional level. The hundreds of conflicts that dotted the region would remain, at their core, fairly localized affairs. The fact that they were occurring everywhere at the same time did not necessarily translate into a larger movement, at least not in the sense of one with the capacity to shape the broader contours of state power. To be sure, peasants drew on support from regional-national organizations and learned from the examples of those who had come before them, but this was a politics that was fundamentally localized due in large part to the contradictory nature of agrarian reform during this period.

On the one hand, during and after the crisis in banana production in the mid-1960s, a central goal of the Ecuadorian state was to revive the banana industry and export agriculture more broadly. Here, the interests of domestic capitalists and the state coincided to ensure that the kind of large-scale land invasion we saw in Tenguel, whereby hundreds of workers seized control over thousands of hectares of high quality land, would not be repeated. Such efforts were contained partly by repression. Even in the case of Tenguel, where workers had the benefit of media attention and foreign ownership, the police forcefully took control of the property in 1963 after a military regime came to power on the national level and sought to "restore order." Workers were then incorporated into cooperatives that, over the next two decades, essentially collapsed, forcing cooperative members to sell their lands to surrounding capitalists who then reestablished banana plantations. Even under the best of circumstances, the power of well-connected landowners, combined with the state's need for export revenue, insured that peasants were not going to acquire the best land.

On the other hand, and part of the reason repression was relatively limited, sectors within the state did signal there was a more progressive side to agrarian reform, one that was to be carried out by the landless themselves through the invasion of marginal lands. Agrarian reform in Ecuador never "gave" land to the rural poor in the coast in the sense of the state identifying uncultivated or underused land and turning it over to those who needed it. Rather, an unspoken formula, shaped by laws and policies, emerged. Peasant-workers would identify vacant land; organize; occupy the land; legally form a commune, colonia, cooperative, or whatever the latest vehicle for acquiring land happened to be; and push their cause. If they selected marginal land owned by a weak or absentee landowner, could quickly establish a physical presence on the property, had good connections, and knew how to navigate the political system, then they stood a chance of success. If, however, they miscalculated, and occupied the land of an owner who was well connected, then their removal could be swift and violent.

The point here is less about understanding why and how certain groups of peasants successfully acquired land, and why others failed, than it is about the mode of politics embodied in this emerging process. Most peasants correctly saw the state as a potential ally. It could be unresponsive, even repressive, but it could also be supportive and was the place peasants turned to when trying to acquire land and other resources. The state's relative receptiveness was, of course, the product of a long history of struggle by peasants and others.

In this sense, agrarian reform in Ecuador's coast accomplished what many of its moderate designers intended. It routed political unrest through reformist channels managed by the state and, as a result, had the effect of undermining revolutionary impulses. The question for most peasants during this period revolved around not how to capture state power in the revolutionary sense but rather how to access sectors within the state in order to facilitate the acquisition of land. Had the Ecuadorian state simply been repressive, or entirely unresponsive to peasant demands, in effect making access to state power impossible or meaningless, it is quite possible such conflicts could have led down more revolutionary paths. This did not happen. Agrarian reform led local groups of peasants to organize in relatively small numbers to occupy (marginal) land, but it did not encourage large-scale organizing against the state or the region's landed class. Instead, by establishing a fairly formulaic, if difficult and uncertain, path toward land acquisition, it drew peasants further into—and invested them in—a state that could at times tip the scales in their favor.

Nevertheless, the fact that this conflict-laden process of agrarian reform would ultimately deliver fairly firm control over the best land to domestic capitalists while containing peasant political unrest was far from clear between the mid-1960s, when democracy returned to Ecuador, and the late 1970s, when agrarian reform had largely lost momentum. In the southern coast, land invasions would continue through the mid-1970s, often under the guidance of leaders from Mollepongo and Shumiral. This meant not only that many of the region's peasants were formally organized but also that, by the mid-1970s, one of the most militant regional peasant organizations in the country would emerge from the region—the Union Regional de Organizaciónes Campesinas del Litoral Ecuador (Regional Union of Peasant Organizations of the Litoral, Ecuador—UROCAL).

Yet, as UROCAL grew in importance, with respect to both local organizations and its ability to make demands on the state, the regional movement itself weakened. More peasants were organized than ever before, but cooperatives, communes, and workers' associations weakened as their overall orientation, internal dynamics, and relationships with outside groups were transformed. The focus of these local organizations no longer revolved around the acquisition of land but instead centered on the struggle to obtain resources to cultivate crops and build communities.

In trying to meet the needs of its base organizations, UROCAL, now led by a younger generation of professional leaders, consciously struggled against several problems, including the disintegration of base organizations, their control by the state, the bureaucratization of leaders, and internal stratification. The leaders focused on a concrete set of problems—credit and commercialization—to strengthen not only UROCAL and the base organizations/communities it served but also broader efforts at political transformation. Nevertheless, whereas a local politics of land invasion could be tied to a broader politics of liberation, the translation between local needs and large-scale political mobilization became much more difficult as peasants became enmeshed in state development projects and the politics of credit and commercialization. As a new model of state-led development emerged, peasants went from being reluctant rebels struggling for land to state clients petitioning for credit and other resources.

In the end, then, this contradictory model of development would transform both the region's agrarian proletariat and its landowning/middle peasantry. On the one hand, agrarian reform—and the class struggle embodied in it—delivered the best land to domestic capitalists who reestablished (smaller) banana plantations that contracted with multinationals such as United Fruit and Standard Fruit (now Chiquita and Dole). Contracting had a variety of impacts, not least of which was allowing multinationals to retain control of the industry without assuming any of the risks associated with direct production. But perhaps most importantly, by putting banana production in the hands of domestic producers, and insuring labor unions would not reemerge on much smaller plantations, the system of contracting produced a labor force that was both highly exploited and politically fragmented. Former United Fruit workers, then, who had invaded the hacienda, acquired land, and subsequently lost that land through a failed agrarian reform process, now saw their sons and daughters working on local plantations under conditions far worse than they experienced on Hacienda Tenguel in the 1940s and 1950s. By the end of the 1960s, there were almost no agrarian labor unions in Ecuador's coast, a condition that has not changed much in the ensuing decades. Wolf's description of a dependent landless class without much tactical power vis-à-vis their employers was sadly prescient in the case of Ecuador's coast (1969: 290).

On the other hand, agrarian reform, which in many ways was implemented by Ecuador's rural poor, also produced something of a "middle" peasantry with reasonably secure access to (marginal) land and a degree of autonomy from large landowners. In the coast, however, such autonomy did not so much translate into tactical power vis-à-vis large landowners, as Wolf might suggest. Instead, peasant autonomy translated into a deepening marginality characterized by the small-scale production of cacao and food crops, which in itself required constant appeals to the state. This model become increasingly untenable under neoliberalism from the 1980s onward, largely because what few state resources flowed into agriculture went toward the capital-intensive export sector. Peasants were left fighting over crumbs and were not so much battling against large landowners—who operated in an almost distinct agricultural sphere—as they were struggling to get basic resources from the state in order to sustain small-scale production and maintain their tenuous hold on the land.

And they were not alone, which partially explains why much of the Latin American countryside was (relatively) subdued politically in the 1980s and early 1990s. Neoliberalism produced an economic crisis in the countryside that might have produced more immediate unrest had it not also generated a political paralysis that undermined the type of revolutionary politics analyzed by Wolf in *Peasant Wars*—that is, a politics aimed at taking state power. Agrarian reform in Ecuador during the 1960s and 1970s provided peasants with resources and (inconsistent) allies within the government while drawing them into the state and nation. This was an uneven and conflict-filled process, but one that could provide important resources, including access to land.

With neoliberalism, however, the positive (if inconsistent) role played by the state eroded, a process that was bolstered by an ideological project aimed at denigrating and dismantling the state. The broad and hegemonic nature of neoliberalism in the 1980s and 1990s not only made it difficult to analytically connect the series of forces that were destroying the Latin American countryside but also impeded the ability of social actors to name the problem, shape the contours of the debate, and forge an anti-neoliberal bloc. This project was also inhibited by the widespread disillusionment with the state as a potentially positive force in people's lives. Put another way, working to influence or capture state power seemed not only far-fetched in the absence of viable social movements (Wolf's "outside leadership") but also pointless in a context where neoliberalism retained an air of inevitably and the state had lost much of its capacity to intervene on behalf of working people. This was certainly true of Ecuador's coast.

Yet, this process also helps explain why, starting in the mid-1990s, there was such a powerful backlash against neoliberalism. In Ecuador, as in much of Latin America, this uprising would not be limited to the countryside and would be infused by an ethnic-indigenous politics that would have been difficult for Wolf to imagine in the 1960s, but is nonetheless only understandable in terms the "complex field of power" in which it evolved over the course of several decades. In the case of Ecuador, this did not produce a peasant revolution, but it did generate an anti-neoliberal bloc that partially captured state power and rolled back some of the excesses of the neoliberal period. What the rise of this Left in Ecuador and much of Latin America required—as Wolf suggested—was leadership in the form of organizations and parties with the capacity to mobilize, shape state power, and challenge capital at the national level. As *Peasant Wars* suggests, and as the case of Ecuador demonstrates, this level of political cohesion only happens rarely.

Steve Striffler is Director of the Labor Resource Center and Professor of Anthropology at the University of Massachusetts Boston. He writes on labor and the Left in Latin America and the United States. His first book, *In the Shadows of State and Capital* (2001), examines the United Fruit Company and peasant-worker struggle in Ecuador. His second book, *Chicken: The Dangerous Transformation of America's Favorite Food* (2005), explores the history of the poultry industry and Latin American immigration into the Southern United States. His latest book is *Solidarity: Latin America and the US Left in the Era of Human Rights* (2019).

Notes

1. Velasco Ibarra was Ecuador's ultimate populist and was elected president five times between 1934 and 1968. Though he was by no means a leftist, his rhetoric, energy, and policies could nonetheless briefly open up space for popular mobilization.
2. UFC refers to a small collection of United Fruit Company correspondences.
3. The Confederación de Trabajadores del Ecuador (CTE) was formed in 1944 and was the Communist Party's trade union. The Federación Provincial del Trabajadores del Guayas (FPTG) was essentially the coastal/regional expression of the CTE and one of the most militant working-class organizations in Ecuador at the time.
4. It was leaders from the CTE and the FPTG who helped the peasants form a commune and then pushed their case through several different bureaucracies. It is important to note that all these organizations—the CTE, the FPTG, and the Mollepongo

Commune—formed during the organizing surge surrounding the May Revolution of 1944 and Velasco's return to power. It was no coincidence that the key moments of the Mollepongo conflict coincided with Velasco's second administration (1945–1947).

5. A tentative agreement was reached, the peasants remained on the disputed territory, and the commune was finally legalized in 1955.

References

Barsky, Osvaldo. 1984. *La reforma agraria ecuatoriano*. Quito: CEN-FLACSO.

Chiriboga, Manuel. 1980. *Jornaleros y gran propietarios en 135 años de exportación cacaotera (1790–1925)*. Quito: Consejo Provincial Pichincha.

Larrea M., Carlos, ed. 1987. *El Banano en el Ecuador: Transnacionales, modernización y subdesarrollo*. Quito: FLACSO.

Striffler, Steve. 2002. *In the Shadow of State and Capital: The United Fruit Company, Popular Struggle, and Agrarian Restructuring in Ecuador, 1900–1995*. Durham, NC: Duke University Press.

Torre, Carlos de la. 1993. *La seducción velasquista*. Quito: Ediciones Libri Mundi.

Wolf, Eric. 1969. *Peasant Wars of the Twentieth Century*. New York: Harper & Row.

— Chapter 3 —

AT THE CROSSROADS OF POWER
Lesley Gill

For those on the left, the countryside was where the revolution would be made . . . How this would happen, through what organizational channels, with what alliances, with what leadership, and with what strategies, were subjects of acrimonious debate. That a revolution was possible, that it would include the peasantry, and that much of it would be fought in the countryside was, however, not a subject for serious doubt.
—William Roseberry, "Beyond the Agrarian Question in Latin America"

Peasant Wars of the Twentieth Century appeared in a moment of social and political ferment, following the success of the Cuban Revolution and during the Vietnam War and decolonization movements around the world. Although Wolf viewed peasants as fundamentally tragic figures, he was optimistic about their capacity to force power holders everywhere to yield "to human effort to widen participation and knowledge" (1969: 301). As the epigraph suggests, many academics, policy makers, and Latin American leftists shared his 1960s-era confidence in the revolutionary potential of peasants and the possibilities of social transformation, even as violence and the expansion of agrarian capitalism pushed the imagined support base of rural revolutionaries into the cities. Their optimism stands out against the contemporary eclipse of revolution, which is nowadays widely perceived as neither possible nor desirable.

Wolf located peasants within spatially and historically constituted fields of capitalist power in which various categories of people played different parts in revolutionary movements. He focused on the relationships between diverse groups—peasants, merchants, workers, landlords, soldiers, and so forth—and the connections that

entwined them in "webs of group relations" within states and un-
evenly developing capitalist economies (Wolf 1956) in which "the
coexistence of old and new strata, of regions dominated by the past
and regions in the grip of the future, spell trouble for society as a
whole" (1969: 283). "Rootless intellectuals," for example, linked rural
people to political parties and social movements beyond the confines
of villages; reformist Islam and urban migration brought Algerian
peasants and town-based elites together, while returning labor migrants imported socialist thinking from France to Algeria; and the
combustible mix of industrial worker strikes, peasant uprisings, and
soldier desertions from the army ignited the Russian Revolution.
Wolf understood the importance of broad-based alliances for scaling
up protest, and he suggested, "It is probably not so much the growth
of an industrial proletariat . . . which produces revolutionary activity,
as the development of an industrial workforce still closely geared to
life in the villages" (292). Such analytic and political commitments
stood in contrast to many nonanthropologists who ignored peasants and deployed teleological understandings of Marxism to privi-
lege the urban working class as the protagonist of revolution. They
also differed from his peers in anthropology who turned away from
politics and proffered analyses of the putatively timeless, bounded
"cultures" of non-Western peoples, with scant concern for the larger
social formations in which their lives unfolded.

Wolf wanted to nudge anthropology into a deeper engagement
with power, and his emphasis on fields of power and webs of social relationships suggested ways to move beyond many of the dichotomies that framed mid-twentieth-century social science, such
as peasant/proletarian, rural/urban, and domestic/foreign spatial
divides. Yet, as a peasant insurgency battled the United States in
Vietnam and the "agrarian question" loomed on the Latin American
political agenda after the 1959 Cuban Revolution, Wolf, like state
officials, academics, students, political parties, militaries, and guerrillas in Latin America and the United States, was most attuned to
the countryside. He did not draw out a deeper analysis of the connections between rural rebels and urban dwellers or examine forms
of protest adopted by people in the towns and cities. Similarly, although questions of boundaries were central to his work, and he recognized the significance of regional differences, Wolf devoted little
attention to how capital accumulation configured distinct regional
webs of power, how regions were related, or what sorts of coalitions
across space and economic sector were central to advancing transformative social change.[1]

The sociologist Jeffrey Paige subsequently took Wolf to task. He insisted peasants were too individualistic and competitive to act collectively and that agricultural workers in export enclaves represented the vanguard of Third World revolutions. Because they labored together, agricultural workers could only challenge employers by organizing collectively, and they were, according to Paige, more radical than their industrial counterparts in developed capitalist countries (1975: 1–71). Paige's concern with rural proletarians and export enclaves raised questions about the heterogeneity of existing social relations, their political implications, and regional variation. Yet his economic determinism, which assigned a political consciousness to workers based on their role in the economy, undermined his discussion of enclaves and social movements. *Peasant Wars of the Twentieth Century* never capitulated to economism. It addressed fundamental political concerns, especially how the organizational and material base of social life facilitated the cultivation of solidarity and collective resistance. Wolf also remained open to contingency, fluid social relationships, and changing alliances within historically and spatially created fields of power.

This chapter builds on that legacy. It focuses on the making and unmaking of a militant, heterogeneous working class in Barrancabermeja, an oil export enclave in Colombia's Middle Magdalena region, and how shifting class dynamics shaped modes of struggle and forms of organization. It argues that foreign-dominated export enclaves and their working people, who typically had ties to the countryside, were important, albeit overlooked, sources of militancy in mid-twentieth-century Latin America. As several scholars have shown, export enclaves formed the bedrock of radical movements whose influence was felt well beyond isolated zones of commodity production (Bergquist 1986; Forster 2001; John 2009; Santiago 2006), and the social life of enclaves was always much richer than the clash of foreign bosses and male proletarians described by modernization theory and the dependency school.[2] Several studies demonstrate the first generation of workers moved in and out of subsistence agriculture, and subsequent generations engaged in "informal" economic activities in enclaves that had become urban centers, complicating understandings of labor as limited to an industrial proletariat (Forster 2001; Gill 2016; LeGrand 1998; Salas 2009; Striffler 2002, 2004). My focus is therefore not on peasants or proletarians but on labor, understood as differently labeled working people engaged in making, unmaking, and remaking social relationships within interconnected fields of state, capital, and imperial power that transcend rural-urban dichotomies. Labor is conceptualized as a political formation, one that includes multiple ways of working (e.g., rural petty commodity producers, urban waged and unwaged workers), as well as the power-laden process by which working people are categorized, unified, and divided (Carbonella and Kasmir 2014).

The chapter asks how the struggles and compromises between labor, dominant groups, and the state shaped forms of protest and configured space in Barrancabermeja, probing how power-laden social relationships become entwined more tightly in some places than others, and how novel combinations of people, places, and power give rise to different political possibilities (Kasmir and Gill 2018). It then examines how, following the nationalization of the Colombian oil industry, working people initiated a new protest modality—the civic strike—that built on older forms of struggle. Civic strikes cut across the grain of social fragmentation and laid the groundwork for a powerful civic-popular movement in the 1970s that spanned the city and the country. Just as this movement was attaining more institutional representation and starting to scale up its power, however, it was destroyed in the early twenty-first century by a violent, far-right counterinsurgent movement that ushered in neoliberalism.

The chapter first places Barrancabermeja within the context of the development of other late-nineteenth- and early twentieth-century foreign-dominated export enclaves in Latin America. It considers how these places were connected to larger fields of power, how new labor arrangements formed that transcended peasant/proletarian dichotomies, and how working people mounted resistance with sometimes far-reaching implications. It then examines the mid-twentieth-century emergence of the "civic strike" as a new form of popular protest and explores the demise of Barrancabermeja's militant social movement at the turn of the millennium amid a maelstrom of political violence and neoliberal restructuring. Although the devastation wrecked in Barrancabermeja was extreme, it was not unique, and its experience raises concerns about the future Wolf could not have foreseen.

Spaces of Power

In early twentieth-century Colombia, new export enclaves emerged amid a tenuous peace following the conclusion of the Thousand Days' War (1899–1902) and spurred the growth of commodity production, exemplifying the uneven spread of capitalist development across

Colombia. Coffee cultivation exploded in the central and western highlands; cattle ranching expanded on the Caribbean coast; sugar cane developed in the Cauca Valley; and foreign-controlled banana and oil enclaves arose on the Caribbean coast and in the Middle Magdalena Valley, respectively. The commodity boom and the Conservative government's willingness to finance road, rail, and port projects gave rise to new spatial configurations of land, labor, and power that were tied to regional dynamics. The configurations represented variegated forms of spatial enclosure and concentrations of people and capital investment, where intense social struggles over the control of space, the nature of work, and the quality of life operated through uneven connections to wider networks of political control and violence. They exemplify what Frederick Cooper calls "lumps"—places where power coalesces and where social relations are dense (2005: 91–92), and where different political processes unfold through combined forms of interdependence (Kasmir and Gill 2018).

Before the twentieth century, Barrancabermeja was a sleepy hamlet on the middle stretch of the Magdalena River, surrounded by dense tropical forest. The Colombian government transformed it forever when, in 1919, it awarded a concession of more than three hundred thousand hectares to the Tropical Oil Company (TROCO), a subsidiary of the Standard Oil Corporation, which developed it as a major oil export operation.[3] The emergent enclave drew impoverished peasant migrants—mostly young men and some single women—and itinerant merchants in search of a future. They came initially from the Afro-Colombian Caribbean coastal provinces and the Antioquian highlands, where lighter-skinned individuals were considered "more robust of body and keen of mind" than the local population (Gibb and Knowlton 1956: 374). While young men cleared jungle, opened access roads, constructed infrastructure, and eventually labored in the oil fields, women typically worked as laundresses, cooks, and sex workers. Working people increasingly found themselves pitted against the managers and supervisors of the corporation over labor relations, living conditions, land tenure, and petty commerce.

For the first generation of peasants who migrated to Barrancabermeja between the 1920s and 1950, the rupture between subsistence agriculture and wage labor was not complete. Capitalist discipline had not yet become an integral and "normal" part of their lives, as it would become for male children who followed their fathers into the oil industry. First-generation male migrants combined wage labor for the oil company with subsistence agriculture on small parcels carved from frontier land. The cultivation of food crops kept proletarianization at bay. It served as a defense against unstable working conditions, acted as a buffer against high prices in company stores, and permitted settlers to retain a modicum of control over their labor and daily lives. Migrants' occupation of frontier lands, however, immediately brought them into conflict with the corporation, which claimed exclusive access to the subsoil. TROCO sought to guarantee itself a workforce by driving cultivators off and depriving them of the opportunity to feed themselves. To do so, it instructed corporate overseers to issue passes to those settlers whose land rights it recognized and to persecute those who defied corporate domination. Not surprisingly, constant conflicts erupted between the company and rural people over land claims.

Migrants also protested the abysmal labor and living conditions they endured in the oil fields and work camps. Diseases, lack of adequate health facilities and housing, and arduous working conditions, which began and ended with the blow of a whistle, exacted a heavy toll that was exasperated by the stark differences that separated impoverished Colombians from a small, transient group of white US and Canadian staff. TROCO's foreign managers and skilled workers lived in well-appointed neighborhoods—complete with swimming pools, a golf course, a social club, and a hospital—that were segregated from the rudimentary accommodations for Colombian migrants. The lines of segregation demarcated deep class, race, and national divisions, and they stoked resentment of the gringo overlords.

The enclave quickly became a symbol of national subservience to a foreign power and attracted itinerant labor organizers, such as Maria Cano, Raúl Eduardo Mahécha, and Ignacio Torres Giraldo, who were motivated by the chance to target the domination of a US corporation. They founded labor unions, organized strikes, and spoke out in defense of working people up and down the Magdalena River, from the United Fruit Company banana zone on the Caribbean coast through the oil fields of Barrancabermeja to the Girardot dockworkers hundreds of miles inland. The activists were in touch with various political currents such as socialism, communism, liberalism, and anti-imperialist nationalism, which began to circulate among working people. In Barrancabermeja, the lawyer Eduardo Mahécha, a member of the Partido Socialista Revolucionario, reached out to peasant colonizers by opening a store where they could purchase low-cost necessities and circumvent TROCO's high-priced company store. He also offered his legal services to oil workers and, in 1922, founded the Unión Sindical Obrera (USO), a labor union that soon attracted thousands of people and became a defining force in both Barrancabermeja and Colombia. These early organizational initiatives built on the entanglements of subsistence cultivators and oil workers and drew the working population of Barrancabermeja into a broader web of popular power.

Subsistence cultivators, wage laborers, and petty merchants from different regional backgrounds united around a common desire to exercise control over the conditions of work—how, when, with whom, and where. Together, they shaped the modes of struggle and oppositional thinking that undergirded the first major strikes that rocked Barrancabermeja in 1924 and 1927. Oil workers advanced a series of demands through the USO, including wage increases, improvements in food and hygiene, an eight-hour workday, and Sunday as a day of rest, but they also supported the land rights of rural cultivators and backed the desire of petty merchants to sell consumer goods in the enclave, rejecting TROCO's claim to monopolize land and commerce. In turn, rural cultivators donated food—yuca, plantains, squash, and rice—to soup kitchens set up to feed striking workers, and merchants contributed to a strike fund. Sex workers, who often formed long-term relationships with oil workers, also worked in soup kitchens and participated in food distribution during strikes. Thus, even as some migrants organized as "workers" and rattled the central government with their labor demands, they projected their growing power in support of peasants and merchants, whose interests they shared (Vega et al. 2009). Backing the land claims of rural cultivators blended easily with demands for labor rights because oil workers were either semi-proletarianized peasants or recently dispossessed from the land. Similarly, because oil workers—like other working people in Barrancabermeja—objected to the high prices charged in the company store, they easily supported the efforts of petty merchants to sell their goods in the enclave.

The occupational and regional differences among migrant workers were less fraught than the divisions between Colombians and gringos. The disparity between Colombians engaged in hard, dirty, dangerous work, housed in overcrowded works camps, and controlled by passes and North American supervisors cosseted within a sumptuous residential setting nurtured opposition. Yet the first generation of working people did not have a common set of traditions and practices on which to draw. They had to build new relationships and understandings in Barrancabermeja. Their task was facilitated by the rotating TROCO personnel who spoke Spanish poorly, if at all, participated little in the social life of Colombians, and did not share the same cultural beliefs and assumptions as rural migrants, all of which freed migrants from the ties of deference, obedience, clientelism, and religious moralism that undermined working-class solidarity elsewhere (e.g., Bergquist 1978; Farnsworth-Alvear 2000). The castigating sermons of the Catholic Church were largely absent in the oil port, and there was no entrenched rural oligarchy wielding authority. In addition, the Liberal-Conservative diarchy that controlled patronage networks in many regions of the country was less important in Barrancabermeja, where TROCO enjoyed the support of both parties. Consequently, political groups and ideologies marginalized from the halls of state power found bases of support among working people and more political space in which to operate.

Barrancabermeja was clearly more than a place where an industrial proletariat battled with corporate bosses. It was a simmering stew of diverse working people from different regional backgrounds who engaged in various forms of subsistence agriculture, petty commerce, and wage labor. Archila argues the mixing and mingling of migrants from many parts of the country in the crowded work camps of a foreign corporation and in the bars and brothels of the oil port generated an openness to different ways of life and to new ideas that laid the basis for a cosmopolitan culture to emerge in plebeian Barrancabermeja. As Luis Rojas, an early migrant, told him, "They never rejected me here; people from here were good. Better said, the people here are good because [Barranca] is a very cosmopolitan town . . . A highlander [or] a Venezuelan comes here and nobody is rejected. Very cosmopolitan. That is why in a strike, nobody says, 'You, why are you getting involved here'" (quoted in Archila 1978: 113, my translation). The acknowledgment and taken-for-grantedness of cultural differences and the general absence of kinfolk to perpetuate values and traditions made Barrancabermeja an experiment in working-class cosmopolitanism that was represented by a powerful union tied to the concerns of rural cultivators and petty merchants.

Working people expressed themselves in terms of anti-imperialist nationalism, articulated most powerfully through the USO, which insisted on the national control of natural resources. Imperialism was not an abstract concept in Barrancabermeja and United Fruit's coastal banana zone, as it likely was for artisans and peasants in the region known as the "coffee axis," where the production and marketing of coffee was under national control. Labor organizers readily translated it into the exploitation, indignities, and forms of exclusion that arose from the omnipresence of TROCO and that working people experienced in their daily lives. It was also stimulated by the twenty-one-year US occupation of Nicaragua (1912–1933) and the 1903 loss of Panama to the United States, which prompted fears that TROCO would steal Barrancabermeja and claim it as a US possession. A 1928 massacre of hundreds of United Fruit banana works further enflamed anti-imperialist sympathies, as the banana zone suffered from many of the same social and economic problems as Barrancabermeja.

The struggles between diverse working people and the managers and supervisors of TROCO over working conditions, daily life, and visions of the future molded the socio-spatial contours of Barrancabermeja. The enclave made manifest a specific set of social and spatial configurations required by TROCO to generate profits, which were highly dynamic. On the one hand, the corporation drew on its ties to the United States, as well as Colombian state officials, the police, and the military, to create and maintain its power, blurring the boundaries between "foreign" and "domestic." On the other hand, by concentrating thousands of people in a remote frontier outpost, the oil company simultaneously created the conditions for labor organizers to reach thousands of people with their messages. Working people pushed back against overweening corporate power by producing and controlling space through the extension of their relationships, institutions, and alliances, demonstrating that corporate dispositions could never be taken for granted.[4] They did so most memorably in 1948, following the assassination of the leftist political leader Jorge Eliécer Gaitán[5] and a fifty-day oil worker strike in which the USO called for the nationalization of the oil industry. *Barranqueños* declared the national government illegitimate and set up a revolutionary junta composed of communists, liberals, and supporters of Gaitán that ruled the enclave for ten days. Along with the Caribbean banana enclave, Barrancabermeja represented a unique configuration of militant class power in Colombia.

The organizational and political trajectory of Barrancabermeja's laboring people reflected those of other Latin American export enclaves, where the struggles of wage laborers were also tied to the countryside and resonated well beyond specific regions. For example, Bolivian tin miners, who lived and worked in remote highland encampments, played a leading role in the 1952 Bolivian Revolution, which deposed a clique of mine owners and rural landlords—the so-called *rosca*. Most miners had grown up in Quechua- or Aymara-speaking homes and maintained close ties to family members in peasant communities, where they returned during layoffs or after firings from the mines. The presence of politicized miners in the villages facilitated the spread of revolution in the countryside by transforming local strikes into the seizure of landlords' estates (John 2009: 138–141). Similarly, Guatemalan wage laborers and peasants in two markedly different plantation zones—the highland coffee belt and United Fruit's lowland banana region—united around demands for economic justice during work stoppages and shaped the course of Guatemala's revolutionary decade of the 1940s (Forster 2001: 120). In Ecuador, the opening of a United Fruit–controlled banana zone also attracted migrants to a tropical frontier and generated conflicts over natural resources in which migrants were intermittently peasants and proletarians, depending on the corporation's labor demands and their capacity to resist (e.g., Striffler 2002). And, like Barrancabermeja, the banana enclaves in Colombia, Ecuador, and Guatemala drew highly motivated outside organizers, inspired by anti-imperialist sentiments and socialist notions of the common good, whose close attention helped to unionize workforces that subsequently rattled the chains of empire.

The diverse labor formations in export zones represented unique arrangements of people, places, and power that arose from highly uneven patterns of capitalist development. As Charles Bergquist observed, working people were "sometimes more 'industrial' and 'urban,' sometimes more 'agricultural' and 'rural,' sometimes pure wage workers" (1986: 8), and their social reproduction depended on the maintenance of networks that linked export zones, rural communities, small towns, and cities. Similarly, their popular struggles muddied clear distinctions between rural/urban and foreign/domestic. Yet, while working people in several enclave economies energized radical labor and popular movements, the struggles, alliances, and agendas of working people in export enclaves were not always progressive.

Despite the importance of the Colombian oil industry and the rebelliousness of working people, Barrancabermeja—much like the coastal banana zone—remained a radical outpost of class power in Latin America's most conservative country. Unlike in other parts of Latin America, the militancy of its working people never transcended the Middle Magdalena region. This was due in part to the long shadow cast by coffee over the process of labor and class formation in Colombia, complicating efforts to scale up alliances beyond the confines of Barrancabermeja and the Magdalena River Valley. Collective organization failed in the coffee axis for several reasons. First, the emergence of a new, regionally based entrepreneurial class of Colombian coffee producers and marketers never provoked the development of anti-imperialist sentiments as in the oil and banana zones. Second, the social organization of coffee cultivation rested on family-centered, labor-intensive production arrangements on smallholdings. It was characterized by exceptionally high levels of exploitation, which drove a violent struggle for land among small-scale producers, sharecroppers, and workers, and between them and elites, to avoid proletarianization. Finally, rural cultivators and workers channeled their grievances through clientelist networks of the Liberal and Conservative parties. By so doing, they pursued individual values, reinforced the status quo, and undermined the emergence of a combative, national labor movement (Bergquist 1986). As the struggle for land grew increasingly violent, Colombia erupted into a prolonged period of partisan civil war, known simply as La Violencia (1948–1958), that was centered in the coffee axis but affected much of the country.

The diverse regional trajectories that made up the social fabric of capitalism in Colombia demonstrate how the historical struggles of capital and labor gave rise to highly uneven fields of power that shaped the limits of political possibility in very different ways. These configurations of power were inherently unstable, and the early twentieth-century struggles that molded Barrancabermeja contributed to its transformation mid-century, when an intensifying Cold War, an exclusionary government, the nationalization of the oil industry, and changing class dynamics in the countryside reshaped the organization and direction of popular resistance in Barrancabermeja.

From Labor Strikes to Civic Strikes

Following World War II, Barrancabermeja shifted from a foreign-dominated export enclave to an increasingly urbanized, "state-controlled company town" (Van Isschot 2015). Growing nationalism and concerns about the Mexican government's expropriation of foreign oil corporations had moved TROCO and worried Colombian industrialists to reevaluate how Colombia produced oil and dealt with restive workers. In 1951, TROCO relinquished its oil concession, and the Colombian government subsequently nationalized the oil industry and created, in 1961, a new state-run oil company, Empresa Colombiana de Petróleos (ECOPETROL), that fulfilled one of the oil workers' principal demands. Although the creation of ECOPETROL demonstrated that working people could modify the rules on which contests over capital accumulation took place, Barrancabermeja remained a gritty, working-class outpost without a hospital, schools, decent roads, electricity, and especially potable water, and relations with the state soured over the provision of public services as the urban population exploded in the 1960s. To pressure government authorities, a new protest modality—the "civic strike"—emerged that paralyzed economic activity for days.[6] It linked neighborhood-based livelihood struggles, peasant demands for land, and oil worker protests over working conditions at the point of production.

Long before the Bolivian Water War and the Coalition in Defense of Water and Life (Coordinadora) captured international attention in 2000, citizens in Barrancabermeja were producing a complex, multidimensional form of resistance that spanned the city and the countryside and articulated its class character through demands made in the name of *el pueblo*, the people. The first civic strike for improvements in public services erupted in 1963, and it was followed by major strikes in 1975 and 1977. Although the USO was politically, culturally, and organizationally indispensable to these mobilizations, peasants, students, and urban squatters energized the strikes by blocking transportation and occupying public space. Barrancabermeja became a prototype for similar civic strikes in other Colombian cities. To understand this oppositional form, let us briefly review the social processes and emerging alliances that gave rise to a radical-left synthesis distinct from the previous era.

In mid-twentieth-century Colombia, small-scale, rural cultivators found themselves under growing pressure. The expansion of agrarian capitalism, supported by the US Alliance for Progress, was eroding subsistence agriculture and displacing peasants in some regions of the country, and the Colombian state's failure to enact significant agrarian reform provoked rising peasant protests. In the Middle Magdalena, the development of the agricultural frontier had followed the same pattern that unfolded in other tropical hinterlands (LeGrand 1986). First, peasant settlers fleeing La Violencia cleared forest and planted subsistence crops, increasing the land's value. Then, speculators and cattle ranchers moved in, concentrated property in large holdings, gained formal title (often fraudulently), and converted the lands to cattle pastures and cotton, rice, and soybean fields (Molano 2009: 37; Zamosc 1986: 28). As the agricultural frontier closed, unclaimed lands were less available than in the past. In the immediate vicinity of Barrancabermeja, ECOPETROL was also undermining peasant livelihoods by developing new oil fields without delineating "industrial" from "rural" areas, and erecting barriers that hindered travel between rural villages and urban centers. And much like TROCO, it routinely evicted peasants without adequate compensation for improvements they made (Havens and Romieux 1966: 101–124).

Peasants formed leagues to protect their interests and forged ties to the USO and leftist political parties, especially the Colombian Communist Party (PCC). In addition to Barrancabermeja, the PCC enjoyed considerable influence around the towns of Puerto Berrío and Puerto Boyacá to the south of Barrancabermeja and around Puerto Wilches to the north. Its support for rural small holders grew out of a radical vision of agrarian democracy, articulated by rural people themselves, that focused on land rights, participation in local organizations, control over the market, freedom from onerous labor obligations, and education and other rights of citizenship (Chernick and Jimenez 1993; Pizarro Leongómez 1989). Despite its worker discourse, the PCC was less a vanguard of the working class than an educator of peasants (Medina 1989), and pockets of rural cultivators in the Middle Magdalena and elsewhere on the fringes of Colombian society developed lasting loyalties to it.

Yet the PCC was shut out of government by a 1957 power-sharing deal between the Liberal and Conservative parties to end La Violencia. Known as the National Front, the agreement stipulated the two parties would alternate the presidency and divide public offices between them. The new bipartisan order quelled La Violencia and enabled business as usual to continue under the two-party system, but the legitimacy of the National Front rested on shaky pillars in the countryside, where peasant frustration with the slow pace of agrarian reform frequently erupted into land invasions such as the 1967 takeover of 160,000 hectares that once belonged to Shell Oil Company, across the river from Barrancabermeja (Zamosc 1986).

The emergence of several guerrilla insurgencies in the aftermath of the 1959 Cuban Revolution only heightened government worries about peasant radicalism. The PCC-affiliated Revolutionary Armed Forces of Colombia (FARC) emerged in central Colombia in 1964, after the US-backed bombing of peasant "independent republics" established by refugees fleeing the violence of the coffee axis. The Cuban-inspired National Liberation Army (ELN) followed soon after in Barrancabermeja's rural hinterland. Unlike the peasant-based FARC, it was more closely tied to urban intellectuals, students, and liberation theology. The Maoist-oriented Popular Liberation Army (EPL) was yet another group that arose at the time. Although other guerrilla insurgencies would also appear over the years, these three were the largest and most important; all initially believed social transformation would start in the countryside and that mobilizing peasants was a key task, and all would establish bases of support in the Middle Magdalena, and eventually Barrancabermeja.

Yet, as Colombian guerrillas fomented revolution in the countryside, the steady march of agrarian capitalism and enduring violence pushed their peasant support bases to the cities in a rising flood. The urban population of Barrancabermeja doubled in the 1960s, demonstrating the city was not exempt from the upheavals taking place in rural areas. Migrants were not separated from capitalism or from the so-called formal economy. Their casual labor as part-time construction workers, domestic workers, and itinerant vendors produced value and kept the city running, yet migrants were excluded from many of the rights of citizenship (e.g., health care and education) that the oil workers had already won. Many chased dreams of work with ECOPETROL, but the oil company could no longer provide a job to everyone, and a second generation of oil workers, who had grown up in the city and received some education, filled most of the positions in the company. The newcomers invaded lands on the urban periphery, sometimes with the help of the insurgents and political parties who hoped to win votes at election time. The shantytowns that popped up like mushrooms were bereft of social services. The juxtaposition of these impoverished neighborhoods and a profitable oil company with its well-paid workforce laid bare the state's role in the production of inequalities and the differential entitlements of citizenship.

New social and political networks between squatters, oil workers, and others found initial expression in the 1963 civic strike, which focused on improvements in public services, especially the pressing need for potable water in a city where the average daytime high temperature hovered near 100 degrees. The strike's coordinating committee embraced a cross-class coalition of former municipal functionaries, church representatives, and merchants, as well as leaders from the USO and Providencia, an urban shantytown of uprooted peasants organized by the PCC, which had prior experience in peasant organizations. The strike lasted three days, and it was followed by a forty-three-day labor strike. Fighting between protesters and security forces that broke out in the streets highlighted the government's heavy-handed response, which led to the firing of dozens of oil workers, the imposition of a state of siege, and the installation of a military mayor. Yet the strike produced some concrete results: the government initiated a new water project and a public hospital, reinstated fired oil workers, and began construction on a new high school and technical school for oil workers' children (Van Isschot 2015). Nevertheless, the repression eroded relationships with the National Front government, which many *barranqueños* had once understood as a constructive attempt to restore peace and democracy in Colombia, and it set a precedent for the future in which "communist subversion" became a justification for the suppression of popular protest. As the Cold War heated up, many residents of Barrancabermeja and the Middle Magdalena understood it as a pretext, elaborated by the United States and its Colombian allies, to repress efforts to expand social well-being and democratic processes. When major civic strikes exploded again, in 1975 and 1977, both the government and the insurgencies believed a national insurrection was imminent. Barrancabermeja had become a hotbed of leftist political projects and ideas that provided the accelerant for a popular civic movement that had grown angrier and better organized.

Building solidarity was not easy. Oil workers lived more comfortable lives than their parents' generation or the legions of destitute peasants settling the urban periphery, whom they often characterized as less modern than themselves. They were also better educated and enjoyed more social security. Yet, despite the differences between a full-time, well-paid oil proletariat linked to a strategic global industry and the underemployed and displaced peasants of the urban periphery, a common thread linked both groups: the desire to control their work and the products of their labor and to reside in neighborhoods in which potable water, electricity, schools, health clinics, and paved roads were available to everyone.

The USO downplayed the differences between its members and urban squatters; indeed, some oil workers lived side by side with immigrants in underserved neighborhoods, where they suffered from the same lack of services as everyone. State repression had also radicalized the USO, which declared itself an alternative political project rooted in the defense of natural resources and tied to "the people" — oil workers, peasants, urban squatters, students. The USO created unity through a political program that contributed funds to the development of infrastructure in poor neighborhoods, supported peasants affected by oil exploration, and advocated for the extension of benefits to temporary ECOPETROL workers (Delgado 2006). These actions made the USO an important reference point for urban residents and rural cultivators who felt a claim to the country's oil wealth, which many of them had produced with their land and labor, and who demanded that a larger share of ECOPETROL profits return to them in the form of public services. Moreover, the presence of unionized workers in immigrant neighborhoods, or their connections to friends and relatives in these settings, provided a core of established, politicized individuals with ties to leftist political parties and movements.

The radicalization of the USO was accompanied by a shift in the organization and doctrine of the Catholic Church. The creation, in 1962, of the diocese of Barrancabermeja, which embraced fourteen municipalities on each side of the Magdalena River, initiated a new era of Catholic activism. A surge of progressive priests and religious established residences in poor urban neighborhoods and the small towns that dotted the riverbanks. Energized by the teachings of liberation theology—a movement within the Catholic Church spurred by the second Vatican council (1962–1965) that declared "a preferential option for the poor"—they advocated social change and contributed to an upsurge in political organization. They built new connections between Barrancabermeja and its hinterland, provided peasant and urban squatters with political support, and shielded them from military repression when possible. Together with the USO, the progressive Church represented the most important non-state presence in Barrancabermeja's poor neighborhoods, sparking the formation of neighborhood organizations such as the Organización Femenina Popular (OFP), which brought together poor urban women to advocate for housing and public services and forged ties to peasant women in the countryside, as well as the residents of small towns and hamlets along the Magdalena River. The OFP's neighborhood leaders played a key role in mobilizing urban dwellers and bringing rural people to the city to support protests. Activist priests and religious, who resided in poor neighborhoods, also facilitated relationships between squatters and the USO and bridged some of the differences and factionalism that divided groups with similar goals.

Finally, the homegrown ELN had chosen the Middle Magdalena as a staging ground for its revolutionary struggle because of the tradition of popular resistance, especially the close ties between the oil workers and the peasantry around Barrancabermeja (Medina 2001: 78–79), and it built alliances with oil workers of the USO and university students in Bucaramanga, the provincial capital. Yet, for most of the 1970s, the ELN remained isolated in the countryside, where it was almost annihilated by the army in 1973. Although trade unionists sent supplies to the insurgents and organized the theft of weapons for them (Gill 2016: 77), the ELN envisioned urban working-class organizations like the USO as a support base for a revolution that would take place in the countryside. It virtually ignored the burgeoning shantytowns and vibrant popular organizations of Barrancabermeja until the 1980s.

New and remade relationships between oil workers, urban squatters, and peasants, as well as between them and progressive clergy, students, and political parties, formed the substratum of a powerful social movement that arose from the 1975 and 1977 civic strikes.[7] This movement was full of tensions, but it embodied a modality of protest, appropriate for mid-twentieth-century Barrancabermeja, that built on past struggles, connected diverse working people, and pushed the Colombian state to take more responsibility for the welfare of its citizens. It also gave birth to the Coordinadora Popular de Barranca-bermeja, an umbrella organization conceived as a permanent link between Barrancabermeja's expanding immigrant neighborhoods, the USO, peasant movements, and leftist political parties. The Coordinadora became the regional interlocutor with the national government. Its representatives, as well as the leaders of other civic movements, began meeting with government officials in Bogotá, the national capital, to discuss public services and unemployment, and because of its deep popular roots and political clout, the Coordinadora provided visibility and respectability to peasant mobilizations that took place under its umbrella (Molano 2009: 56). Indeed, the Coordinadora had expanded the geography of working-class power by the early 1980s and opened possibilities for broad forms of struggle—some with far-reaching political horizons.

For many urban and rural working people, the experience of solidarity through involvement with a network of grassroots organizations provided a sense of dignity and entitlement—a feeling that they were making history and pushing back against the violence and indifference of the state. Men and women saw hope for change through the power of popular protest, and they developed a new sense of self rooted in a larger social collectivity, as they tied personal aspirations to local, national, and international concerns. Yet this intricate fabric of working-class solidarity would come under increasing strain, and by the end of the century, the combined pressure of economic restructuring and relentless state and paramilitary violence tore it apart.

Unraveling

Beginning in the 1980s, the growing strength of the insurgencies, heightened popular militancy, and the birth of a vicious counter-revolution unleashed a maelstrom of violence that unspooled the threads of popular solidarity in Barrancabermeja. A vicious counterinsurgent war had been intensifying since the 1960s—first in the countryside and then in Barrancabermeja—and military strategists increasingly defined the Middle Magdalena as a national security threat. Although many *barranqueños* believed, because of the strength and militancy of their organizations, the right-wing counterrevolution sweeping the countryside would never touch the city, they were mistaken. It was precisely because Barrancabermeja was a bastion of popular power, the center of the Colombian oil industry, and, by the 1980s, a guerrilla stronghold that the counterinsurgency movement—a complicated alliance between agrarian elites, drug traffickers, traditional politicians, and sectors of the security forces—targeted it. The wholesale divestment of social relations, the disarticulation of rural-urban connections, and the destruction of organizations through which working people crafted their livelihoods and channeled their demands to the state were central to the defeat of Barrancabermeja's popular movement by the beginning of the millennium.

The takeover of Barrancabermeja did not happen immediately; rather, paramilitaries aided and abetted by the state security forces slowly encircled the city as they morphed from roving death squads in the 1980s to standing armies in the late 1990s. Death squads emerged in the southern Middle Magdalena in the early 1980s to combat the FARC, which had used the early proceeds from the coca/ cocaine traffic to expand out of its southern stronghold into the Middle Magdalena and dedicate itself to kidnapping and extorting landowners, some of whom were newly rich drug traffickers who had acquired land in the region. Regional elites claimed the state was not doing enough to protect them from the FARC. They financed Muerte a Secuestradores (MAS)—a paramilitary group tied to the security forces that served as a prototype for similar groups elsewhere—to defend them from guerrilla harassment. But rather than engaging the guerrillas, the paramilitaries took aim at softer targets—unarmed peasants, leftist political parties, trade unionists, and others believed to be the support base of the insurgency.

Regional elites wanted to suppress any possibility that popular concerns about land reform, public services, infrastructure, and public education would receive serious attention, after the government of Belisario Bentancur (1982–1986) "opened" the political system and initiated peace negotiations aimed at incorporating the insurgencies into the political process. Although the talks never enjoyed the full backing of the agrarian elites or the security forces, they resulted in two important reforms that represented a concession to the guerrillas and threatened regional power holders: new electoral laws enabled the direct election of previously appointed mayors and governors, and guerrillas gained the right to establish legally recognized political parties to compete in elections without first laying down their arms. The Unión Patriótica, A Luchar, and the Frente Popular—tied to the FARC, the ELN, and the EPL, respectively—quickly formed and, in the case of the Union Patriótica, performed well in municipal and provincial elections. Because the political reforms threatened the prerogatives of regional power holders, increased political competition served only to intensify regional conflict in the context of a dirty war.

Rural cultivators were the first to experience the full force of paramilitary violence when, in the early 1980s, MAS carried out a series of massacres in the southern Middle Magdalena around the small towns of Puerto Boyacá and Puerto Berrío, an area where drugs lords from the Medellin cartel had amassed large estates, the FARC had developed bases of peasant support, and the Union Patriótica had performed well in local elections. Paramilitaries then threatened survivors with death if they remained on the land, forcibly displacing those they did not murder. More rural massacres followed over the years in response to intensifying peasant militancy. Of the ten Colombian municipalities with the most peasant protest in the 1980s, eight were in the Middle Magdalena (Van Isschot 2015: 92). In June 1987, for example, the Northeast Civic Strike brought out tens of thousands of peasants who marched on major cities and shut down rural commerce in five provinces. Although stigmatized as subversive, the strike demonstrated a high degree of coordination between rural and urban activists. Thousands of peasants entered Barrancabermeja, where they occupied a church for five days and received the backing of the Coordinadora, which organized a solidarity march, and urban civic groups who blocked roads and brought business to a halt (Van Isschot 2015).

Peasants warned urban activists about the spreading paramilitary threat, and the influx of traumatized refugees changed the political dynamics of the city. Politicized peasants, displaced from areas under guerrilla control, moved the insurgents to follow their support base into the city, after the guerrillas had largely ignored Barrancabermeja. The ELN and the FARC also organized urban militias in the northeastern and southeastern districts of Barrancabermeja. Composed mostly of young people, the militias supported the insurgencies with information about the movement of security forces, logistics, and the organization of political activities. The guerrillas also coopted, took over, and worked with or around neighborhood organizations and unions, with varying degrees of popular support. Moreover, their controversial decision to combine legal and illegal means of struggle (*la combinación de todas las formas de lucha*) had individuals acting on behalf of the insurgencies in trade unions, neighborhood groups, political parties, and civic organizations. This practice lent credence to accusations that guerrillas operated within legal organizations, and it enabled the military to justify targeting popular organizations and exposing unarmed civilians to state repression. It was not long before the distinction between rural and urban violence and legal and illegal protest blurred. Mercenaries attacked peasant activists living in Barrancabermeja, as well as prominent labor leaders and journalists. The USO, in particular, suffered heavy losses: between 1977 and 2004, eighty-nine oil workers were murdered in Barrancabermeja (Valencia and Celis 2012: 125).

The rising force of paramilitarism provided the leverage for the neoliberal restructuring of the economy, which began in earnest under the administration of César Gaviria (1990–1994). The one-two punch of counterinsurgent violence and economic transformation dealt a severe blow to both rural cultivators and wage laborers in Barrancabermeja, where state workers represented a substantial sector of the workforce. In the countryside, the end of government subsidies and protective tariff barriers undercut domestic food production and fueled the growth of new extractive enclaves—coal, gold, and oil—and export crops such as African palm, as well as the expansion of the coca/cocaine industry, which absorbed ruined and displaced peasants with no viable alternatives. Organized violence lubricated the rise of new development poles, as paramilitaries took control of social and political life in these emergent nodes of mineral and agricultural expansion. It achieved a profound rearrangement of space and global commodity flows that undergirded a changing, highly uneven, balance of power.

In Barrancabermeja, new labor laws and the partial or complete privatization of ECOPETROL and other state entities hollowed out the hard-won popular gains of earlier rounds of class struggle and aimed to make workers—especially those in the oil industry—more "manageable." Privatization led to job loss or new contracts on less favorable terms, and the cost of public services increased. The rising of subcontracting diminished the power of the USO and other unions and opened the door for private contractors with ties to the paramilitaries to exert greater control over the labor process. Unemployment, economic precariousness, and insecurity increased, substantially weakening what urban workers could do alone and with others. Because of mounting violence, demands for land, public services, and better working conditions gradually gave way to a focus on "human rights," especially the right to life, and civic strikes took on a more defensive character.

Paramilitaries attacked working people who opposed the economic reforms, the theft of their lands, and the assassination of their leaders, serving as the midwife of neoliberalism through predation and dispossession. By the late 1990s, they had morphed into standing armies that collaborated with the state security forces and occupied and controlled territory, and several of these armies federated, in 1997, under the umbrella of the United Self-Defense Forces of Colombia (AUC). The peak of paramilitary power coincided with the enactment, in 2001, of Plan Colombia, a $1.3 billion mostly military aid program officially described as a counter-narcotics initiative. Yet Plan Colombia targeted the FARC's coca-producing strongholds in the south, rather than the Caribbean coast, where drug traffickers exported refined cocaine, and it strengthened paramilitarism by channeling money and arms to the mercenaries' main ally—the Colombian security forces.

One AUC affiliate—the Bloque Central Bolívar (BCB)—seized control of Barrancabermeja in 2000, routing the guerrillas and driving the final nail in the coffin of a once vibrant working class. With the collusion of state security forces, the BCB dismantled the relationships, practices, and institutions that tied working people together and stunted popular demands that the state care for its citizens through the provision of decent wages, safe and democratic working conditions, and public services; protect natural resources from foreign despoliation; and enact agrarian reform. The fear and lack of trust that spread under the four-year BCB reign of terror, as well as widespread impunity that protected the mercenaries, made it nearly impossible for working people in the city and the countryside to stop what was happening to them.

Insurgent divisions and guerrilla betrayals of each other and their support networks solidified popular resentment that had been growing for years and facilitated the paramilitary takeover, making a bad situation worse. Guerrilla extortion and resort to kidnapping and bombings in heavily populated civilian areas had long raised questions about the political projects the insurgents claimed to represent. Increasingly arbitrary "justice" meted out to presumed informants further alienated the population, as did the behavior of young guerrilla militia members, who acted less like the vanguard of a political alternative than as degenerate thugs who took advantage of people like themselves. Because of the inability or unwillingness of local commanders to control criminal behavior within their own ranks, thuggery overwhelmed any remaining vision of revolutionary transformation. Barrancabermeja changed from a city that had long received displaced victims of the violence to one that became a source of displacement—a city where the degradation of the insurgencies, a paramilitary victory that rested on savage violence, and the imperatives of neoliberalism defeated the understanding and practice of solidarity that had characterized its working-class political culture for decades.

Conclusion

For much of the twentieth century, Barrancabermeja was a combative center of working-class power in one of Latin America's most conservative countries. Differently labeled working people shaped changing practices of popular struggle, forcing us to acknowledge that, in specific moments, peasants, oil workers, urban squatters, and petty merchants joined together not because they had identical conditions of labor but because they experienced broadly similar social circumstances. Grasping this commonality is difficult if we do not acknowledge the hybrid rural-urban experiences of working people and the wide variety of forms of employment—industrial, agricultural, retail, waged, and unwaged—in which they engaged. Although the oil workers and the USO gave unrelenting power to Barrancabermeja's popular civic movement, what emerged was not just a "workers" movement but a class struggle rooted in an ethos of belonging to the "people." The valences of this struggle shifted as working people came together and were pulled apart in different ways, and as TROCO gave way to the Colombian state. For a brief moment in the mid-twentieth century, the popular movement reached beyond regional political horizons and took tentative steps toward scaling up its power.

Nowadays, however, Barrancabermeja bears witness to the devastation unleashed by paramilitary counterinsurgent violence and decades of neoliberal restructuring, backed by the Colombian and US governments. Terror has forced people to turn inward to deal with their problems, and it has reorganized popular memory by creating a present in which devastating memories serve less to fire collective mobilization than reinforce a legacy of painful defeat and a denial of the future. It has also attenuated calls for redistributive justice. The USO is a shadow of its former self. After decades of government stigmatization, many *barranqueños* associate it with the discredited insurgencies and view it as a problem, rather than a solution. Criminal gangs and paramilitary successor groups control the urban periphery, where displaced peasants have been incorporated into new, authoritarian hierarchies and enjoy neither rights nor protection. Threats and harassment greet any expression of protest or nonconformity.

Although the experience of Barrancabermeja is extreme, it has much in common with the setbacks experienced by working people elsewhere during the late twentieth and early twenty-first centuries. Unlike the mid-twentieth century, when many *barranqueños*, as well as activist intellectuals around the world like Eric Wolf, thought social transformation was possible—even likely in their lifetimes—we look back on that era from nonrevolutionary times. Revolution nowadays has lost its appeal, and Wolf's belief that an informed citizenry would act in the interest of the majority has crashed on the rocks of authoritarian nationalism around the world. Connections between the past when transformative change seemed possible and the present have been severed, and defensive struggles, reformist initiatives, and appeals to human rights have taken the place of an earlier generation's "freedom dreams" (see Kelly 2002). Rekindling hope in an era of pessimism is important to the reconstruction of "webs of group relations" that once allowed working people in Barrancabermeja to reach beyond their differences and build bonds of solidarity.

Lesley Gill teaches anthropology at Vanderbilt University. She is the author of *A Century of Violence in a Red City* (2016) and *The School of the Americas* (2004).

Notes

This chapter draws on Gill (2016).

1. The importance of regional differences was developed much more fully in his later work (e.g., Wolf 1982).
2. See LeGrand (n.d., 1998) for a critique of such portrayals.
3. Over the course of the twentieth century, other foreign oil companies also received a government concession to drill for oil in the Middle Magdalena, including Texaco and Shell.
4. See Herod (2011) for more discussion of how labor and capital make space in enclave economies.
5. Gaitan was a labor lawyer whose national stature rose after the infamous 1928 massacre of banana workers in United Fruit's Caribbean enclave. As an emerging politician, he championed the rights of workers and supported agrarian reform.

Backed by workers, peasants, and sectors of the middle class, Gaitan rose to power on the left wing of the Liberal Party and would likely have been elected president.
6. See Giraldo and Camargo (1986) for more discussion of Colombian civic strikes.
7. Although in both Barrancabermeja and other Colombian cities, these strikes were notable for their cross-class character, Barrancabermeja was a working-class city, and working people constituted the indispensable core of its civic movements.

References

Archila, Mauricio. 1978. *Aqui nadie es forastero*. Bogotá: CINEP.
Bergquist, Charles. 1978. *Coffee and Conflict in Colombia, 1886–1910*. Durham, NC: Duke University Press.
———. 1986. *Labor in Latin American: Comparative Essays on Chile, Argentina, Venezuela, and Colombia*. Stanford, CA: Stanford University Press.
Carbonella, August, and Sharryn Kasmir. 2014. "Introduction: Toward a Global Anthropology of Labor." In *Blood and Fire: Toward a Global Anthropology of Labor*, ed. Sharryn Kasmir and August Carbonella, 1–30. New York: Berghahn Books.
Chernick, Michael, and Michael Jimenez. 1993. "Popular Liberation, Radical Democracy, and Marxism: Leftist Politics in Colombia, 1974–1991." In *The Latin American Left: From the Fall of Allende to Perestroika*, ed. Barry Carr and Steve Ellner, 127–149. Boulder, CO: Westview Press.
Cooper, Frederick. 2005. *Colonialism in Question: Theory, Knowledge, History*. Berkeley: University of California Press.
Delgado, Alvaro. 2006. "El conflicto laboral en el Magdalena medio." In *Conflictos, poderes, e identidades en el Magdalena medio, 1990–2001*, ed. Mauricio Archila and Ingrid Johanna Bolivar, 85–164. Bogotá: CINEP/COLCIENCIAS.
Farnsworth-Alvear, Ann. 2000. *Dulcinea in the Factory: Myth, Morals, Men, and Women in Colombia's Industrial Experiment, 1905–1960*. Durham, NC: Duke University Press.
Forster, Cindy. 2001. *The Time of Freedom: Campesino Workers in Guatemala's October Revolution*. Pittsburgh, PA: University of Pittsburgh Press.
Gibb, George Sweet, and Evelyn H. Knowlton. 1956. *History of Standard Oil Company (New Jersey): The Resurgent Years, 1911–1927*. New York: Harper & Row.
Gill. Lesley. 2016. *A Century of Violence in a Red City: Popular Struggle, Counterinsurgency, and Human Rights in Colombia*. Durham, NC: Duke University Press.
Giraldo, Javier, and Santiago Camargo. 1986. "Paros y movimientos cívicos in Colombia," *Controversia* 128: 11–42.
Havens, A. Eugene, and Michel Romieux. 1966. *Barrancabermeja: Conflictos sociales en torno a un centro petroleros*. Bogotá: Universidad Nacional.
Herod, Andrew. 2011. "Social Engineering through Spatial Engineering: Company Towns and the Geographical Imagination." In *Company Towns in the Americas: Landscape, Power, and Working-Class Communities*, ed. Oliver J. Dinius and Angela Vergara, 21–44. Athens: University of Georgia Press.
John, S. Sándor. 2009. *Bolivia's Radical Tradition: Permanent Revolution in the Andes*. Tucson: University of Arizona Press.
Kasmir, Sharryn, and Lesley Gill. 2018. "No Smooth Surfaces: An Anthropology of Unevenness and Combination." *Current Anthropology* 59 (4): 355–377.
Kelly, Robin D. G. 2002. *Freedom Dreams: The Black Radical Imagination*. Boston: Beacon Press.

LeGrand, Catherine C. 1986. *Frontier Expansion and Peasant Protest in Colombia, 1830–1936*. Albuquerque: University of New Mexico Press.

———. 1998. "Living in Macondo: Economy and Culture in a United Fruit Company Banana Enclave in Colombia." In *Close Encounters of Empire: Writing the Cultural History of US-Latin American Relations*, ed. Gilbert M. Joseph, Catherine C. LeGrand, and Ricardo Salvatore, 333–368. Durham, NC: Duke University Press.

———. n.d. "Recent Trends in the Interpretation of Banana and Other Enclaves in Latin America." Unpublished manuscript.

Medina, Carlos. 2001. *Elementos para una história política del Ejéricto de Liberación Nacional*. Bogotá: Rodríguez Quito Editores.

Medina, Medofilo. 1989. *Historia PCC, Tomo II:Orígenes de la violencia (1949–57)*. Bogotá: CEIS-INEDO.

Molano Brazo, Alfredo. 2009. *El medio del Magdalena medio*. Bogotá: CINEP.

Paige, Jeffrey. 1975. *Agrarian Revolution: Social Movements and Export Agriculture in the Underdeveloped World*. New York: Free Press.

Pizarro Leongómez, Eduaro. 1989. "Los origenes del movimiento armado comunista en Colombia, 1949–1966." *Análisis Politico* 7: 7–31.

Roseberry, William. 1993. "Beyond the Agrarian Question in Latin America." In *Confronting Historical Paradigms: Peasants, Labor, and the Capitalist World System in Africa and Latin America*, ed. Frederick Cooper, Allan Isaacman, Florencia Mallon, William Roseberry, and Steve Stern, 318–368. Madison: University of Wisconsin Press.

Salas, Miguel Tinker. 2009. *The Enduring Legacy: Oil, Culture, and Society in Venezuela*. Durham, NC: Duke University Press.

Santiago, Myrna. 2006. *The Ecology of Oil: Environment, Labor, and the Mexican Revolution, 1900–1938*. New York: Cambridge University Press.

Striffler, Steve. 2002. *In the Shadow of State and Capital: The United Fruit Company, Popular Struggle, and Agrarian Restructuring in Ecuador, 1900–1995*. Durham, NC: Duke University Press.

———. 2004. "Class Formation in Latin America: One Family's Enduring Journey Between Country and City." *International Labor and Working Class History* 65: 11–25.

Valencia, León, and Juan Carlos Celis. 2012. *Sindicalismo asasinado: Reveladora investigación contras los sindicalistas colombianos*. Bogotá: Random House Mondadori.

Van Isschot, Luis. 2015. *The Social Origins of Human Rights: Protesting Political Violence in Colombia's Oil Capital, 1919–2010*. Madison: University of Wisconsin Press.

Vega, Renan, Luz Angela Nunez, and Alexander Pereira. 2009. *Petroleo y protesta: La USO y los trabajadores petroleros en Colombia*. Bogotá: Corporacion Aury Sara.

Wolf, Eric. 1956. "Aspects of Group Relations in a Complex Society." *American Anthropologist* 58 (6): 1065–1078.

———. 1969. *Peasant Wars of the Twentieth Century*. New York: Harper & Row.

———. 1982. *Europe and the People Without History*. Berkeley: University of California Press.

Zamosc, Leon. 1986. *The Agrarian Question and the Peasant Movement in Colombia, 1967–1981*. New York: Cambridge University Press.

— Chapter 4 —

THE CATHOLIC CHURCH, PEASANTS, AND REVOLUTION IN NORTHERN MORAZÁN, EL SALVADOR

Leigh Binford

❦

In *Peasant Wars of the Twentieth Century*, Eric Wolf analyzed the roles that peasants played in six successful or relatively successful revolutions. He characterized those revolutions as involving "peasant wars," although, as was noted in the introduction, peasants played a much larger role in some of them (Vietnam, China, and Mexico) than in others (Cuba, Russia, and Algeria) where their activity assumed more of an ancillary role. Wolf noted how "peasants are often merely passive spectators of political struggles or long for the sudden advent of a millennium" but that "ultimately, the decisive factor in making a peasant rebellion possible lies in the relation of the peasantry to the field of power which surrounds it" (1969: 290), a relationship that landlords, merchants, political bosses, and priests mediated.

This chapter examines peasants from northern Morazán in the Salvadoran Revolution (1980–1992), which was eventually terminated through a Peace Accord between the government and the rebel Farabundo Martí National Liberation Front (FMLN), composed of five leftist politico-military organizations that united in October 1980. The People's Revolutionary Army (ERP) of the FMLN controlled northern Morazán from the early 1980s until the end of the war. I am particularly interested in the role of the priests who promoted liberation theology and served as the initial contacts between rural peasants and the urban-based ERP leadership. I argue that "middle peasants" were indeed the first people in the region to affiliate with the rebels, but I also maintain that as the revolution gathered steam, recruitment to the ERP broadened and economic status became a less meaningful guide to political affiliation. As Joaquín Chávez (2017) noted for Chalatenango, early relations between northern Morazanian peasants and urban-based ERP guerrilla leaders tended to be relatively horizontal; relations between peasants and the guerrilla leadership became more vertical when the latter left the cities for rebel camps being established in rural areas. But even as they subordinated themselves to the ERP High Command, peasants trained previously in liberation theology served in units that specialized in political organization, health care, supply acquisition, cultural diffusion, and other noncombat functions key to the maintenance of fighting capacity and morale. A final section of this chapter discusses the ravages of several decades of postwar neoliberal political economy and the waning of peasant organization in the postwar.

By Way of Background

El Salvador is a small but densely populated country that in 1970 packed more than 3.7 million inhabitants into an area the size of the state of Massachusetts. Coffee was introduced into the country early in the nineteenth century and led to land concentration, land struggles, and even peasant rebellions, the most notable of which occurred in 1932, when indigenous peasants in western El Salvador rose up following depression-related declines in wages and employment. The rebellion was supported by the nascent Salvadoran Communist Party under Agustín Farabundo Martí. However, the army quickly routed the poorly armed rebels, after which civil guards organized by the agrarian bourgeoisie cold-bloodedly murdered thousands of unarmed men and women (Anderson 1995; Gould and Lauria-Santiago 2008). Thereafter, *la Matanza* (the Slaughter) provided ample fodder for the paranoid equation of organized peasants with communist subversion (see Lindo-Fuentes et al. 2007). In its wake, urban-based oligarchs ceded administration of government to the military, retaining control over the coffee economy. By this point, capitalism in some form had penetrated most rural areas of El Salvador more thoroughly than most cases discussed by Wolf, and the state maintained social control over the countryside through the selective violence of security forces.

This was also true of northern Morazán, a rugged, mountainous area in El Salvador's extreme northeast. Historically, this roughly two hundred square mile region, bordered on three sides by Honduras and on the fourth (south) side by the Torola River, served as a refuge for peasants fleeing land dispossession and unemployment elsewhere. As of 1980, a few small coffee plantations around the town of Perquín were the only regional buds of agrarian capitalism, though land had long been commoditized and money mediated most exchanges. Merchant capitalists skimmed off much of the peasants' surplus by renting land and purchasing crops forward at discounted prices, and poor peasants had little to guard them against market downturns and poor weather.

Most of the fifty thousand residents (approximately ten thousand households) grew corn, beans, and sorghum for personal consumption; many landholding households in lower, hotter areas near the Torola River also cultivated henequen from which they extracted fiber they bundled and sold in regional markets or worked up into rope, carrying bags, hammocks, lassos, and bridles. But many landless workers and land-poor peasants had to migrate seasonally (November to January) to agro-export zones in El Salvador's south and west, where they worked harvesting cotton, cutting sugar cane, or picking coffee. A 1908 Agrarian Law outlawed rural unions, and small contingents of National Guardsmen or Treasury Police enforced social "peace" in and around most municipal centers. The scant availability of education meant that the Catholic Church served as the most effective instrument of ideological control, spreading a message of fatalism that explained poverty on earth as poor people's destiny and a glorious afterlife as the reward for passive acceptance of that earthly fate.

Liberation Theology

Following the 1959 Cuban Revolution, the Salvadoran Communal Union (UCS) developed as an initiative of US President John F. Kennedy's Alliance for Progress and the AFL-CIO's Institute for Free Labor Development to establish a pro-government, anti-communist bulwark in rural El Salvador. A few years later, in 1965, the Federation of Christian Peasants of El Salvador (FECCAS) formed in the Aguilares region of Cuscatlán department.[1] Though initially linked to the conservative wing of the Catholic Church, within a decade FECCAS shed its ties to conservative Catholicism and mobilized around demands for agrarian reform, higher wages for landless field workers, and other measures resisted by the state and agrarian bourgeoisie. Soon, this more militant instantiation of FECCAS was joined by the Rural Workers Union (UTC) in Chalatenango and San

Vicente (Golita and Galdámez 1993; Montgomery 1983; Pearce 1986). Conditions for rural workers deteriorated when plantation owners expelled resident laborers (*colonos*) and when tens of thousands of Salvadorans who had migrated to Honduras in search of land and/or employment were forcefully repatriated to El Salvador in 1969 in the wake of a brief, "hundred hours" war between the two countries. The war also ended the short-lived Central American Common Market, curtailing the growth of light industry that was supposed to provide an urban alternative to rural poverty and underemployment.

The radicalization of FECCAS in central El Salvador can be attributed to the growing influence of liberation theology, the specifically Latin American response to the papal encyclicals of the Second Vatican Council (1962–1965). In 1968, some 130 bishops (of a total of 600) from throughout Latin America met in Medellín, Colombia, to apply Vatican II to Latin America. Catholic theologians developed liberation theology through study and discussion that took place before, during, and after the Medellín meeting. Christian Smith treated liberation theology as a "movement" and wrote it "is not only a set of theological ideas or beliefs, but an attempt to mobilize a previously immobilized constituency for collective action against an antagonist to promote social change" (1991: 25). He explained:

> Liberation theology essentially is an attempt to reconceptualize the Christian faith from the perspective of the poor and oppressed. At heart it contends that the Christian gospel, the "good news," is that God is working—and that God's people should therefore be working—in history to combat and eradicate all forms of oppression and domination, whether social, cultural, political, economic, or spiritual. (27)

Liberation theology, also mentioned by Lesley Gill in this volume, differentiated the poor who passively made peace with their poverty from those who struggled in solidarity with others to overcome it. The latter were defined as the poor-with-spirit "who accept their situation as the foundation for creating the new human being" (Ellacuría 1991: 70). Through their exposure to liberation theology, many Salvadorans became convinced change was both possible and sanctioned by God and that they had the obligation to work toward the creation of a just world.

Liberation theology challenged the weak hegemony that supported oligarchical rule and the military-controlled state in areas characterized by scant presence of educational institutions and poorly funded municipal administrations. However, it developed differently in the archdiocese, where Archbishop Chávez y González lent his support, then in the four provincial dioceses controlled by conservative bishops, who regarded the new doctrine as a threat to social peace and the financial support that large landowners had historically rendered to the church. The archdiocese was headquartered in San Salvador, the nation's capital, and administered Catholic parishes in San Salvador, Chalatenango, Cuscatlán, and La Libertad. In 1965, these four departments contained 40 percent of the country's population and an estimated 54 percent of El Salvador's clergy, as well as a high percentage of the 750 male and 350 female members of religious orders, many of them assigned to parochial schools in the capital (Richard and Meléndez 1982: 59). Catholic clergy in El Salvador's remaining ten departments labored at the behest of bishops administering dioceses centered (from west to east) in the cities of Santa Ana, San Vicente, Santiago de María, and San Miguel (Cardenal 1992: 263).[2]

The Archdiocese and the Rest

The introduction and spread of progressive Christianity in working-class neighborhoods of San Salvador and select rural areas of the archdiocese coincided with struggles for land and higher wages in west and central El Salvador, and many catechists and Delegates of the Word trained by progressive priests participated in these struggles. Most progressive priests took a "pastoral approach" to liberation theology practice in which clergy "could (indeed, were obliged to) accompany their people, but . . . could not take a political stance" (Montgomery 1983: 69; see Berryman 1984: 332–33, 337–341; Gould 2015). However, about a third of the younger priests identified with a more radical, Marxist-influenced version of liberation theology that "emphasized the need for the people to transform reality" (Montgomery 1983: 69). Priests associated with the pastoral current supported people's right to participate in organizations like FECCAS and the UTC struggling for land, higher wages, and access to credit. Over time, FECCAS radicalized and in 1974 linked up with the UTC to form the Rural Workers Federation, the maximum expression of prewar peasant organization in west and central El Salvador. In 1975, FECCAS-UTC joined the Popular Revolutionary Bloc, the largest of several "mass organizations" that linked a growing popular movement to nascent guerrilla organizations.

Through the Catholic Church, peasants and workers (urban and rural) living in and around the archdiocese could participate in seminars, training programs, radio schools, and a Catholic Church–sponsored cooperative movement that provided critical literacy skills, leadership training, and experience in collective organization. Liberation theology informed many if not most programs, which received encouragement and financial assistance from Archbishop Chávez y González (see Cardenal 1992: 263; Chávez 2017; Richard and Meléndez 1982: 54–55).

However, none of the aforementioned educational initiatives were available to the residents of the four departments, organized into two Catholic dioceses (Santiago de María and San Miguel), east of the Lempa River. The church's low profile in the east likely resulted from the confluence of several factors. On one hand, western and central areas exhibited greater economic development; they contained the political capital, most industry, and a preponderance of El Salvador's valuable coffee land. On the other hand, provincial bishops tended to be socially and politically conservative; they maintained close ties to the army and administered dioceses heavily dependent on the financial largess of wealthy landowners. The progressive educational mission in the East—which includes northern Morazán—fell *exclusively* to peasant training centers such as the Centro Reina de la Paz (El Castaño) in Chirilagua, San Miguel, and Centro Los Naranjos in Jiquilisco, Usulután. Most of the nine regional centers for peasant formation and promotion—"peasant universities," as they came to be called—were scattered along El Salvador's southern tier, often near the Pan-American Highway. Jesuits and members of other Catholic orders founded the centers beginning in the late 1960s. Until closed down by the military government in the late 1970s, they trained thousands of catechists in liberation theology and provided them the tools to establish Christian Base Communities (*Comunidades Eclesiales de Base* or CEBs) and pursue community-based development initiatives (Binford 2004; Chávez 2017; Montgomery 1982, 1983; Peterson 1997). In a few years, the peasant universities became loosely organized into a national network of Catholic schools specializing in the formation of adult, mostly male, leaders. Eastern, central, and western regions contained peasant universities, but they exercised close to a monopoly on peasant and workers' leadership training east of the Lempa River.

Peter Sánchez provides a useful description of the Los Naranjos training center in *Priest Under Fire*, which recounts the life of Fr. David Rodríguez. Based on interviews I conducted in northern Morazán in the early to mid-1990s, the pedagogical approach in Los Naranjos was similar to that in other centers. Rodríguez was born in 1940 to a prominent landholding family in the department of San Vicente. Following studies at the San José de la Montaña seminary in San Salvador, he entered the priesthood in 1963 and then went to study in Europe before being recalled to El Salvador by San Vicente Bishop Pedro Aparicio, who assigned him to Toluca parish, located a mere seven miles from the departmental capital (Sánchez 2015: 38–40, 49). Rodríguez embraced liberation theology around 1970 and soon thereafter entered into conflict with wealthy landowners, which provoked clashes between him and Bishop Aparicio. In 1973, the bishop transferred Rodríguez to San Carlos Lempa, a poor, malaria-infested community in cotton country near the Pacific coast. From San Carlos Lempa, Rodríguez sent peasants to the Los Naranjos center that had opened across the Lempa River in nearby Jiquilisco, Usulután. Fr. Juan Macho founded Los Naranjos in the early 1970s. Based on his interviews with Rodríguez, Sánchez summarized the arrangement there as follows:

> The teachers at Centro Naranjos offered courses principally to lay leaders (Delegates of the Word and catechists) who had been identified by their priests as "natural leaders." The individuals selected showed themselves to have not only leadership potential but also a commitment to the new pastoral mission. The priests who ran the center would send letters to various parishes letting them know that a course was going to start on a certain day, and then the parish priest would let the center know how many campesinos [peasants] had the proper qualification to attend that specific course. Once they had enough students, twenty to thirty, the center would enroll them and prepare everything to commence the course, which would last up to four weeks. The Passionist order financed most of the cost, meaning that neither the campesinos nor the home parishes had to pay tuition, food, or lodging. (89)

One northern Morazanian catechist explained his early experience in the El Castaño center, located in the department of San Miguel, as follows:

> When I arrived at the center [El Castaño], I was a bit concerned and I asked myself, "What are we going to do here?" At that time the schedule for each day had been written up, and I was looking at it. Well, at such an hour [one class] and such an hour another class. They had themes on community development, health education, agriculture and free themes. I asked myself, "To combine these things as a Christian, how's it going to happen?" I [had] thought they were going to teach us things about the Bible and to pray . . . The other thing that bothered me a bit is that I was accustomed to seeing priests dressed in pants and cassocks. But as I watched them wearing tee-shirts and playing soccer with the masses . . . well one has a preconception, all that is a bit strange. (Cited in Binford 2004: 112–113)

By the mid-1970s, the training centers had achieved sufficient coordination to develop and share didactic materials, such as *Conozcamos nuestra patria* ("Let's get to know our country"), an eighty-page mimeographed textbook produced in 1974 by the Centros Rurales de la Iglesia en El Salvador (Rural Centers of the Salvadoran Church). Lengthy sections of the textbook dealt with the history and economic and social development of El Salvador, as well as the nation's physical and human geography. The longest chapter (5) treated "Means of Production," a term straight out of Marxian political economy, with subsections devoted to land, capital, labor, industry, and commerce. As in other chapters, a "reflection" prodded readers to ponder questions such as "Do you think that the system of land tenure is just?" (*¿Crees tú que la tenencia de la tierra es justa?*), "Does Minifundism cause rural unemployment?" (*¿Ocasiona el Minifundismo un desempleo rural?*), and "What do you see as the solution for the unjust system of land tenure?" (*¿Cuál sería para ti la solución de la injusta tenencia de la tierra?*) (CRIS 1974: 76).[3] Priest-teachers used social analysis "to both explain and deplore human suffering" in a theology that, as Paul Farmer observed, draws connections that "bring into relief not merely the suffering of the wretched of the earth [but] also the forces that promote that suffering" (2004: 287). These ideas presented a frontal challenge to fatalistic explanations of the social order that rationalized suffering on Earth as a manifestation of God's will and promised the poor recompense in the hereafter. Real life exercises reinforced the lessons in which students—mostly adult men, married and with children—were transported to the hovels of plantation workers and the plush homes of absentee landowners. Afterward, the students reflected as a group on the meaning of what they had seen and heard. It seems pretty clear the priest-teachers identified more with the radical approach to liberation theology than the pastoral approach.

When the students returned to their communities in San Vicente, Usulután, Morazán, and elsewhere, many dedicated time and energy to developing CEBs through which they spread a message of dignity, respect, and the obligation of poor people to struggle against oppression. For a time, conservative Catholic bishops may have been unaware of the theological bent of the centers, for they instructed priests to recruit students in the expectation that trained lay catechists would relieve some of the pressure on understaffed clergy. Before the war, the dioceses outside the archdiocese recorded ratios of between ten and twenty thousand Catholic parishioners to each priest. (The ratio in the Archdiocese was a nominally lower four thousand parishioners per priest. See CH, n.d.) According to Tommie Sue Montgomery, the rapid growth of popular organizations cannot be understood without considering the role of CEBs "in organizing and concienticizing the people." She goes on to note: "Similarly, the strength of the revolutionary leadership at the grass roots cannot be explained without recognizing that dozens, if not hundreds, of revolutionary leaders acquired their organizational skills through their training as catechists and delegates" (1982: 220).

Liberation Theology and Peasant Organization

Many early peasant leaders, whether in western, central, or eastern areas of El Salvador, were economically better off than most residents of their communities (Binford 2004; Chávez 2017). They may not have been "self-sufficient middle peasants"—a term favored by Wolf to designate those peasants most likely to rebel, but most owned land, in many cases enough to produce and set aside resources to maintain their households during the time—a few days to a month—they attended a seminar in the capital or a course in one of the peasant universities.[4] Also, greater access to resources endowed them with the freedom to travel around their home areas forming and working with CEBs. Poorer members of the rural social order struggled to scrape out a living by farming rented land, working locally for others, and/or migrating seasonally to agro-export zones. To put the matter in Eric Wolf's terms, these poor peasants (and landless laborers) lacked the "tactical power" that came with control over land (1969: 290). Those with tactical power composed a small portion of the peasantry overall but were disproportionately represented among the prewar rural leadership. While not rich or even particularly well off, they enjoyed a degree of the tactical mobility (enhanced in the case of northern Morazán by rugged terrain and a relatively remote location) that Wolf found to be an important factor in revolutions in Mexico, China, Cuba, and elsewhere during the first six decades of the twentieth century.

In northern Morazán, the conservative priest Fr. Andrés Argueta recruited and sent local peasants to El Castaño and other centers several years before his young, radical nephew Fr. Miguel Ventura arrived to preside over the newly formed Torola parish. Shortly after assuming his post, Ventura encountered lay catechists whom he knew from El Castaño, where he had given classes before his ordination. Once settled in northern Morazán, Ventura even organized catechism training locally to make it available to peasants whose poverty prevented them from attending the centers (Binford 2017).

In essence, the centers acted as transmission belts, bringing aspects of "the training of the cities" (Germaine Tillion, cited in Wolf 1969: 292) to the countryside. Not only did would-be catechists learn about liberation theology (and many other things) from priests, but they also learned from one another, exchanging information about social and economic conditions and the repressive actions of the state in different areas around the country. Returning home, they adapted their training to local conditions. For instance, a group of peasants in the Agua Zarca area of Torola municipality, inspired by liberation theology and probably drawing on rudimentary training in coopera- tive development offered by some centers, elected to work the land collectively, as Ventura explained after the war to Fina Rubio and Eduard Balsebre (2009: 81–82):

> Within the *caseríos* [hamlets], some people cultivated a bit more maguey than others. Those who produced more shared their fields communally. That meant that everyone in the *caserío*, fifteen or twenty people, were working this maguey plantation collectively. If one plot was not very large, they fin- ished the day's work in maybe three hours and then moved on to another plot. That's how the week progressed. On Saturday, they sold the product that they had extracted in the market, and in the afternoon the community divided up the money among all. Then on Sunday, they purchased basic consumption goods. It was a really collective way of working and living. I'm talking about the years 1974–1975.

In this way, some resource-poor peasants hoped to avoid seasonal labor migration to agro-export zones. The objective of the collective labor was more autarkic than socially transformative in that the par- ticipants had the object of evading rather than restructuring relations between merchants (and labor recruiters) and peasants. But even be- fore the Agua Zarca cooperative experiment, Treasury Police and National Guard agents were surveilling church meetings, and some catechists, concerned for their safety, expressed to Ventura their need to organize politically. Thus, Ventura introduced carefully selected catechists to Rafael Arce Zablah, a founder of the ERP, who was radi- calized while a student at the Jesuit-run and private Central Ameri- can University. During several clandestine meetings, Arce posited the need of preparing for armed struggle against the state, which he viewed as an inevitability. Some catechists responded positively to Arce's message, joined the ERP, and recruited others to the or- ganization—starting with family members and trusted friends and relatives. They maintained links with the leadership in San Salvador and took charge of the work in northern Morazán, organizing security when urban-based ERP militants arrived from San Salvador and San Miguel to clandestinely impart rudimentary military training (Binford 2017; Henríquez 2010: 53).

Rafael Arce Zablah died in combat during an armed activity in El Carmen, La Unión, in 1975, the same year Bishop Eduardo Álvarez, who administered the diocese of San Miguel, transferred Ventura from Torola to Delicias de Concepción, located a few miles south of the Torola River, to remove him from northern Morazán. However, catechists crossed the river to visit Ventura in Delicias and invited him to meetings in the north. Two years later, in 1977, a shootout at an army checkpoint at the entrance to Osicala, near the Torola River bridge, resulted in the deaths of four soldiers and the former catechist Ramón Sánchez, who had become an ERP militant. The army arrested Ventura and shortly thereafter catechist Fabio Argueta, accusing them of involvement in armed activities. Both were severely tortured for several weeks until public protests forced their release. Ventura went into exile, spending time in the United States before slipping back into Morazán in April 1982. Argueta abandoned religious work and went underground, organizing on behalf of the ERP.

Ventura and Argueta were fortunate to have survived capture in 1977, because that year marked a sea change in the modality of repression. According to Michael McClintock, "the traditional style of repression—prolonged imprisonment and exile—was gradually transformed until, by 1977, 'disappearance' and extra-judicial executions became the accepted way of dealing with the opposition" (1985: 172). However, growing repression did not prevent peasants and rural workers from joining mass organizations covertly linked to armed rebel groups committed to overthrowing the state. The earliest mass organization in El Salvador developed in 1974, but the ERP, which privileged armed struggle over popular organization, formed the 28 February Popular Leagues (LP-28) only in 1978. Mass organizations drew hundreds and sometimes thousands of peasants and rural workers to San Salvador, San Miguel, and other cities where they protested, chanted, and marched alongside students, slum dwellers, factory workers, teachers, and others at rallies, and occupied churches, factories, and government offices. Protesters demanded land reform, wage increases, the cessation of repression, and an end to military government—all key demands taken up by the FMLN later in its revolutionary platform. When police and soldiers harassed, threatened, arrested, and shot protesters, they reinforced the basic lessons of liberation theology by tying the present to biblical tales of the suffering of the Jews at the hands of Egyptians and the repression of early Christians by Romans. Moreover, many peasants from northern Morazán and elsewhere came to see themselves as part of a national movement for social justice and democracy.[5]

On returning to their communities, increasingly radicalized peasants and rural workers were pursued by National Guardsmen, Treasury Police, and paramilitaries from the Nationalist Democratic Organization, composed of civilians who served as the "eyes and ears" of the intelligence system in rural areas (McClintock 1985: 66, 204–209). In northern Morazán, Corporal Mata and the guardsmen in his charge worked from their base in the market town of Jocoaitique to gather information from a network of spies and kidnapped, tortured, and murdered people over a wide area. Other paramilitary groups worked out of Joateca, San Fernando, and Perquín. For security, organized peasants took turns manning lookout posts high up on mountainsides and warned those working fields below when soldiers or guardsmen entered the area on foot or in vehicles. Small groups that had joined the ERP assaulted local National Guard posts and destroyed military vehicles with homemade mines, sometimes recuperating weapons; others entered town centers under the cover of darkness to plaster buildings with anti-government propaganda. As the repression intensified, northern Morazán became increasingly polarized politically, and many men began sleeping in the bush for safety.

Up to this point, relations between rural and urban militants, peasants and ex-students, and the like had been relatively horizontal. The ERP leadership, weighted toward ex-university students based in San Salvador, set overall strategy, but peasants in northern Morazán—some occupying sensitive positions of great responsibility—implemented the strategy based on their knowledge of local conditions. Urban militants who visited northern Morazán before the war traveled largely by night under the care of local guides and disguised themselves as cattle merchants when it was necessary to move about during daylight hours (Medrano and Raudales 1994: 73–78). Urban militants supplied military training and taught peasants about organizational compartmentalization and other matters, but their ignorance of regional social relations and cultural mores left broad areas to be filled in by the local peasant leadership: Who to approach? How to approach people without arousing suspicion? Which peasants were allied with the authorities and which were not? No urban intellectual, no matter how committed to the struggle, could answer these questions. But as I discuss in the next section, peasants and rural workers ceded control to urban militants once war broke out in El Salvador and the latter left the cities for the countryside. They continued to fulfill critical roles, but their radius of decision-making shrank as urban militants took over.

In October 1979, after several years of surging mass movements, escalating repression, and growing economic, social, and political instability, young, "progressive" army officers in San Salvador staged a coup in a last-ditch effort to prevent a leftist overthrow. They formed a Civilian-Military Junta—an intermediate step toward democratic elections—but older, conservative, and high-ranking officers who favored repression over reform quickly outmaneuvered them. As government repression escalated, most civilians on the junta resigned and a new junta was formed. Under pressure from the United States and fearing a cutoff of military assistance, this junta sponsored an agrarian reform in March 1980 that the United States hoped would divide the Left. But the reform came too late and provided too little to prevent war. While Phase I of agrarian reform Decree 153 was enacted, albeit under military supervision and accompanied by repression, the reform's Phase II, which would have affected 30 percent of the nation's valuable coffee land, was postponed and eventually canceled because of staunch bourgeois opposition. Meanwhile, the junta proved powerless to reduce urban repression, which intensified as the army, police, and death squads linked to them kidnapped, tortured, and murdered thousands of people (AWC and ACLU 1982). The volcanic fields of Devil's Gateway above San Salvador gained international notoriety as a death squad body dump.

By mid-1980, militants were leaving the dangerous cities for the countryside and organizing training camps in remote areas of northern Chalatenango, northern Morazán, and elsewhere. Repression was intense in many rural areas too, and many people fled northern Morazán, especially following a full-scale army invasion in October 1980, the same month the FMLN formed out of the ERP and four other political-military organizations. As atrocities perpetrated by government forces piled up and open war approached, liberation theology less often served as a motivating force for joining the guerrillas, though it might have rationalized some people's decisions to do so. When ERP leaders with university and union backgrounds repaired to northern Morazán, they took charge of ERP military camps, established a chain of command, made personnel assignments, set daily routines, and enforced discipline. Peasant volunteers entered the ranks as line troops, though the most astute, daring, and experienced among them rose to become field commanders and direct troops in battle. However, few northern Morazanian natives acceded to the ERP High Command, which designed battle plans and set overall strategy. Many former catechists entered political, logistical, health, or cultural units that drew on literacy skills, self-discipline, and organizational experiences nurtured in peasant universities and sharpened through work with Christian Base Communities. Most young recruits learned how to handle weaponry and comport themselves in battle, but only those assigned to a noncombat unit acquired skills that might ease their reinsertion into civil society once the war ended. At this point, Wolf's "middle peasant" thesis—which refers mainly to the early stages of political involvement—breaks down.

The 1992 Peace Accord that ended the twelve-year revolutionary war mandated a reduction in the size of the army and replacement of militarized security forces with a National Civilian Police force under civilian direction. The FMLN disarmed and became a legal political party. It acknowledged the legitimacy of the reigning conservative Nationalist Republican Alliance (ARENA) government and began to compete for power through the ballot box. Most urban-origin leaders returned to San Salvador to organize the new party in the capital. Given a political conjuncture that included the breakup of the USSR (1990) and diminished Cuban support, this may have been the best deal the FMLN could strike. However, the Peace Accord did not alter the overall distribution of economic power beyond the establishment of a toothless and short-lived Social and Economic Forum, empowered to study the postwar situation and make nonbinding recommendations. The most significant redistributive act involved a Land Transfer Program (PTT) that provided land to a limited number of ex-FMLN combatants, FMLN social base, and ex-Salvadoran soldiers—a transparent effort to dissuade frustrated ex-combatants on either side from again taking up arms. However, the land was not expropriated from landowners, as in the case of Decree 153 of 1980, but instead transferred from "willing sellers" (private landowners) to "willing buyers" (program beneficiaries)—who received loans from a Land Bank capitalized by the US Agency for International Development (USAID). Because landowners were able to choose whether to sell and negotiate prices, the PTT closely followed the neoliberal playbook.

Postwar Dissolution

Northern Morazán was among the principal theaters of the revolutionary war. At least five thousand people died there, and repeated combat, aerial bombing, and shelling damaged or destroyed much infrastructure: the road system; electricity and telephone networks; and churches, schools, health centers, and municipal buildings. The war also resulted in massive internal population displacement and spurred international migration, setting the stage for the postwar "remittance economy." The open-air camps, forced marches, and exposure to death by any number of means (bullets, mines, air force bombs, accident, disease, etc.) left physical and mental marks still visible more than a quarter-century later (Binford 2016; see Silber 2011).

Many beneficiaries of the postwar Land Transfer Program had not acquired knowledge of agriculture; others lacked the capital to initiate a small-scale farming enterprise. The PTT required recipients to organize themselves into groups, pool individual loans, purchase land collectively, and form cooperatives. However, northern Morazanians had little experience in collective agriculture (Binford 2016: 98–100). By the mid-1990s, the US government was advocating *parcelación* (subdivision) and individual titling as necessary steps toward the creation of a land market that, according to USAID experts, would enable more efficient producers to concentrate resources at the expense of less efficient ones.[6] With individual titling, the FMLN's hopes of drawing on peasant cooperatives as bases of postwar political support dissipated, and within a decade much PTT land had been sold off. Cooperatives disbanded entirely or remained cooperatives in name only. With a few exceptions, peasants worked the land as private property. With the five-year grace period on loan repayment about to end in the mid-1990s, tens of thousands of peasants faced the possibility of losing land acquired through the PTT.

The most far-reaching postwar change involved the adoption of neoliberal reforms promoted by the USAID-funded Salvadoran Foundation for Development and supported by the ARENA governments that controlled the administrative branch from 1989 to 2009. Under ARENA, the government privatized the banking sector, TACA airlines, telecommunications, electricity distribution, the pension system, and coffee and sugar export; eliminated the Institute of Regulatory Supplies (which regulated consumer prices) and the Urban Housing Institute; reduced or eliminated many government subsidies and regulatory bodies; and sliced import duties. In 2001, ARENA rammed a currency change through El Salvador's unicameral Legislative Assembly, replacing the Salvadoran colón with the US dollar; three years later, in 2004, the government ratified the Central American-Dominican Republic Free Trade Agreement, better known as CAFTA-DR. Many newly privatized companies came under the control of transnational capital (Moreno 2004; Robinson 2003; Spalding 2014).

As a result of these policies, cheap, imported goods flooded the country. US companies were guaranteed protection under trade laws with disputes settled by international tribunals rather than Salvadoran courts, and the Salvadoran government ceded control over monetary policy to the US Federal Reserve in Washington, DC (see Garni and Weyher 2014; Moreno 2004; Towers and Borzutzky 2004). Raúl Moreno (2004: 32–33) explained that government cutbacks and the privatization of public enterprises had led to thousands of lost jobs and

> . . . provoked the destruction of labor organizations and the erosion of social gains won in the past. On the other hand, the privatization of public enterprises has led to the institutionalization of the subcontracting of services from other enterprises, which under the modality of "concession of services" for cleaning, private security, canteen . . . provide minimal labor benefits—even below those [legally] permitted—which stimulate the creation of jobs under precarious conditions.

In 1995, ARENA increased the regressive value added tax (IVA) from 10 to 13 percent, benefiting from the votes of federal deputies previously allied with the ERP, which earlier that year had split from the FMLN and formed the liberal Democratic Party (PD). This betrayal of the ERP's rural base, hit hard by the rise in the IVA, sent shock waves through northern Morazán. Most sitting PD mayors lost municipal elections in 1997, and over the course of several election cycles, the party's influence diminished nationally to the point that the National Electoral Commission revoked the PD's electoral accreditation and the party was dissolved.

Tariff reduction and price liberation resulted in higher costs of production and lower prices for small farmers. Cheap surplus grain dumped on the Salvadoran market depressed domestic market prices, at times below the cost of production (Garni and Weyher 2014: 68). By 2009, El Salvador was importing 42 percent of the corn consumed nationally. Even before the war ended, the agrarian bourgeoisie had shifted much of its capital into urban finance, commerce, and services. People living in rural zones like northern Morazán and those contemplating returning to them after 1992, often left (the first group) or stayed away (the second) because of limited economic opportunities. I estimate northern Morazán contained roughly thirty-five thousand inhabitants in 2010, down 30 percent from approximately fifty thousand in 1975.

Many northern Morazanians not linked to the ERP-FMLN spent the war in cities, towns, and displaced persons' camps under government control, exposed to pro-government radio and television stations that labeled FMLN fighters "terrorists" and "criminal delinquents," blamed the insurgents for the war, and represented them as puppets of Cuba and Fidel Castro. Thus, it is not surprising that after the war they supported ARENA or another conservative political party and not the FMLN. The postwar political sentiments of ex-combatants and the ERP's rural peasant-worker base were complex and shifting. Most voted for FMLN candidates, but a minority opted for ARENA or another party, while many others eschewed politics altogether and dedicated themselves to rebuilding household economies. The FMLN's postwar image was also damaged by corruption accusations leveled against some postwar FMLN mayors, as well as public discussion of the darker features of irregular warfare: wartime executions, insurgent appropriation of civilian property, occasional forced recruitment, and FMLN solicitation of "donations" (of corn, money, cattle, etc.) from peasants who remained in the zone during the conflict. Recriminations, revisionist history, and social and political conflict were inevitable consequences of a peace agreement that left conservatives in control of the government and the stewardship of the national economy in the hands of a small group of wealthy capitalists (see Binford 2002; Bourgois 2001; Silber 2011; Wade 2016). This was a new and different field of power on which the FMLN and its adherents would have to learn to maneuver.

The electoral victory of FMLN presidential candidate Mauricio Funes in 2009 broke ARENA's two-decade chokehold on the presidency. Funes continued a program begun under the outgoing ARENA president to supply peasants with free seed and fertilizer; he also provided elderly people with small pensions, mandated free school uniforms for children, and expanded Red Solidaria (Solidary Network), a World Bank–style targeted poverty alleviation program for people residing in more than seventy of the country's poorest municipalities, most located in former conflict zones. Though appreciated by recipients, the redistributive policies did not improve the rural economic climate overall or address the root causes of international migration (Garni and Weyher 2014: 68). The tens of thousands of Salvadorans who sought refuge in the United States during the revolution established beachheads for more expansive postwar migratory waves and northern Morazán became a major sending area.[7] Many contemporary northern Morazanian households have become veritable transnational units with people living in El Salvador dependent for their economic wellbeing on remittances from international migrants.

Cell phones have become ubiquitous in rural areas since the turn of the millennium. Small-scale commercial farmers use them to track product prices in urban markets; criminals extort money from truckers and bus drivers; families implore relatives living in the United States to send money for food, clothing, school quotas, fertilizer, and other things (see Alarcón 2015). The educational infrastructure has been rebuilt and even improved. As a result, more northern Morazanians are obtaining secondary and even postsecondary educations, but they are also discovering that high levels of urban un- and underemployment lead to the devaluation of educational credentials and depress wages. Few youths are interested in working in agriculture, where wages are so low—four to six dollars daily in many areas of northern Morazán in 2012—that some producers employ Nicaraguan and Honduran migrants attracted by payment in US dollars.

The instability of relationships (within families and communities)—induced in part by the revolutionary war and its inconclusive end—combined with the corrosive effects of neoliberalism to problematize the imagination of an alternative reality. As of 2012, northern Morazán was still hemorrhaging young people to the United States, despite the six to eight thousand dollars charged by smugglers and the great danger the journey involves. A sufficient amount of money entered northern Morazán in the form of remittances to warrant opening a branch of Western Union in Perquín, a small town high in the mountains near the Honduran border. Finally, it is important to note the Catholic Church suffered a double whammy in the postwar, its ideological influence eroded by a government campaign, begun in the 1970s, to "blame" liberation theology for the conflict, and its political clout reduced by the rapid postwar growth of evangelical movements that promote messages of individual salvation compatible with neoliberal capitalism.[8]

Rural social movements were most effervescent during a brief period in the mid- to late 1990s when recipients of land in the 1980 Phase I and 1992 PTT reforms mobilized through the Democratic Peasant Alliance (ADC) and the Forum for the Defense and Recuperation of the Agricultural Sector (FORO) for cancellation of the agrarian debt. The ADC was created by major peasant organizations in 1989, three years before the war ended, to form a united front against ARENA, whose presidential candidate, Alfredo Cristiani, won that year's election. The FORO, a looser organization of hetero-geneous membership (including some former ADC member organi-zations and ex-rebel soldiers), arose in 1995 when the debt struggle began. Initially competitive, the ADC and FORO eventually joined forces to create a short-lived Agrarian Front that successfully pres-sured the Legislative Assembly to pardon 85 percent of the debt and create a special line of credit for land reform recipients unable to repay the remaining 15 percent (Flint 2000; Kowalchuk 2003). Argu-ably, the debt cancellation stands as the major accomplishment of the peasant movement over the past twenty-five years. There exist plenty of studies documenting the deleterious impacts of free market re-forms on Salvadoran agriculture (e.g., CNAF 2014; CONFRAS 2009), but peasant organizations, reduced in size and without significant political clout, have had little success in taking them on.

Marc Edelman concluded an analysis of peasant struggles in the Central American Isthmus by noting how generally "the peasant struggles that, from the 1970s to the 1990s, sustained pressure for agrarian reform and better production conditions have diminished in size and frequency" (2008: 230). Specifically, Edelman was referring to the rise—detailed in an earlier article (Edelman 1998)—and demise of the Communitarian Association for Development, a region-wide association of peasant organizations linked to Vía Campesina, the transnational peasant coalition that promotes sustainable agriculture on an agro-ecological model. Edelman pointed to the negative ef-fects of "internal organizational weaknesses," but I am interested in highlighting the increasingly unfavorable external environment for peasant political mobilization that he summarized as follows:

> Political opportunities have diminished, as has the importance of agricul-ture in the region's economies; conditions for smallholders, particularly basic grains and coffee producers, have deteriorated; and massive migration from the countryside has transformed rural households, cultural expectations and political aspirations in ways that do not bode well for peasants' organizations. (2008: 238–239)

As Edelman makes clear, the decline of peasant political clout is a region-wide phenomenon; it has not been limited to northern Morazán or even El Salvador but can be documented in Nicaragua, Honduras, Costa Rica, and elsewhere. However, the Salvadoran case is complicated by the lingering effects of death, displacement, destruction, and psychological trauma wrought by the war and the processes that followed the incorporation of the FMLN into institutionalized politics, as well as the state's assault—to date relatively successful—on liberation theology. Most FMLN supporters and sympathizers, uninterested in a return to the chaotic seventies' period of militant protests and violent state repression, were relieved to see the fighting end and expected the FMLN to successfully represent their interests—though now through legal channels. With the opening of political competition (nominal electoral democracy) after the war and the weakening of the national military and its marginalization from politics, there *seemed* to be less need for independent, contestatory social movements—movements that were absent in northern Morazán during most of the 1970s. However, by the time the FMLN won presidential elections in 2009, the party found itself saddled with the legacy of seventeen years of neoliberal reforms that locked El Salvador into the global role of supplier of cheap labor to the United States.

At particular moments over the course of the past fifteen years, rural workers and peasants joined an array of urban-based groups to fight the privatization of water distribution and quash government efforts to privatize that part of the Salvadoran Institute of Social Security that "serves as a national public health care system for workers under formal contract in larger public firms and in the private sector" (Almeida 2008: 194; see Smith-Nonini 2010). Broad coalitions of rural and urban inhabitants have also succeeded in halting the incursion of transnational mining organizations. At least for the moment, struggles for access to the means of reproduction that affect most people in El Salvador—health care, water, public education, transportation, and public safety—outweigh those related to production, which is to say, struggles over matters related to employment (wages and salaries, the working day, working conditions, etc.). In El Salvador and elsewhere, future social movements for transformative change will require closer collaboration than ever between people in the countryside and those in the cities.

Finally, I would note that, as Wolf suggested, better-off peasants, which he referred to as "middle peasants," were among the main rural protagonists at the beginning of the Salvadoran revolutionary war in northern Morazán, northern Chalatenango, and probably other regions where the FMLN developed deep roots. It is less clear that they were involved in a strictly defensive struggle, given that radicalization of many rural dwellers responded (in part) to the repressive activity of state forces and paramilitaries linked to them. Though liberation theology was less about the restoration of a peasant utopia than about the configuration of a society of justice, equality, and brotherhood, it is clear some of the early social experimentation—such as the collective agriculture practiced by a small group of people in Torola—did involve efforts to evade rural merchant capitalists rather than change the system *dans son ensemble*.

The postwar period (1992–present) has entailed a progressive deepening of neoliberal capitalism, which had yet to take hold or even be introduced at the time Wolf wrote *Peasant Wars of the Twentieth Century*. If Wolf acknowledged the tragedy of the postwar peasantry, then he also held out hope, with the argument that "for the first time in millennia, human kind is moving toward a solution of the age-old problem of hunger and disease, and everywhere ancient monopolies of power and received wisdom are yielding to human effort to widen participation and knowledge" (1969: 301). That was, perhaps, 1960s optimism talking, though there was reason to be optimistic about the future in the 1960s, as noted in the introduction to this book. Neither Wolf nor others could have predicted on the basis of what had gone before the nature of the changing field of force or the speed and depth of commodification that would accompany neoliberal globalization and the challenges that rampant commodification would entail.

Acknowledgments

Some of the material on which this chapter is based was obtained during fieldwork supported by the National Science Foundation under Grant No. BCS-0962643 from the Cultural Anthropology Program.

Leigh Binford is Professor Emeritus at the College of Staten Island of the City University of New York. He writes on rural social economies, international migration, and struggle in Mexico and El Salvador. He coauthored (with Scott Cook) *Obliging Need: Rural Petty Industry in Mexican Capitalism* (1990) and wrote *The El Mozote Massacre: Anthropology and Human Rights* (1996, published in an enlarged edition in 2016) and *Tomorrow We're All Going to the Harvest: Temporary Foreign Worker Programs and Neoliberal Political Economy* (2013).

Notes

1. The UCS was designed as a conduit for state assistance to select groups of peasants. Despite the name, the UCS lacked the power of collective representation and negotiation. With the UCS, FECCAS, and others, the state sought to occupy organizational space in rural El Salvador that might otherwise be filled by more radical groups.
2. Since 1987, the number of dioceses has been increased from five to eight.
3. Minifundism refers to access to an amount of land insufficient to maintain the household. Minifundists had to supplement their incomes through some other means: petty commerce, petty commodity production, and/or wage labor (often including seasonal wage labor).
4. The peasant universities covered students' travel and living costs but provided no assistance to students to maintain family members that remained behind.
5. For instance, Antonio Vigil Vázquez (n.d.) narrated his experience of protest and repression during prewar mass LP-28 actions carried out in San Salvador and San Miguel.
6. In most cases, cooperative members owned the land in common but cultivated plots individually. In a few cases, areas planted in export crops like coffee were worked collectively.
7. The US Census Bureau estimated the number of Salvadoran migrants to the United States increased 2.5 times between 1990 (465,433) and 2004 (1,201,002) and that the amount of money remitted by all Salvadoran migrants (US-bound and otherwise) grew from $800 million to more than $3.2 billion annually. (Currently it is estimated at $4.5 billion.) After the war, the Morazán department became an important source of migration and one of El Salvador's principal recipients of remittances, which play an important role both in balancing national accounts and sustaining household economies (CEMLA 2009).
8. Perhaps wary of the baggage of the past and its potential effects on Catholic influence in the present, the institutional Catholic Church–appointed Fernando Sáenz Lacalle, a former military chaplain and member of Opus Dei, as archbishop in 1995. On 18 November 2000, the eleventh anniversary of the Jesuit assassination, Sáenz announced, "Liberation theology no longer has any place" (cited in Johnson 2000). When Sáenz retired in 2008, the Vatican, which took a conservative turn after the death of Pope John XXIII, replaced Sáenz with another conservative bishop, José Luis Escobar Alas, who closed down Tutela Legal, the Catholic Church's wartime human rights office and repository of "the most comprehensive archive of El Salvador's bloody history" because it was, according to him, "no longer relevant" (cited in Lakhani 2013). Liberation theology remained active but on the defensive in northern Morazán through the work of Fr. Rogelio Ponceele, a Belgian priest who accompanied rebels and civilians during the war (see López Vigil 1987), but Ponceele retired in 2015. Fr. Miguel Ventura partnered during the war and left the church after it, eventually being appointed Morazán governor in 2009 by President Funes. Ventura served as governor until Funes left office in 2014; Funes was succeeded by the FMLN's Salvador Sánchez Cerén (2014–2019).

References

Alarcón Medina, Rafael. 2015. "Peasant Warriors in an Electronic Social-Formation: From Rural Communities to Transnational Circuits of Dependence in Post-war El Salvador." *Convergence: The International Journal of Research into New Media Technologies* 21 (4): 474–495.

Almeida, Paul D. 2008. *Waves of Protest: Popular Struggle in El Salvador, 1925–2005*. Minneapolis: University of Minnesota Press.

Anderson, Thomas P. 1995. *Matanza*. Willimantic, CT: Curbstone.

AWC (Americas Watch Committee) and ACLU (American Civil Liberties Union). 1982. *Report on Human Rights in El Salvador*. New York: Vintage.

Berryman, Phillip. 1984. *The Religious Roots of Rebellion: Christians in Central American Revolutions*. Maryknoll, NY: Orbis.

Binford, Leigh. 2002. "Violence in El Salvador: A Rejoinder to Philippe Bourgois's 'The Power of Violence in War and Peace: Post–Cold War Lessons from El Salvador.'" *Ethnography* 3 (1): 177–195.

———. 2004. "Priests, Catechists, Revolutionaries: Organic Intellectuals in the Salvadoran Revolution." In *Landscapes of Struggle: Politics, Community, and the Nation-State in Twentieth Century El Salvador*, ed. Aldo Lauria-Santiago and Leigh Binford, 105–125. Pittsburgh, PA: University of Pittsburgh Press.

———. 2016. *The El Mozote Massacre: Human Rights and Global Implications*. Tucson: University of Arizona Press.

———. 2017. "Fabio's Story: Peasant Intellectuals in the Salvadoran Revolution." Unpublished manuscript.

Bourgois, Philippe. 2001. "The Power of Violence in War and Peace: Post–Cold War Lessons from El Salvador." *Ethnography* 2 (1): 5–34.

Cardenal, Rodolfo. 1992. "The Church in Central America." In *The Church in Latin America 1492–1992*, ed. Enrique Dussel, 243–270. Maryknoll, NY: Orbis Books.

CH (Catholic hierarchy). n.d. "The Hierarchy of the Catholic Church: Current and historical information about its bishops and dioceses." *Catholic Hierarchy News*. http://www.catholic-hierarchy.org.

CEMLA (Centre for Latin American Monetary Studies). 2009. "International Remittances in El Salvador." Mexico City: Inter-American Development Bank. http://www.cemla-remesas.org/informes/report-elsalvador.pdf.

Chávez, Joaquín M. 2017. *Poets and Prophets of the Resistance: Intellectuals and the Origins of El Salvador's Civil War*. Oxford: Oxford University Press.

CNAF (Comité Nacional de Agricultura Familiar). 2014. *Caracterización de la Agricultura Familiar en El Salvador: Políticas y Resultados Obtenidos — 1989/2014*. San Salvador: CNAF and CONFRAS.

CONFRAS (Confederación de Federaciones de la Reforma Agraria Salvadoreña). 2009. *Situación de las cooperativas y asociaciones agropecuarias afiliadas a Federaciones y CONFRAS*. San Salvador: CONFRAS.

CRIS (Centros Rurales de la Iglesia en El Salvador). 1974. "Conozcamos nuestra patria." Mimeo.

Ellacuría, Ignacio. 1991. "Utopia and Prophecy in Latin America." In *Toward a Society That Serves Its People: The Intellectual Contribution of El Salvador's Murdered Jesuits*, ed. John Hassett and Hugh Lacy, 44–88. Washington, DC: Georgetown University Press.

Edelman, Marc. 1998. "Transnational Peasant Politics in Central America." *Latin American Research Review* 33 (3): 49–86.

———. 2008. "Transnational Organizing in Agrarian Central America: Histories, Challenges, Prospects." *Journal of Agrarian Change* 8 (2–3): 229–257.

Farmer, Paul. 2004. "On Suffering and Structural Violence: A View from Below." In *Violence in War and Peace: An Anthology*, ed. Nancy Scheper-Hughes and Philippe Bourgois, 281–289. Malden, MA: Blackwell.

Flint, Adam. 2000. "The Reemergence of Social Movements in an Era of Neo-liberal Democracy in El Salvador." Paper prepared for the panel "Popular Responses to Political Transformation: The Importance of the Local for Understanding the Global" at the annual meeting of the Latin American Studies Association, Miami, FL, 16–18 March.

Garni, Alisa, and L. Frank Weyher. 2013. "Dollars, 'Free Trade,' and Migration: The Combined Forces of Alienation in Postwar El Salvador." *Latin American Perspectives* 40 (5): 62–77.

Golita, Alfonso, and Ernesto Galdámez. 1993. "El movimiento campesino en El Salvador: Evolución y lucha." Fundación Nacional para el Desarrollo, Documento de Trabajo no. 14, San Salvador.

Gould, Jeffrey. 2015. "Ignacio Ellacuría and the Salvadorean Revolution." *Journal of Latin American Studies* 47 (2): 285–315.

Gould, Jeffrey L., and Aldo Lauria-Santiago. 2008. *To Rise in Darkness: Revolution, Repression and Memory in El Salvador, 1920–1932*. Durham, NC: Duke University Press.

Henríquez Consalvi, Carlos [pseud. Santiago]. (1992) 2010. *Broadcasting the Civil War in El Salvador: A Memoir of Guerrilla Radio*. Austin: University of Texas Press.

Johnson, Marianne. 2000. "The Hand of Opus Dei in El Salvador." Opus Dei Awareness Network, 18 November. http://www.odan.org/media_hand_of_od.htm.

Kowalchuk, Lisa. 2003. "From Competition to Cooperation: Threats, Opportunities, and Organizational Survival in the Salvadoran Peasant Movement." *Revista Europea de Estudios Latinoamericanos y del Caribe* 74: 43–63.

Lakhani, Nika. 2013. "El Salvador shutters historic rights clinic." *Al Jazeera*, 13 October. http://www.aljazeera.com/indepth/features/2013/10/el-salvador-shutters-historic-rights-clinic-20131010112129327660.html.

Lindo-Fuentes, Hector, Erik Ching, and Rafael A. Lara-Martínez. 2007. *Remembering a Massacre in El Salvador: The Insurrection of 1932, Roque Dalton, and the Politics of Historical Memory*. Albuquerque: University of New Mexico Press.

López Vigil, Mario. 1987. *Muerte y vida en Morazán: Testimonio de un sacerdote*. San Salvador: University of Central America.

McClintock, Michael. 1985. *The American Connection, Vol. 1: State Terror and Popular Resistance in El Salvador*. London: Zed Books.

Medrano, Juan Ramón, and Walter Raudales. 1994. *Ni Militar Ni Sacerdote (de seudónimo Balta)*. San Salvador: Arcoiris.

Montgomery, Tommie Sue. 1982. "Cross and Rifle: Revolution and the Church in El Salvador and Nicaragua." *Journal of International Affairs* 36 (2): 209–221.

———. 1983. *Revolution in El Salvador*. Boulder, CO: Westview.

Moreno, Raúl. 2004. *La globalización neoliberal en El Salvador: Un análisis de sus impactos e implicaciones*. Barcelona: Fundación Món-3.

Pearce, Jenny. 1986. *Promised Land: Peasant Rebellion in Chalatenango, El Salvador*. London: Latin America Bureau.

Peterson, Anna L. 1997. *Martyrdom and the Politics of Religion: Progressive Catholicism in El Salvador's Civil War*. Albany: State University of New York Press.

Richard, Pablo, and Guillermo Meléndez, ed. 1982. *La Iglesia de los pobres en América Central: Un análisis socio-político y teológico de la iglesia centroamericana (1960–1982)*. San José: Departamento Ecuménico de Investigaciones.

Robinson, William. 2003. *Transnational Conflicts: Central America, Social Change, and Globalization*. London: Verso.

Rubio, Blanca, and Eduard Balsebre. 2009. *Rompiendo silencios: Desobdiencia y lucha en Villa el Rosario*. San Salvador: Red de Solidaridad para la Transformación Social y Museo de la Palabra y la Imagen.

Sánchez, Peter M. 2015. *Priest Under Fire: Padre David Rodríguez, the Catholic Church, and El Salvador's Revolutionary Movement.* Gainesville: University Press of Florida.

Silber, Carlota. 2011. *Everyday Revolutionaries: Gender, Violence and Disillusionment in Postwar El Salvador.* New Brunswick, NJ: Rutgers University Press.

Smith, Christian. 1991. *The Emergence of Liberation Theology: Radical Religion and Social Movement Theory.* Chicago: University of Chicago Press.

Smith-Nonini, Sandy. 2010. *Healing the Body Politic: El Salvador's Popular Struggle for Health Rights from Civil War to Neoliberal Peace.* New Brunswick, NJ: Rutgers University Press.

Spalding, Rose. 2014. *Contesting Trade in Central America: Market Reform and Resistance.* Austin: University of Texas Press.

Towers, Marcia, and Silvia Borzutsky. 2004. "The Socioeconomic Implications of Dollarization in El Salvador." *Latin American Politics and Society* 46 (3): 29–54.

Vigil Vázquez, Antonio [pseud. Quique]. n.d. Untitled memoir. Unpublished manuscript.

Wade, Christine J. 2016. *Captured Peace: Elites and Peacebuilding in El Salvador.* Athens: Ohio University Press.

Wolf, Eric. 1969. *Peasant Wars of the Twentieth Century.* New York: Harper & Row.

— Chapter 5 —

PEASANTS, CRIME, AND WAR IN RURAL MEXICO

Casey Walsh

The Mexican Revolution (1910–1920) continues to generate a tremendous amount of interest. In part this is because most Mexicans view the event as their own, an insurgent peasant upwelling that challenged neocolonial exploitation of the sort that continues to define life in that country and across the Global South. The rebellions led by Pancho Villa and Emiliano Zapata were eventually defeated by a bourgeois state party, but they were nonetheless successful in forcing the passage of a constitution that defined material resources such as water and oil as property of the nation, and the institutionalization of a new social pact that involved the redistribution of land, the nationalization of oil, free lay education, health care, and other elements of social welfare. The prosperity of the post–World War II period, known as the Milagro Mexicano, was experienced as an outcome of the revolution and the product of the government that formed in its wake. The Institutional Revolutionary Party, which ruled Mexico for almost eighty years, contributed to its own popularity and to the image of the revolution as a popular uprising with a clientelism fueled by that prosperity, and by controlling the narrative about what the revolution was through schoolbooks, murals, and other media.

This chapter traces the historical arc that links the uprising of the revolution, through mid-century developmentalism, to the current expressions of class struggle in neoliberal Mexico. It is inspired by the work of Eric Wolf, especially his *Peasant Wars of the Twentieth Century,* in several ways. First, Wolf's materialist historical anthropology insisted on the importance of understanding peasant politics within a longer temporal frame than that used by social scientists and even historians. In his explanation of the Mexican Revolution, for example, he argues:

> Many of the causes of the revolution had their origins not in the period of the Diaz dictatorship [1880–1911, just before the revolution], but in an earlier period, when Mexico was still New Spain and a colony of the Spanish mother country . . . all these problems derived ultimately from the original encounter of an Indian Population with a band of conquerors who had taken possession of Middle America in the name of the Spanish Crown. (1969: 3)

This deep history allowed him to identify fundamental, in addition to proximate, causes of social conflict, especially those having to do with the social organization of land and labor. In this chapter, I consider current forms of violence and conflict in rural Mexico to be expressions of dynamics of capital accumulation and class formation that have unfolded since the late nineteenth century.

Second, Wolf approached the six revolutions in *Peasant Wars* with attention to all their material complexity rather than through schematic outlines based in abstract categories. From the beginning of his career in the 1940s, Wolf worked with the anthropological category of "peasant," which he defined as a rural social class practicing autonomous subsistence cultivation and structurally engaged with markets and states. In the introduction to *Peasant Wars*, he distinguishes the peasant from both the forager and the farmer, for the first does not cultivate much, and the latter "enters the market fully, subjects his land and labor to open competition, explores alternative uses for the factors of production in the search for maximal returns, and favors the more profitable product over the one entailing the smaller risk" (xv). He also notes the important difference between peasants and rural proletarians such as the laborers working for wages on Cuban sugar plantations (257). But while peasantries can be differentiated from other groups based on (among other things) their social relations of production, they, like the fields of production and power in which they form, are always diverse and historically specific. Wolf viewed the twentieth-century peasantries that rose in rebellion as local "precipitates" (276) of global processes of industrial capitalism, not unrelated to, but certainly not the same as, those peasantries that formed in the context of previous states—such as the Mexican or Spanish empires—and pre-capitalist or mercantile capitalist economies.

Some thirty years later, Michael Kearney (1996: 3) argued that because of migration, globalization, and the spread of wage relations, "peasants are mostly gone," so we should also bid farewell to the peasant concept with its binary oppositions between rural and urban, peasant and proletarian, tradition and modernity. But Wolf's anthropology had already begun to break down those rigidities without discarding the idea that classes-in-themselves exist and that they condition subject positions. In *Peasant Wars*, Wolf conceptualized the class status of rural groups, but he did so through the detailed examination of local social formations and fields of power. "The anthropologist," he argues in the introduction to *Peasant Wars*,

> with field experience in small-scale communities, knows that there are differences in behavior and outlook between tenants and proprietors, between poor and rich peasants, between cultivators who are also craftsmen and those who only plow and harvest, between men who are responsible for all agricultural operations on a holding they rent or own and wage laborers who do their work under supervision of others in return for money. He also knows that one must distinguish between peasants who live close to towns and are involved in town markets and urban affairs and those living in more remote villages; between peasants who are beginning to send their sons and daughters to the factories and those who continue to labor within the boundaries of their parochial little worlds." (1969: xviii–xi)

Wolf's analysis of rural politics hinges on fine distinctions, especially between rich peasants who benefit from the status quo, poor peasants who lack land and thus have no margin of autonomy from state and market, and those "middle" peasants who are "tactically mobile" because they command economic resources and activities—land, casual labor, livestock, smuggling—that provide them "some latitude of movement" (290–291). This approach is descriptive more than prescriptive, so at the same time it insists on treating "peasant" as a material social reality more than a category, it also presages a shift in anthropological political economy away from structural typologies toward a focus on processes (Kearney 1996; Roseberry 1989). This is a third way Wolf's work shapes this chapter.

To productively evaluate rural politics in Mexico today, I suggest we push even further in this direction, understanding the crucial issue to be, as Wolf himself recognized, the political-economic processes that constitute the livelihoods and subjectivities of individuals, and the solidarities and identities of groups. Despite critical attention to the constructedness of the concepts of peasant and revolution in Mexico, I use Wolf's own words from *Peasant Wars* to point out the importance of asking "just what kinds of peasants we refer to when we speak of peasant involvement in political upheaval" in Mexico today (1969: x–xi). Who are the rural dwellers who are rising up as Zapatistas, or forging short and brutal careers in the narco-economy?

How are they articulated with processes of capital accumulation and state formation? In this chapter, I offer some preliminary answers to these questions, derived mostly from secondary literature but also from fieldwork I carried out in northern Mexico, on the border with Texas, between 1998 and 2008. I first review the literature on the Mexican Revolution and its aftermath, before focusing on the Zapatista rebellion and the violence associated with organized crime. I argue these latter two social conflagrations are not captured in any simple way by either the concept of peasant or that of war and that Wolf's historical materialism can be used to understand them in those terms.

The Mexican Revolution

In *Peasant Wars*, Eric Wolf provided an insightful analysis of the Mexican Revolution and its long unfolding. That revolution involved a complex set of movements by varied social groups, the character of which had a good deal to do with the environmental conditions of two large regions, the tropical south and the desert north. Each macro-region of Mexico gave rise to an army. The southern army was centered in the state of Morelos and led by Emiliano Zapata. Morelos was, like much of highland southern and central Mexico, a verdant landscape home to peasant agriculture for thousands of years. Wolf takes a very long perspective, finding continuity in peasant rebellions to secure land and livelihoods from the fifteenth to twentieth centuries. Peasants in highland Mexico had sustained tributary relationships with states long before the arrival of the Spaniards, but beginning in the colonial era, livestock and sugar plantations moved into this region, seizing land, channeling spring waters, and circling villages (Melville 1994; Warman 1976). Household economies thus came to integrate wage labor, as well as subsistence production, in proportions that shifted depending on the demands of capitalist agriculture, which increased steadily through the mid- and late nineteenth century. Sugar was, from the beginning of its transatlantic history in the 1500s, particularly modern and industrial in the organization of its production (Mintz 1985; Ortiz 1995). So, while the peasants of Morelos were deeply integrated into capitalism, this agonistic relationship gave these communities a particular, "closed, corporate" (Wolf 1957) character—defensive, solidary, and inward looking. They became, Wolf argues, "veritable fortresses of peasant tradition within the body of the country itself . . . sizzling pressure cookers of unrest" (1969: 294). For this reason, John Womack (1970) argued the peasants of Morelos fought a revolution in order to re-main the same—to resist the changes wrought by capitalism.

The other popular army of the Mexican Revolution formed in the north, principally in the state of Chihuahua, although the leaders that eventually triumphed and formed the postrevolutionary state were largely from the state of Sonora. Northern Mexico is a land of scant rainfall and wide expanse of dry land with occasional springs and streams. Agriculture was very uncommon in this region before the arrival of the Spaniards and could be practiced only by European and Mesoamerican colonists using irrigation technology. Ranching and mining defined the colonial economy throughout the north, and large-scale agriculture and industries emerged strongly in the late nineteenth and early twentieth centuries, just before the revolution erupted in 1910.

Wolf identifies three important groups in *norteño* society that com-bined to forge the military movement of the revolution. A bourgeoi-sie got its start in commerce but strengthened with the glass, textile, and steel industries, as well as large-scale irrigated commercial agri-culture. This stratum generated leaders such as Francisco Madero, Álvaro Obregón, and Plutarco Calles, who eventually won the fight-ing and forged a new state. The men (and some women) who formed the rank and file of the armies were, in Wolf's (1969: 35) analysis, "cowboys and bandits" typical of the region. Often they were fiercely independent descendants of the mestizo and criollo colonists sent by the Spanish Crown to secure its northern borderlands from highly mobile indigenous groups such as the Apaches, Comanches, and Kickapoos (Alonso 1995; Nugent 1996). Others were peasants from the center of the country who migrated to the north after the railroads were built in the 1880s to work for wages in mines, industries, and plantation agriculture in both the Mexican north and the Southwest United States (Friedrich 1970). Together these formed a vulnerable, mobile, and volatile semi-proletarian, semi-peasant mass (Katz 1988; Meyers 1994). While land distribution was a principal objective of the southern peasant army, the rebels of the north were motivated less by demands for land than by a quest, informed by the radical liberal-ism of northern intellectuals such as the Flores Magón brothers, for political independence, respect, and honor (Hernández Padilla 1988).

While most historians are comfortable with the idea that the Mexi-can Revolution began with the Plan de San Luis—a call-to-arms emitted by the northern businessman and liberal thinker Francisco Madero—there is not much agreement about when the revolution ended. Most would say 1920, with the presidency of Adolfo de la Huerta, or 1924, with the rise to power of the strong President Plutarco Calles. But ongoing rebellions cast doubts on that Whiggish history of the consolidation of the nation-state after the revolution, and point to a dynamic of rule more aptly characterized as a "war of position" (Gramsci 1971). In the 1920s and 1930s, campesinos in western Mexico responded to the new government's agrarian politics and the nationalization of churches with armed rebellions against federal troops and local supporters of the national government (González Navarro 2001; Purnell 1999). At the same time, while the land reform that alienated these *cristero* rebels was a pillar of the government's popular support from 1920 to 1940, many rural folks were actually left out of the land redistribution and welfare state largesse of the postrevolutionary era, which led to another kind of peasant agitation throughout the twentieth century.

The process of nationalizing and redistributing land was negotiated by activist peasants and reformist government employees, and while some private industrial agricultural plantations were broken up in Morelos (sugar), the Yucatán (henequen), and the Comarca Lagunera (cotton), land reform was more easily carried out through the construction of large irrigation systems that brought previously uncultivated ranchlands into intensive agricultural production and allowed the settlement of landless peasants (Aboites 1988; Olssen 2017; Walsh 2008). When this *agrarismo* petered out after the presidency of Lázaro Cárdenas (1934–1940), frustrated peasant activists often turned against the state and large landowners (Werner Tobler 1994). Between 1942 and 1962, for example, Rubén Jaramillo and his followers pressed for land reform and orchestrated land takeovers in Morelos (Padilla 2008), the land of Emiliano Zapata and his southern peasant army of the Mexican Revolution. The Cuban Revolution inspired both peasants and the state to harden their positions, and Jaramillo himself was killed by the army in 1962. It was at that time that Genaro Vázquez, a schoolteacher trained at the teacher's academy in Ayotzinapa, Guerrero, organized the Central Campesina Independiente, which, together with the Central Independiente de Obreros Agrícolas y Campesinos, pushed back against the Mexican state's official peasant organizations, most notably the Confederación Nacional Campesina. In Mexico's more developed north, campesinos orchestrated land seizures on the fringes of the irrigated development zones, sometimes successfully. Independent agrarian leaders such as Ramón Danzós were thrown in jail by a government intent on stopping campesinos from getting the upper hand in the protracted war of position in rural Mexico.

Alongside these relatively peaceful movements, a good number of armed groups kept the peasant "war of maneuver" alive in Mexico over the last century (Avina 2014; Bartra 1985; Carr 1996; see Gramsci 1971 for a discussion of the concept). These groups gained mainstream moral and tactical support when the Mexican government sent the army to squash student demonstrations in the Plaza de Tlatelolco in 1968, massacring hundreds of young people and killing eleven more in another demonstration in Mexico City in 1971. The next decade witnessed armed conflict in both urban and rural Mexico between revolutionaries and the state, while the federal government rolled out populist measures to win hearts and minds with a renewed program of land reform and welfare-state spending, financed by petrodollars. President Luis Echevarria (1970–1976) pushed through a distribution of lands in the coastal regions, the northern deserts, and the southern forests, and his successor, José López Portillo, focused state resources on rural development projects (Harvey 1998: 125–127). Unimpressed by these measures, the ranks of radical organizers swelled in the 1970s with young people and intellectuals, who took their work to the more marginal peasant communities, many of them in heavily indigenous "regions of refuge" (Aguirre Beltrán 1967) in the center and south of the country.

The Zapatistas who rose in the southern state of Chiapas are heirs to this long history of peasant struggle after the Mexican Revolution. On 1 January 1994, a few thousand indigenous peasants carrying arms took over several regional towns in Chiapas, declaring themselves the Zapatista Army of National Liberation (EZLN). They proclaimed opposition to the Mexican state, to the exploitation of capitalism, to the recently negotiated North American Free Trade Agreement (NAFTA), and to five hundred years of racist, colonial rule. Driving the rebellion forward, however, were shortages of and conflicts over land, which had simmered in the region for decades but reached a crisis point in the early 1990s (Harvey 1998: 190–193). While the motivations and goals of the rebels were aimed at securing dignity and respect as indigenous people, they were also quite literally fighting for their survival as peasants: small-scale, self-sufficient, indigenous agricultural producers.

Chiapas in 1990 was an extremely complex social situation in which multiple independent and state-affiliated peasant organizations had been involved in land conflicts for decades. Private landowners and colonization programs had displaced indigenous peasants from the densely settled highlands to more remote areas of the rainforest, where they formed new communities with more independence and horizontal power structures. Nevertheless, they still encountered the same problems of land concentration, this time in the hands of mestizo cattlemen, and serious shortages of land for a growing population of peasant agriculturalists. In many of their communications these rebels were represented by Subcomandante Marcos, an urban intellectual from northern Mexico who began to live and work with peasant communities in Chiapas in 1983. Along with Marxist-inspired radical intellectuals, missionaries of the Catholic Church propagated liberatory concepts among these communities, contributing to a radical political culture with roots in indigenous ontologies and practices (Harvey 1998). At the same time, the indigenous identity constructed by the Zapatistas and those they have inspired must also be understood as part of a long engagement between indigenous people, the state, and radical activists (Gledhill 2008; Saldívar Tanaka 2008).

Although the Zapatistas quickly retreated from the towns they took in January 1994, the government mobilized the army and local paramilitary groups, who were responsible for, among other atrocities, the massacre of dozens of members of a pacifist group in the town of Acteal, Chiapas, and the displacement of thousands more Zapatista sympathizers. Peasant groups elsewhere in southern Mexico rallied to the example of the Zapatistas, demanding autonomy from the state and the removal of military forces from their communities. In the state of Guerrero, the Southern Sierra Peasant Organization (Organización Campesina de la Sierra del Sur) received the wrath of police retribution at the Aguas Blancas massacre in which seventeen people were killed. This led to the formation of the other notable peasant guerrilla of the 1990s in Mexico, the Popular Revolutionary Army.

Under the leadership of the high-profile Subcomandante Marcos, the EZLN regrouped and entered into a critical dialogue with the political establishment in Mexico on the one hand and with transnational social movements of liberation on the other. The "détente" established between the EZLN and the federal government has allowed the peasant organization the time and space needed to distribute its message massively on an international stage, to build a protective network of human rights activists and observers (Speed 2004), and to engage with national level politics. From the beginning, this *zapatismo* was conceived to be an indigenous struggle, marking distance with versions of the Mexican revolutionary tradition cast as a national process protagonized by mestizos. Nonetheless, it was never a parochial movement with only localist ambition, for the

EZLN's struggle for autonomy has questioned the very heart of the liberal Mexican state. The indigenous peasant groups of the EZLN have built community organizations and infrastructure throughout highland Chiapas, and they exert a de facto independence that defies a state that only accepts autonomies that fit within a multicultural, constitutional liberalism: cultural expression and language, principally (Harvey 2016).

The Drug War

At the same time that indigenous peasants built regional autonomy on Mexico's southern border, a much messier and less principled conflict broke out in northern and western Mexico amid the "rubble" (Gordillo 2014) of the postrevolutionary welfare state. It is not a rebellion against the state, and it is fought not over access to land but rather over the right to participate in, and profit from, an extremely lucrative trade in narcotics and other controlled commodities, such as migrant labor, sex, and stolen gasoline, as well as extortion and protection rackets. Nevertheless, it is important to evaluate the place of this conflict within the long history of uprisings and violence in Mexico and to consider whether this current round of popular violence can be understood in the terms deployed by Wolf in *Peasant Wars*. I suggest that if we consider the importance of the economic activities carried out by the warring factions of this conflict to the livelihoods and household economies of ordinary Mexicans, and locate most of those involved in the violence in relation to long term processes of state formation and capital accumulation, then we can see that this conflict is a moment in which the long-simmering peasant war of position has emerged once again into open hostilities.

Much of the marijuana, heroin, and methamphetamines that are moved across the border to the United States is produced in Mexico, particularly in the Sierra Madre Occidental from Chihuahua to Guerrero, while cocaine from South America passes through the region. The transnational criminal organizations (TCOs), often called "cartels," that have grown to control this commerce have added to their portfolios a whole range of other prohibited economic activities: trafficking of weapons and migrants, money laundering, prostitution, protection rackets, and the theft from public infrastructures of goods such as gasoline. Regardless, the huge risks and rewards of this commerce derive from the regulatory state structures that create scarcity for these substances, and the ruthless competition among those groups seeking to realize those profits. In this context, the organizations either arm themselves or contract mercenaries to manage the violence required to successfully do business. The violence associated with the illegal economy resulted in a tripling of reported homicides between 2007 and 2011, with rates exceeding those of many war zones in areas such as the northern border cities and the "Golden Triangle" producing region where the states of Sinaloa, Durango, and Chihuahua meet (Shirk and Wallman 2015; Williams 2012). Paradoxically, while the spectacle of public assassinations is a highly visible ideological tactic of the TCOs, many homicides are hidden from view by their perpetrators, and many go unreported and uninvestigated because of the extreme danger involved. All this makes it very difficult to know exactly how large the toll has been, but estimates range from 80,000 to 150,000 lives have been taken.

Is this a "war"? Or just murderous crime? How should we understand the violence of the narco-economy? In an important book published three decades ago, Friedrich Katz (1988) developed a continuum of "riot, rebellion and revolution" to characterize "rural social unrest in Mexico." Katz and colleagues direct our attention to all the manifestations of rural violence that are not framed as efforts to create a new national political order—that is, rural violence that is hard to valorize as revolutionary or prerevolutionary. On the face of things, TCOs and the paramilitary forces that serve them have no apparent political platform, ideology, or commitment that shapes their engagements with the state and society. While not random, this violence might not seem to qualify as motivated by the political reasons that are usually behind revolutions and wars. TCOs are business operations, and the violence they engender is aimed at maximizing profits. In contrast, the Mexican Revolution, as both open and latent conflict, has long been described as a war of peasant and worker liberation, because it was fought over political ideas and principles of radical liberalism (democracy, free elections, effective suffrage, etc.), as well as to secure more narrowly economic elements such as land and wages. Peasant riots and rebellions are usually understood to be guided by the same "hidden transcripts" (Scott 1992), as are much less dramatic forms of resistance.

There are, however, compelling reasons to see TCOs as enacting political projects of rule based in neoliberal political culture, and thus to identify the current violence as "war" (Correa-Cabrera 2017). The businesses involved in the illicit economy are at the same time paramilitary organizations that operate in a space outside the formal boundaries of state institutions. The TCOs shape governments by supporting some state actors for elected office, eliminating others, and purchasing or coercing the allegiance of yet others. While it would be a mistake to draw this boundary between state and TCO too firmly, as people and transactions involved in the narco-economy are lodged within state institutions and operate with the complicity of state actors, the complete failure of the state to monopolize violence places the current conflict in the realm of civil war. Furthermore, the goal of maximizing profits by whatever means necessary should be considered political. Profit-driven business organizations that take on state functions such as violence are the maximum expressions of the political philosophy and practice of neoliberalism, which privileges deregulation, decentralization, and the primacy of the individual and the firm to the organization of society (Harvey 2005; Trouillot 2001). There have also been some efforts by the TCOs to secure the hearts and minds of people through the distribution of goods and services, and they have carried out concerted campaigns to control the media by intimidating journalists and sending their own, often horrendously brutal messages. Perhaps most importantly, both participants and bystanders cast the violence of the narco-economy as a legitimate questioning of hierarchy and inequality that Eric Hobsbawm (1969) defined as social banditry (Joseph 1990). As a result, different criminal business organizations claim obedience, if not support, from the populace in different regions, questioning the state's claim to have a monopoly over the legitimate use of violence and positioning themselves as competitors for sovereignty.

The ways the narco-economy and its violence take shape in the lives of everyday Mexicans comes into focus in the work of anthropologists. In 2005, just before violence spiraled out of control, Shaylih Muehlmann witnessed the pervasive effects and cultural foundations of the narco-economy in a small town in Sonora. In her book *When I Wear My Alligator Boots*, Muehlmann (2014) shows how the risks, rewards, and reasonings of the drug economy shape the lives of ordinary people trying to make a living in rural areas with little other opportunity for social mobility. Oftentimes people are involved tangentially in the drug economy through banal activities such as opening up bank accounts for other people that function to launder money. She notes it is unremarkable that children would make a few bucks running errands for traffickers or unloading drugs from their boats. Sometimes, however, they are directly involved in the transportation and sale of the products, and even in the violence associated with it.

Muehlmann argues that the violence associated with narcotics is rooted in the political culture of rural northern Mexico, where there is an enduring respect for the rebelliousness of illegal economic activity fueled both by the asymmetry and antagonism of the relation with the United States, as well as a deep distrust of the Mexican government:

> The drug trade allows some people, especially young men, to draw on the sense of pride and defiance that characterizes the popular northern Mexican persona of the narcotraficante and the rich cultural matrix from which this figure emerges. The persona of the traficante resonates historically with a legacy U.S.-Mexican antagonism on the border that has been fueled by the militarization of the region and the lack of other viable routes of upward mobility. (2014: 20)

The appeal of the cultural trappings of the drug economy—ostentatious clothing, narco-*corridos*, military armament, and a blasé embrace of violence and death—is rooted in a society composed historically, as Wolf put it, of "cowboys and bandits" (1969: 35). Although the framing of this culture of class conflict in terms of "cowboys and bandits" is perhaps a bit clumsy, there is nevertheless a deeply gendered ideal that men in rural northern Mexico should be independent, honorable, and brave—*valiente*, in local parlance (Alonso 1995: 231; Nugent 1996: 23). And this political culture is certainly rooted in the material history of the north as a frontier of conquests and colonizations, cattle raising, and rustling (Duncan Baretta and Markoff 1978; Lopes 2005). In the 1860s, this *norteño* political culture took the form of support for the liberalism of Benito Juárez and around 1900 in the radical liberalism and anarcho-syndicalism of the Partido Liberal Mexicano. Daniel Nugent (1996) and Ana Alonso (1995) noticed this ethic of rebellion in the town of Namiquipa, Chihuahua, and argued it made that locale a focal point of the Mexican Revolution. From this perspective, smoldering within political culture in northern Mexico is a latent rebellious violence that, for Muehlmann, takes its most shocking shape in the figure of Samuel, a young boy who boasts of contract killings for narco-traffickers (2014: 20–21). This *norteño* political culture has very old roots but now forms the basis of the neoliberal order enacted by TCOs in the civil war to control the illegal economy.

But, is this a *"peasant* war"? Not entirely. And that is because there are people from many social positions involved in this violence. As generations of scholars have noted since Marx, peasants self-organize at the scale of the village or clan. Any wider social project, such as a peasant war or revolution, involves intellectual and political leadership, usually by actors of a different class. Consider that there are those who practice subsistence agriculture and fishing who have incorporated the production and trafficking of illegal commodities into their livelihoods. While these folks fit squarely into the peasant category, many of those involved in the violence are city dwellers, and many who lead the TCOs are from middle-class and wealthy backgrounds. But this was also the case of the peasant wars discussed by Wolf. In China, leadership was provided by intellectuals of the gentry and, as in Cuba and Russia, by the Communist Party (1969: 104–105). In Mexico, radical liberal intellectuals provided conceptual orientation for the rebels, and wealthy dissidents led the victorious forces. That it was a bourgeois revolution does not mean it was not a peasant war. Something similar can be said of the current hostilities.

Wolf's "peasant wars" were thus mobilizations both within and across social classes that evolved over time. I, too, would address the question of narco-violence not by starting with the political nature of the peasantry as a class-in-itself outside of history or even at any given time but rather in terms of how different groups emerge, interact, and decay over time. The "epochal" analysis of Raymond Williams (1977) emphasizes that people inhabit shifting mixtures of emergent and residual class positions as they navigate changing regimes of accumulation (Harvey 1990). Like the rebellions of the Zapatistas and other peasant groups in southern Mexico, the drug war is an armed conflagration fought among those people abandoned by the neoliberal state when it dismantled a mid-century regime of accumulation based on green revolution technology and postrevolutionary land distribution and social organizations. However, the combatants in the illegal economy emerge not always from a clearly definable peasant class or fraction but rather more generally from the "rubble" (Gordillo 2014) of socioeconomic positions and social structures of accumulation erected by the developmentalist postrevolutionary Mexican state.

From its beginnings in the 1920s, the new Mexican state envisioned an industrialized and technified rural Mexico populated by small farmers who would drive the political, economic, and cultural development of the country (Walsh 2008). Although collective farms were created, even during the presidency of Lázaro Cárdenas (1934–1940), the preferred organizational model for these farms was industrial rather than peasant. And while land was owned by the state and managed collectively, much of this *ejidal* enterprise was dedicated to industrial export products such as sugar, henequen, and cotton and formed the productive foundation of state capitalism. After 1940, the green revolution furthered this process by providing technological packages and advice with the goal of turning peasants into small farmers, even those producing the traditional Mesoamerican food-stuffs, such as maize, beans, and chili. This project was successful, especially in northern Mexican irrigation districts in Tamaulipas and Sonora, where *ejidatarios* in the 1960s and 1970s were able to pro-duce twelve metric tons of hybrid maize per irrigated hectare (none of it for subsistence) in support of government objectives such as food sovereignty. Of course, these visions of development were often not realized, especially in the more marginal areas of central and southern Mexico, where peasant socioeconomic organization and production continued to be strong. In fact, the growth of capitalist agriculture articulated with the peasant sector, which subsidized the accumulation process by removing many of the costs of social repro-duction from the wage relation (Kearney 1996; Palerm 2008).

By 1980, the agrarian development model was collapsing, creat-ing the relative surplus population that would find employment in the illegal economy that gained strength in the 1990s and erupted in violence in the 2000s. Across the country, the federal government implemented a neoliberal restructuring plan that removed subsidies for products and supports for producers, and in 1992 privatized the *ejidal* sector, allowing land to be bought and sold. NAFTA, in 1994, was another piece of this plan, for it placed Mexican producers in direct competition with US corporate agriculture. The strategy was to use a market shock to make rural Mexicans more productive and effi-cient or force them to sell their land to others who could be (Warman 2001). This was no longer about turning peasants into farmers but rather was aimed at inducing the shift from farmer to agribusiness that unfolded in most dramatic fashion in the rural United States during the course of the twentieth century. In Mexico's industrial agricultural zones, especially in the north and west, this strategy was indeed successful, for it built on a process of land concentration that was already under way, including in the supposedly inalienable so-cial lands of the *ejidos*. On the other hand, in the more indigenous southern and central regions of the country, the collapse of agrarian development led to the "re-peasantization" of rural production, with rural producers returning to subsistence agriculture complimented by wage work and remittances (Sesia 2003).

This process was in full swing when I conducted fieldwork in the irrigation districts of northern Tamaulipas in the late 1990s. Like many other river drainages across northern Mexico, the Rio Bravo and Rio San Juan were built into agricultural emporiums during the

1930s and 1940s, a period when international cotton prices were kept strong by domestic agricultural policy in the United States, with the Commodity Credit Corporation buying cotton surpluses and retiring them from the market. The US produced most of the world's cotton, so US prices were in effect everywhere, providing an incentive for governments such as that which took over after the Mexican Revolution to focus agricultural development on that crop. Cotton grew particularly well in the irrigation districts of arid zones such as the Mexican north, so landless peasants and agricultural workers were allotted parcels of ten to twenty hectares, an amount that could be farmed with household labor and would produce enough cotton to provide for a stable middle-class life. In fact, colonists in the Valle Bajo Rio Bravo irrigation district were required to plant cotton, and the regional economy and infrastructure were completely devoted to that crop. This regime of accumulation was very successful, and cotton became the biggest earner of foreign currency in Mexico in the 1950s (Aboites 2013; Almaráz and Cerutti 2013; Walsh 2008).

For about twenty years, *ejidatarios* and private landowners enjoyed the bounty of the green revolution in cotton—a time now known as the era of "white gold." And, in many places in Mexico, peasants were converted into farmers. Men and women who were subsistence producers, or whose parents had been just a few years before, drove tractors and managed systems of improved seeds, pesticides, fertilizer, and irrigation to bring in harvests of the world's most industrialized cash crop. They built houses, sent kids to college, bought trucks, had vacations, and enjoyed the bounty of the green revolution. They responded to the dynamics of agricultural policy and international commodity markets. Matamoros was eponymous with the cotton boom and the modern prosperous rural Mexico. When the United States stopped supporting cotton prices and began dumping surpluses on the market, northern Tamaulipas switched to corn and sorghum, and cotton moved to Sonora, Michoacán, Chiapas, and Central America, where it was still profitable for another short while. It was the end of the prosperity of "white gold," and although in the 1970s rural domestic economies were supported by government subsidies linked to a national food system project, the staple crops like maize that took over required almost no labor, and unemployment grew. In the 1990s, a wave of neoliberal reforms privatized *ejidal* lands, decentralized irrigation management, and reduced or eliminated subsidies for agriculture (Weaver et al. 2012).

The end of government developmentalism had disastrous repercussions in Mexico's countryside, as the prosperity and progressive redistribution of the mid-twentieth century crumbled. The "social sector" of Mexico's agriculture—the vast system of collective farms known as *ejidos*—was dismantled and privatized, leaving peasants and rural producers to fend for themselves. Salvador Maldonado noticed that in the Tierra Caliente region of Michoacán, "the post-revolutionary State tried to resolve [social conflict] undertaking large-scale public works. But those projects were suspended or abandoned in the 1980s with the advent of neoliberal politics, and drug-trafficking and other illicit activities quickly moved in to fill the void" (2013: 47). The crisis of rural Mexico led to unemployment and poverty, and propelled migration and the illegal economy. As James McDonald (2005: 121) wrote about another area of rural Michoacán:

> the unfortunate reality in this part of rural Mexico is that young people, primarily men, have three options. First they can be farmers with little or no land who can only aspire to a life that will result in poverty. Second they can migrate, most likely to the United States, in search of jobs and higher wages. Third, they can get involved with the local narcoeconomy, sometimes in conjunction with being a migrant.

In the 1970s, the migration of young Mexicans from the country to the cities spiked sharply, as did their employment in the industrial production of high-value agricultural commodities such as broccoli, lettuce, strawberries, and mangoes, mostly in the United States (Álvarez 2005; Palerm and Urquiola 1993; Wells 1996). In northern Tamaulipas, the countryside began to empty out. The children of many of the families who settled lands in the irrigation districts went to work in Matamoros, Brownsville, or farther north in Texas. Like most of rural Mexico, the small towns and settlements became sites of social reproduction, home mostly to young and old (Kearney 1996). At the same time, contraband, which had always been present in the borderlands, surged anew as people sought ways to make ends meet. While in the 1920s alcohol was smuggled northward, during the "age of white gold" money was to be made crossing goods from the United States such as radios and refrigerators southward to relatively prosperous consumers in Mexico. With the crisis, smuggling resumed its south-north flow, this time focused on drugs, with arms and cash traveling in the opposite direction.

These shifts shaped the lives of young people such as Pablo, whom I met while living in the town of Valle Hermoso, Tamaulipas, in 1998. Tired of walking around town in the blazing sun and humid heat, I went to a small bicycle shop looking for a more comfortable option. Pablo was a bit surprised to see me show up in what was definitely not a tourist destination, but like many people in the Mexico-US borderlands, he was pretty comfortable talking to gringos in Spanish or English. His family was from Valle Hermoso, where he was raised, but he did not complete high school and instead went to work in the agricultural fields of the Valley of South Texas. When I asked him about the extensive line tattoos on his arms, he told me he had spent a few years in jail in Texas after being caught smuggling drugs into Brownsville. He was paid to cross a small package through customs, and as luck would have it, he related, he got caught. Displaying neither bitterness nor guilt, he viewed both the drug business and jail as a normal part of life in the borderlands, something that many young men such as himself had to deal with as they sought out a living. He did not articulate the kind of *norteño* masculine rebelliousness noticed by Muehlmann, Nugent, and Alonso but rather seemed quite done with playing the game of high risks and rewards and had returned home to live with his parents, importing, and reselling used bicycles bought at yard sales in Texas. Whatever small amount he earned contributed to the household expenses.

Conclusion

Is the drug war in Mexico a peasant war? Not in any simple way, but simple discussions of peasants and politics had been eclipsed even before Wolf penned *Peasant Wars*. Those who are fighting that war are not primarily rural producers with goals of securing land and maintaining a peasant way of life but are often urban dwellers with weak ties to the countryside (Campbell 2009). Furthermore, those who are managing the illegal commerce are principally businessmen. and the violence that has been generated by these transnational crime organizations is directed toward the goal of maximizing profits. At the same time, however, among those who are involved at all levels within these TCOs are people with peasant livelihoods or those who come from peasant backgrounds. As was the case with Pablo, many are part of that surplus population thrown off by the demise of a regime of accumulation organized around industrialization, commercial agriculture, and the welfare state. On the other hand, those growing the drug crops in remote mountain areas in Sinaloa, Chihuahua, Durango, Guerrero, and Michoacán are often indeed peasants, and the cash from drug production complements traditional subsistence food production (Maldonado 2013; Malkin 2001). However, while their goals do include securing land, machinery, cattle, and horses (for example), they grow or trade drugs to make the cash needed to finance a life as a prosperous farmer or rancher, rather than that of a peasant engaged in subsistence cultivation (McDonald 2005). These are remarkably conservative political struggles aimed at conserving "a dying way of life" (McDonald 2005: 120), similar perhaps to those rebellious peasants in Morelos who fought a revolution to keep from changing. The nostalgic goal of recovering a mythic *ranchero* lifestyle animates the violence of many young men participating in the narco-economy.

The fleeting encounters anthropologists have had with the narco-economy and its violence suggest it should be conceived of as another moment of open hostilities in a very long struggle of social classes in Mexico. It is indeed a civil war, for it pits TCOs against the armed forces of the state, forcing the TCOs to openly battle the government's police and soldiers, or less openly bribe them into compliance. Whatever arrangement is made, these two large organizational groups are vying for sovereignty: the monopoly over the legitimate use of force in Mexico, as well as the support or at least the obedience of the population. Following Charles Tilly (1985), we could conclude that, in this case, organized crime is indeed state formation, and it emerges from the rubble of state-led twentieth-century developmentalism. The violence deployed by TCOs is not simply a bloody business tactic but rather a popular political project to assert a vision of individual and national identity with deep roots in peasant and rancher rural livelihoods.

Of course, those who lead both sides of this conflict are not peasants but rather fractions of a bourgeoisie thrown up by the dynamism of a deregulated, neoliberal regime of accumulation. In this way, it is similar to the Mexican Revolution a century ago, which was a peasant war that shifted political power to a new fraction of the bourgeoisie. As Eric Wolf established in his *Peasant Wars*, the class status of those who are fighting and those who are leading this civil war is important, for the structural position of these different actors affords them different kinds of political, economic, and cultural resources and different amounts of room to maneuver. At the same time, however, this class status can be understood only through an examination of how larger political-economic movements are lived by real individuals, for it is these movements more than a typological category that constitute social actors in a material sense. As was the case with the Mexican Revolution, it may be that we learn more about the importance of peasant positions in the current wave of violence when we emerge from it. Whatever new social pact emerges from the rubble of the neoliberal regime of accumulation and its associated violence, it will consolidate socioeconomic positions that reflect both the past and future of rural Mexico.

Casey Walsh is Professor of Anthropology at the University of California, Santa Barbara. His research centers on commodities, the social use of water, and the history of anthropological thought. His first book, *Building the Borderlands* (2008), focused on the political economy of cotton to show how and why society and culture in the borderlands of northern Mexico took shape in the twentieth century. His second book, *Virtuous Waters* (2018), is a long history of mineral springs and bathing in Mexico that explores quotidian engagements with heterogeneous waters.

References

Aboites, Luis. 1988. *La irrigación revolucionaria: Historia del sistema nacional de riego del Río Conchos, Chihuahua, 1927–1938*. Mexico City: SEP.

———. 2013. *El norte entre algodones: Población, trabajo agrícola y optimismo en México, 1930–1970*. Mexico City: El Colegio de México.

Aguirre Beltrán, Gonzalo. 1967. *Regiones de refugio: El desarrollo de la comunidad y el proceso dominical en mestizo América*. Mexico City: Instituto Indigenista Interamericano.

Alonso, Ana María. 1995. *Thread of Blood: Gender, Colonialism and Revolution on Mexico's Northern Frontier*. Tucson: University of Arizona Press.

Álvarez, Robert. 2005. *Mangos, Chiles and Truckers: The Business of Transnationalism*. Minneapolis: University of Minnesota Press.

Almaráz, Araceli, and Mario Cerutti, eds. 2013. *Algodón en el norte de México (1920–1970). Impactos regionales de un cultivo estratégico*. Tijuana: El Colegio de la Frontera.

Avina, Alexander. 2014. *Specters of Revolution: Peasant Guerrillas in the Cold War Mexican Countryside*. Oxford: Oxford University Press.

Bartra, Armando. 1985. *Los Herederos de Zapata*. Mexico City: Ediciones ERA.

Campbell, Howard. 2009. *Drug War Zone: Frontline Dispatches from the Streets of El Paso and Juarez*. Austin: University of Texas Press.

Carr, Barry. 1996. *La izquierda Mexicana a través del siglo XX*. Mexico City: Ediciones Era.

Correa-Cabrera, Guadalupe. 2017. *Los Zetas, Inc: Criminal Corporations, Energy and Civil War in Mexico*. Austin: University of Texas Press.

Duncan Baretta, Silvio, and John Markoff. 1978. "Civilization and Barbarism: Cattle Frontiers in Latin America." *Comparative Studies in Society and History* 20 (4): 587–620.

Friedrich, Paul. 1970. *Agrarian Revolt in a Mexican Village*. Chicago: University of Chicago Press.

Gledhill, John. 2008. "Introduction: Anthropological Perspectives on Indigenous Resurgence in Chiapas." *Identities: Global Studies in Culture and Power* 15 (5): 483–505.

González Navarro, Moisés. 2001. *Cristeros y agraristas en Jalisco*. Mexico City: El Colegio de México.

Gordillo, Gaston. 2014. *Rubble: The Afterlife of Destruction*. Durham, NC: Duke University Press.

Gramsci, Antonio. 1971. *Selections from the Prison Notebooks*. New York: International Publishers.

Harvey, David. 1990. *The Condition of Postmodernity: An Enquiry into the Origins of Cultural Change*. Cambridge, MA: Blackwell.

———. 2005. *A Brief History of Neoliberalism*. Oxford: Oxford University Press.

Harvey, Neil. 1998. *The Chiapas Rebellion: The Struggle for Land and Democracy*. Durham, NC: Duke University Press.

———. 2016. "Practicing Autonomy: Zapatismo and Decolonial Liberation." *Latin American and Caribbean Ethnic Studies* 11 (1): 1–24.

Hernández Padilla, Salvador. 1988. *El magonismo: historia de una pasión libertaria, 1900–1922*. Mexico City: Ediciones ERA.

Hobsbawm, Eric. 1969. *Bandits*. London: Weidenfeld & Nicolson.

Joseph, Gilbert M. 1990. "On the Trail of Latin American Bandits: A Reexamination of Peasant Resistance." *Latin American Research Review* 25 (3): 7–53.

Katz, Friedrich, ed. 1988. *Riot, Rebellion, and Revolution: Rural Social Conflict in Mexico*. Princeton, NJ: Princeton University Press.

Kearney, Michael. 1996. *Reconceptualizing the Peasantry: Anthropology in Global Perspective*. Boulder, CO: Westview Press.

Lopes, María-Aparecida. 2005. *De costumbres y leyes. Abigeato y derechos de propiedad en Chihuahua durante el porfiriato*. Mexico City: El Colegio de México / El Colegio de Michoacán.

Maldonado Aranda, Salvador. 2013. "Stories of Drug Trafficking in Rural Mexico: Territories, Drugs and Cartels in Michoacán." *European Review of Latin American and Caribbean Studies* 94: 43–66.

Malkin, Victoria. 2001. "Narcotrafficking, Migration, and Modernity in Rural Mexico." *Latin American Perspectives* 28 (4): 101–112.

McDonald, James. 2005. "The Narcoeconomy and Small-town, Rural Mexico." *Human Organization* 64 (2): 115–125.

Melville, Elinor. 1994. *A Plague of Sheep: Environmental Consequences of the Conquest of Mexico*. Cambridge: Cambridge University Press.

Meyers, William. K. 1994. *Forge of Progress, Crucible of Revolt: Origins of the Mexican Revolution in La Comarca Lagunera, 1880–1911*. Albuquerque: University of New Mexico Press.

Mintz, Sidney. 1985. *Sweetness and Power*. New York: Viking.

Muehlmann, Shaylih. 2014. *When I Wear My Alligator Boots: Narco-culture in the U.S.-Mexico Borderlands*. Berkeley: University of California Press.

Nugent, Daniel. 1996. *Spent Cartridges of Revolution: An Anthropological History of Namiquipa, Chihuahua*. Chicago: University of Chicago Press.

Olssen, Tore. 2017. *Agrarian Crossings: Reformers and the Remaking of the US and Mexican Countryside*. Princeton, NJ: Princeton University Press.

Ortiz, Fernando. 1995. *Cuban Counterpoint: Tobacco and Sugar*. Durham, NC: Duke University Press.

Padilla, Tanalís. 2008. *Rural Resistence in the Land of Zapata: the Jaramillista Movement and the Myth of the Pax Priista, 1940–1962*. Durham, NC: Duke University Press.

Palerm, Angel. 2008. *Antropologia y marxismo*. Mexico City: CIESAS/UAM/UIA.

Palerm, Juan-Vicente, and José Ignacio Urquiola. 1993. "A Binational System of Agricultural Production: The Case of the Mexican Bajio and California." In *Mexico and the United States: Neighbors in Crisis*, ed. Daniel Aldrich and Lorenzo Meyer, 311–366. San Bernardino, CA: Borgo Press.

Purnell, Jennifer. 1999. *Popular Movements and State Formation in Revolutionary Mexico: The Agraristas and Cristeros of Michoacan*. Durham: Duke University Press.

Roseberry, William. 1989. *Anthropologies and Histories: Essays in Culture, History, and Political Economy*. New Brunswick, NJ: Rutgers University Press.

Saldívar Tanaka, Emiko. 2008. *Prácticas cotidianos del estado: una etnografía del indigenismo*. Mexico: Universidad Iberoamericana.

Scott, James. 1992. *Domination and the Arts of Resistance: Hidden Transcripts*. New Haven, CT: Yale University Press.

Sesia, Paola 2003. "Repeasantation and Decommodification of Indigenous Agriculture: Coffee, Corn, and Food Security in Oaxaca." In *The Social Relations of Mexican Commodities: Production, Power and Place*, ed. Casey Walsh and Elizabeth Emma Ferry, 81–126. San Diego, CA: Center for US Mexican Studies.

Shirk, David, and Joel Wallman. 2015. "Understanding Mexico's Drug Violence." *Journal of Conflict Resolution* 59 (8): 1348–1376.

Speed, Shannon. 2004. *Rights in Rebellion: Indigenous Struggle and Human Rights in Chiapas*. Stanford, CA: Stanford University Press.

Tilly, Charles. 1985. "State Formation as Organized Crime." In *Bringing the State Back In*, ed. Peter Evans, Dietrich Rueschemeyer, and Theda Skocpol, 169–187. Cambridge: Cambridge University Press.

Trouillot, Michel-Rolph. 2001. "The Anthropology of the State in the Age of Globalization: Close Encounters of the Deceptive Kind." *Current Anthropology* 42 (1): 125–138.

Walsh, Casey. 2008. *Building the Borderlands: A Transnational History of Irrigated Cotton along the Mexico-Texas Border*. College Station: Texas A&M University Press.

Warman, Arturo. 1976. *Y venimos a contradecir: Los campesinos de Morelos y el estado nacional*. Mexico City: CIS-INAH.

Weaver, Thomas, James Greenberg, William Alexander, and Anne Browning-Aiken. 2012. *Neoliberalism and Commodity Production in Mexico*. Boulder: University of Colorado Press.

Wells, Miriam. 1996. *Strawberry Fields: Politics, Class and Work in California Agriculture*. Berkeley: University of California.

Werner Tobler, Hans. 1994. *La Revolución Mexicana: Transformación social y cambio politico, 1876–1940*. Mexico: Alianza Editorial

Williams, Phil. 2012. "The Terrorism Debate over Mexican Drug Trafficking." *Terrorism and Political Violence* 24 (2): 259–278.

Williams, Raymond. 1977. *Marxism and Literature*. Oxford: Oxford University Press.

Wolf, Eric. 1957. "Closed Corporate Peasant Communities in Mesoamerica and Central Java." *Southwestern Journal of Anthropology* 13 (1): 1–18.

———. 1969. *Peasant Wars of the Twentieth Century*. New York: Harper & Row.

Womack, John. 1970. *Zapata and the Mexican Revolution*. New York: Vintage.

— Chapter 6 —

PEASANT WARS IN BRAZIL

Cliff Welch

$\mathcal{C}\!\!\sim$

Despite numerous peasant uprisings between the late 1800s and the near present, regional peasant revolts in Brazil proved incapable of expanding beyond their boundaries to stimulate the broader national revolutions analyzed by Eric Wolf in *Peasant Wars of the Twentieth Century*. In exploring why, this chapter draws on two factors—mediators and tradition—that Wolf stressed as keys to transforming regional revolts into national wars. Wolf argues both individual and group mediators played "a significant role in peasant involvement in political upheaval." He describes potential mediators as those who "stand at the junctures in social, economic and political relations which connect the village to wide-ranging elites in markets or political networks" (1969: xii). In modern Brazil, mediators of peasant rebels failed to serve the role Wolf projected. In general, they either underestimated or overestimated the revolutionary potential of peasant revolts in Brazil. Only the most recent case of the MST diverges from this general rule.

Wolf also points to ancestral influences and traditional patterns as "causes for persistence or change" (xiii). The persistence of traditional patterns of dominance and submission in rural social relations is a constant theme in Brazilian history. Analysts reference the Brazilian ruling class's remarkable capacity to maintain its hegemony, demonstrated by a plantation system based on African slavery that persisted from 1530 to 1888, the avoidance of a national independence war, and the negotiation of a peaceful transition from slave to free labor. This ruling class hegemony was often filtered through intermediaries—often religious figures—with a proven capacity to manipulate cultural norms, like patrimony, to organize and control the subordinate classes (Faoro [1957] 2000).

In all but the most recent cases, Brazil's peasant wars are best characterized as defensive. In order "to ensure continuity on the land" and protect their "source of livelihood" (Wolf 1969: xiv), peasants rebelled against dramatic changes introduced by liberal governments adopting the capitalist "cultural system," as Wolf calls it (276). Once left undisturbed, they preferred living in autonomy, hoping to be safe, rather than charging out to build alliances or expand their territory. Offensive measures were sometimes taken, such as preemptive strikes on enemy positions, to reinforce an essentially defensive strategy. The cases we call offensive featured mediators with high expectations for mobilizing peasants. In one case, they tried to reproduce the Chinese model of building a peasant revolutionary army. In another, a nonviolent resistance strategy was used to gradually expand peasant territory.

The first two "wars" analyzed are those of Canudos in the 1890s and Contestado in the World War I period. While the Canudos conflict mesmerized Brazil as a nation, receiving extensive media coverage for the era, it was restricted to a single municipality in the Northeast region. The Contestado "war" included skirmishes in a frontier area of the borderlands of two states, but authorities successfully restricted it to this micro-region of southern Brazil. Both took place during the neocolonial period, when capitalist penetration intensified globally in response to the natural resource demands of the second industrial revolution. Messianic leaders mediated both as defensive movements aimed at restoring a pre-capitalist order. Despite their failure to expand, these two bloody conflicts generated powerful stories of Brazilian self-determination that continued to inspire peasant resistance into the twenty-first century.

The next two "wars" examined—Formoso/Trombas in the mid-twentieth century and Araguaia in the 1970s—highlight the interaction of tradition and mediators. Each case involved a peasantry on the move. Fleeing difficult conditions in more developed areas, peasants migrated to wilderness areas in the Center-West, on the outskirts of Formoso, and in the North, along the banks of the Araguaia River. Their very exertion in deforesting and cultivating the land soon made the regions targets for land speculators and state-sponsored projects, helping determine the path of Brazil's ever-expanding agricultural frontier. In the Cold War context, these situations called Communist Party militants to the peasants' defense, stimulating the "wars" analyzed. While many peasants appreciated the mediator's support in defending their territories, agendas clashed, and the conflicts were soon contained. In the Araguaia case, the goals of mediators proved so ambitious that few peasants mobilized, yet it was the peasantry that suffered most from repression.

The fifth case involves Brazil's controversial Movimento dos Trabalhadores Rurais Sem Terra (Landless Workers' Movement—MST). Founded in 1984, the MST quickly established itself as the most vigorous of Brazil's twentieth-century peasant movements. It revived the memory of struggles for radical agrarian reform. It also renewed and repurposed peasant traditions, and rather than serve as a mediator, it cultivated leaders from the peasant population and regularly refreshed them, amplifying leadership capacity to all corners of the country. Rejecting experiments like the Communist Party attempt to form a people's army among peasants in the Araguaia region, it opted for a nonviolent revolutionary strategy of gradual but dramatic change. The case study focuses on part of Brazil's southeast region, where aggressive land and leadership struggles led to the creation of more than one hundred agrarian reform settlements.

These five cases add up to a coherent story about peasant conflicts during Brazil's long twentieth century, a period that coincides with the establishment of republican government in 1889 and continues to the present day. During this entire period, Brazil's ruling class sought to integrate the country in worldwide capitalist development projects, a process that stimulated peasant rebellion. The first two cases involved defensive struggles, while the most recent ones engendered offensive struggles to establish autonomous spaces, one that intended to incite a national revolution, while the others posed little threat to Brazil's territorial integrity. As Wolf argued, resistance to capitalism has consistently stimulated rebellion in the countryside, but for reasons related to tradition and mediation, Brazil's peasantry never managed to foment revolutionary war.

The War of Canudos

The most well-known and influential peasant war of republican Brazil occurred in the Northeast in the 1890s. Frequently described as the War of Canudos, it was amply reported at the time and soon integrated into the nation-state formation story by Euclides da Cunha, a journalist sent to cover the war. His classic book about the conflict, *Os Sertões*, was published in 1902 and translated into English as *Rebellion in the Backlands* in 1944. Partially filtered through Wolf's lens, the Canudos story helps weigh the value of regional differences, traditions and mediators.

The War of Canudos occurred in Bahia state between November 1896 and October 1897. Canudos was the headquarters of a deteriorating plantation when thousands of followers of the millenarian spiritual leader popularly known as Antônio Conselheiro occupied it in 1893. Conselheiro—the Counselor, a Catholic Church–sanctioned designation for especially capable religious laymen—had spent more than twenty years wandering through the semi-arid *sertão* (backlands) of the Northeast, repairing church properties in the region's villages. In the process, he collected a following of thousands of people, nearly all of them peasants. As the millennium approached, Conselheiro called on his flock to settle a "New Jerusalem" to prepare for the Judgment Day predicted at the turn of the century. Canudos, renamed Belo Monte (Lovely Hill) by Conselheiro, became this place until liberal leaders of the new republic began to see it as a threat. Conselheiro viewed republican government critically, condemning the end of monarchy and the advent of liberalism as a transition from "God's law" to "dog's law"—from paternalism to the atomizing, competitive reign of capitalist relations (Cunha 1976: 181–184).[1] Beginning with the state militia and ending with federal army battalions, this backlands New Jerusalem was finally extinguished.

While poorly understood by participants, nearly all were reacting to the increasing insecurity of Brazil's deepening integration into the capitalist world economy. In the North, overseas demand for natural rubber created a new elite. In the northeastern backlands, peasants experienced changes from the construction of railroad corridors, often involving immigrant labor, that stimulated land and power concentration among traditional oligarchs; new laws required census registry, criminalized vagrancy, and taxed even small market transactions. Prices increased, while incomes decreased; neighbors and relatives migrated out of the region and the Catholic Church's influence diminished. As a result, peasant autonomy declined dramatically (Palacios 2009).

Conselheiro was far removed from the anarchist leaders who influenced peasants in the 1910 Mexican Revolution. He represented some of the most traditional and retrograde of Catholic teachings, bemoaning the fall of the monarchy, defending patriarchy, and suppressing the aspirations of his followers. In areas difficult to staff with priests, devout laymen like Conselheiro aided the church in keeping people focused on the afterlife rather than their experiences with misery and injustice (Villa 1997). For the anthropologist Shepard Forman (1975: 217), this belief system supported "an extraordinary sense of submissiveness to authority" among Brazilian peasants.

In this sense, Brazil's first peasant war was a war inspired by a backward-looking, restorationist logic rather than a radical, revolutionary one. By most accounts, Conselheiro was not a good mediator, at least not in the earthly realm. While his followers organized themselves in militias capable of standing off invading armies for nearly a year, Conselheiro kept himself busy restoring the village chapel and orchestrating the construction of a new church. He devoted himself to a spiritual mission, convinced the world was ending and that his flock needed to prove its worth before God in order to be welcomed in heaven. On the other hand, first the local power structure, then the state government, and finally the Republic itself expressed their fears and insecurities about Canudos and the insubordination the *conselheiristas* represented. They saw Canudos as a threat to the fragile new liberal political order.

Locally, the church feared losing their congregation to Conselheiro; regionally, the *coroneis* (landowning local political bosses) complained of dwindling numbers of people available to work on their estates: herding cattle, harvesting, building, cooking meals, and cleaning up. In meeting after meeting with local authorities, Conselheiro showed respect for elites but refused to disband New Jerusalem. He knew little of republican Brazil, but he bemoaned the ouster of Emperor Dom Pedro II, Brazil's second king following independence in 1822. To him, the downfall of the people's protector was just one more sign of a worldwide endgame. His enemies called him a monarchist, which raised the profile of this religious encampment in a little-known corner of Bahia state. Brazilian leaders argued they had to restore order to guarantee the nation's further integration into the international capitalist system.

The peasants of Canudos fought a defensive war. They left the area only to consolidate good relations in the region, sell products, and buy supplies or defend themselves, but never to disrupt the world about them. In November 1896, one such mission, a march of some 500 *conselheiristas* to the town of Juazeiro, came under surprise attack by a squad by 100 state police, who killed more than 150 of the pilgrims. "The peasants used tree branches, old rifles, farm tools, knives and steel bars to defend themselves," wrote the historian Robert Levine (1995: 222), and the police withdrew after suffering ten dead and sixteen wounded. This event is recounted as the first assault on Canudos. Peasants routed two additional military attacks before a final assault, organized in June 1897 by twenty-five battalions from all over the country armed with the latest German canons. The invading army hung, shot, or stabbed to death all the men it captured; burned to the ground more than five thousand houses; and encouraged dogs to hunt down and eat the faithful's cows and goats. Soldiers decapitated Conselheiro, spiking his head on a lance and parading their trophy through interior hamlets as they marched to the coast. It still took them more than two months to destroy Canudos.

The Contestado War

Religious, political, cultural, and anti-capitalist elements were also present in the Contestado War of 1912–1916. The messianic figure José Maria embodied some of the conflict's origins. Allegedly similar to Conselheiro, José Maria adopted the name of the millenarian João Maria de Jesus—who wandered about the interior of southern Brazil offering religious and healing services to backlanders (*sertanejos*) from the 1890s to 1908. In 1912, José Maria attracted a following in the Contestado, a frontier area of contested boundaries between the states of Santa Catarina and Paraná. While the millenarian legacy of João Maria inspired followers, the historian Paulo Pinheiro Machado (2004) argues José Maria never self-identified as a messiah. His followers referred to him as a "monk." They gathered around him because he created a popular pharmacy and taught them how to use natural plant and herbal remedies. Jealous of his popularity, rival power brokers and the press demonized José Maria as a local manifestation of Conselheiro and organized forces to eliminate the threat he supposedly posed to their interests. The monk became a martyr in October when authorities killed him during an attack on his entourage of about forty lightly armed followers. The military commander also died in the fight, helping solidify the skirmish as the first battle of the Contestado War.

At its base, questions of control over material resources, especially land, spurred on the struggle. In 1906, republican leaders advanced a project to construct a railroad from São Paulo to Rio Grande do Sul by contracting with the infamous US capitalist Percival Farquhar, who schemed to monopolize rail transit in Latin America. Farquhar's Brazil Railway Company formed a three-hundred-man security force, larger than that of Paraná state, and demarcated the railroad route between 1908 and 1911 (Dalfré 2008). The investor's immediate return took the form of land grants along the rail line with the final concession of an average distribution of nine miles on each side of the tracks. The Farquhar group also established the Southern Brazilian Lumber and Colonization Company, which built two lumber mills, employing eight hundred full-time workers, introducing not only the first industrial activity in the region but also groups of immigrant colonists from abroad, as well as migrant laborers from elsewhere in Brazil. These activities provoked instability, fear, and conflict. They forced peasants off their land, destroyed forests, flooded crops, and expanded urban areas, stimulating ethnic hostility and deepening the gap between rich and poor (Carvalho 2008).

The peasants, who called themselves *sertanejos* and *caboclos* (a word used to describe their mixed indigenous, African, and European ethnic origins), reacted defensively to the transformation of their world. Growing groups of uprooted peasants sought solace with those associated with José Maria or those who claimed to be oriented by his spirit. A popular Catholicism characterized peasant culture, imbuing believers with the eternal life of the Holy Spirit, upholding righteousness, and reinforcing hierarchy. The pilgrims formed refugee camps that grew to include thousands of capitalism's victims. For their own survival, they planted crops, organized armed patrols and hunting expeditions, and negotiated to acquire meat and other provisions. They understood the railroad and lumber companies as enemies that needed to be contained to defend their own survival. Constantly persecuted by private, state, and federal forces, they attacked railroad and lumber properties. They justified their use of violence as necessary to restore customary rights to use the land to sustain themselves. Take, for example, a revealing message left by an unnamed rebel on the door of a company store during an attack on a railway station in 1914:

> We were in Taquarassú dealing with devotion [and] did not kill or steal, Hermes [Fonseca, president of Brazil, 1910–1914] sent his cowardly forces to bomb us where they killed women and children therefore the cause of all this is the bandit Hermes and therefore we want the law of God that is the monarchy. The government of the Republic herds its Brazilian Sons off land that belongs to the nation in order to sell it to foreigners, we are now willing to make our rights prevail. (Carvalho 2008: 33–34)[2]

The author of the note, apparently writing to express the patrol's motives for attacking the train station, emphasizes the victimization of his group. The republican government attacked without reason, killing innocent women and children. Rebels sought the rule of law defined by God—Monarchy—in contrast with republican law, which they also seemed to experience as "dog's law." Moreover, they accused the Republic of "herding Brazilian sons" off the land in order to sell it to "foreigners," making it necessary for them to fight for their "rights."

The historian Tarcísio Motta de Carvalho convincingly documents the tradition of occupation in the region that privileged *caboclo* slash-and-burn techniques and periodic migration from exhausted to undisturbed areas. For generations, these native sons and daughters of colonization secured and cultivated the land, defending the southwestern advance of Brazil against hostile indigenous nations and neighboring Spanish territories. The economy functioned mainly on an exchange basis with a paternalistic relationship established between *sesmeiros*—the landlords who were granted large expanses of colonial land and whose areas were later recognized by the Empire—and the *posseiros* (squatters), who worked the land almost as if it was their own. The liberal Land Law of 1850, which was rarely implemented until the World War I period, gradually introduced market relations. But it did so in frontier areas like the Contestado mostly through *grilagem*, a practice in which *coroneis* and land title agencies conspired to produce false property titles. In disparate cases, Carvalho's research shows how *posseiros* came to be called *intrusos* (trespassers), representing a profound undermining of their status as land leaseholders (2008: 36–47). The falsified commodification of land spread in a widening swath by the rapacious incursions of Farquhar's railroad, lumber, and colonization operations. As these plans materialized, German, Polish, and Ukrainian immigrants entered the regional mix, and traditional occupations such as that of pack animal traders (*tropeiros*) became obsolete (Machado 2004).

While poverty made the peasants useful in an exchange economy, their lack of cash and collateral made them impediments to capitalist development. The company's security forces burned down their houses and stole their animals. Backed by a private army, the company's lawyers coaxed peasants into signing blank sheets of paper, promising them titles to the land they cultivated. The signed papers soon were used as authorizations to abrogate customary rights and take away peasant access to land that guaranteed their family welfare. In these examples, we find evidence for what Wolf (1969: 276) described as "the world-wide spread and diffusion of a particular cultural system, that of North Atlantic capitalism." This culture promoted a "guiding fiction" in which "land, labor and wealth are commodities, that is, goods produced not for use, but for sale," undermining traditional cultural formations (277). Some peasants were thus forced to seek employment clearing the forest to construct the railway, as peons in Farquhar's lumber mills or even as gunmen for coronels or the company. Desperate for alternatives, many gathered behind mediators like José Maria and his disciples.

A "deep sense of injustice" flourished and resistance grew as the *caboclos* reflected on the "causes for persistence or change" (xiii) in their customary standing, especially their traditional right to cultivate undeveloped land (Diacon 1991; Espig and Machado 2008).

The *caboclos* of the Contestado resisted, but ultimately lost the war. Leaders passed out of favor or died. Rivalries and differences of opinion divided the rebels into smaller groups as the war dragged on. Some factions forced reluctant peasants to join the movement to prevent their forced recruitment by government forces. During peak moments, however, "communitarian social practices," which some later defined as "peasant communism," made the rebellion popular among peasants (Machado 2004: 335–342). By banding together behind leaders of their choosing, they replaced the patron-client relationships that had long typified their subjugation. Men, women, and children participated in the collective defense, while certain members joined offensive patrols, as they sought to guarantee the autonomy of the region. In an era and area where public education did not exist, they created their own pedagogy (Rosa 2011). Untold thousands joined the struggle against republican Brazil. Until 1915, attacks by federal and state troops helped galvanize the solidarity of participants. They fought for their independence, which they connected to customs of land use based on subsistence agriculture, tolerated if not encouraged by traditional power brokers, who benefited from the unpaid labor and support of this subaltern population. By 1916, internal weaknesses combined with the strength of the opposition to undo the rebel stronghold.

Like the Canudos conflict, the Contestado peasant war did not bring revolution to Brazil. Both were fundamentally defensive regional conflicts, whose mediators did not preach social revolution. At most, they aspired to restore the past order of monarchy and effectively established radically different presents in which authorities of their own choosing displaced traditional power elites. They also created systems to guarantee their subsistence, security, and autonomy. They understood their acts as contrary to the liberal, individualistic market conventions then under development, but they did not anticipate the threat such acts posed to the new capitalist order. Their search to escape the transformations underway hastened several changes by enhancing the control exercised by central government authorities over state and local authorities, weakening patron-client relations, compelling the construction of new national security infrastructure, inciting the aspirational expectations of peasants, altering production and supply chains, and creating compelling arguments for the very "modernization" they despised. Wolf concluded, "The peasant's role is essentially tragic: his efforts to undo a grievous present only usher in a vaster, more uncertain future" (1969: 301). But he also quickly defined the peasant's role as "full of hope," as their rebellion means active participation in shaping that future. Both the Canudos and Contestado movements have contributed in this way to Brazilian history, having become rich mines of memory that inspire future generations of rural folk to insist on their inclusion in this ever-unfolding story.

The Formoso and Trombas War

During the 1950s and early 1960s, the Brazilian Communist Party (PCB) became involved in peasant "wars" in diverse locations. These included the Porecatu War in Paraná state (1950–1951), the "peasant war" of Formoso and Trombas in Goiás state (1954–1964) and the "Grass War" (Guerra de Capim) in São Paulo state (1959–1961). In addition to being the largest and lengthiest of PCB-supported peasant struggles, the Goiás war exemplifies conditions in yet another region, the Center-West.

While the conflict's roots are deep, the 1954 start date coincided with the publication of the PCB's agrarian program. Following an analysis of the need to "liquidate latifundia and extinguish the remnants of feudalism and slavery" in Brazil, the program argues the path to national development will advance partly by "delivering to landless peasants and to those with little land the expropriated latifundia areas free of charge and in private property form" (Santos 1954/1955: 143). By breaking up latifundia, PCB leaders imagined achieving several positive results, including improving the lives of peasants, enhancing the popularity of the party, weakening the material power base of rural political bosses, strengthening democracy, and slowing the rural exodus to cities. The plan further determined: "All forms of struggle are good, just and necessary, but must always be struggles of the masses and for the masses. Under these conditions, petitions, small protests and both partial and total strikes are just, even armed struggle" (254). Given this outlook and the broad distribution of PCB militants, it would seem the PCB was poised to become the perfect mediator for turning a variety of regional conflicts into a national revolutionary movement. However, although the PCB Central Committee initially conceived of the armed struggle in Goiás as a step on the way to revolution, most participating peasants viewed their struggle as necessary to defend newfound property rights.

Most of those involved in the conflict were newcomers to the area, landless peasants who aspired to become "existentially involved in cultivation and make autonomous decisions regarding the processes of cultivation" on land they controlled, as Wolf wrote (1969: xiv). This migration was stimulated in part by a government subsidized agricultural colony in nearby Ceres, Goiás, a project Brazilian leader Getúlio Vargas initiated in the 1940s. With promises of subsidized land and services, many poor rural people came to the area, overwhelming the colony's capacity. Facing dashed hopes, some unwelcomed newcomers wandered farther into Brazil's backlands. One who tired of waiting was José Porfírio de Souza. On his return trip home along the Tocantins River, he happened upon the Formoso area. Learning it was a "no man's land" (Carvalho 1978a: 7), he gathered his family and returned to settle there. Others came from the south, as part of the plan for the Ceres colony that included linking it to the Transbrasiliana highway, which wound its way north from Uruguay to the Atlantic port of Belém. Moreover, in 1956, President Juscelino Kubitschek made concrete long-considered plans to construct Brazil's new national capital of Brasília on a nearby plain.

Such growth factors attracted the interest of *grileiros* (unscrupulous land speculators) who organized themselves into cabals. They falsified titles and hired thugs who approached one peasant family after another to explain to them their new status as sharecroppers, describing how they had to hand over 25 percent of their crop as "rent." Peasants were also pressured to sign affidavits declaring recognition of their tenant status and lack of rights to the land (Carneiro 2014: 121; Carvalho 1978a: 7). These intrusions inspired the resistance movement. In response, the *grileiros* became increasingly violent. They tore down and set aflame the peasants' few possessions and structures, and apprehended and tortured men, women, and children. Until 1954, "the *grileiros* made life unbearable in the region," one peasant commented. "It became [a] torture camp, we suffered all sorts of distasteful humiliation," another told a reporter who visited the area in the 1980s (Carneiro 2014: 127). As one of the peasant-migrants' few literate members, José Porfírio offered to investigate the status of property rights in the area. In 1950, supported by his neighbors, he went to check land registries in the state capital of Goiânia, determining they had indeed settled on public lands. Porfírio took advantage of the trip to file official land possession claims for every family he knew (Carvalho 1978a: 7). Thus, Porfírio began to play the role of an organic mediator of peasant demands.

By focusing on defensive tactics, the resisters themselves found ways to persevere in the region while working to establish their rights to the land. Mutual aid arrangements helped defend both the lives and production of those victimized by the *grileiros*. Some dubbed this initial period the phase of "legality," stressing the term as the peasants' own (Carneiro 2014: 130). While authorities behaved like terrorists, the peasants tried to stay "within their legal rights, only defensive," as one participant recalled (155). In 1953, for example, Porfírio "and others" went to the nation's capital to present a letter demanding protection for the peasant-squatters from Vargas (Esteves 2008: 163–164). His populist, labor-oriented government, as well as those of Kubitschek (1956–1961) and João Goulart (1961–1964), preferred pacification to repression, establishing a more favorable political climate for negotiation. By "amplifying the struggle" (Esteves 2008: 161), the peasants sought to enhance their chances for success. In 1953, inspired by the resilience of the Formoso resistance, the PCB sent an emissary to meet with José Firminio Nascimento, a PCB member who lived with his family in Formoso (Carneiro 2014: 132; Cunha 2007: 167–169). In March 1953, *O Estado de Goiás* reported Firminio led a delegation of peasants to meet the governor, who thereafter issued an order protecting their "permanence [on their farms] until the judicial process is resolved with respect to these lands, securely enjoying all their improvements" (Carneiro 2014: 132n16).

In 1954, the PCB directed four militant families to settle in the area and to help support and strengthen the resistance movement. They included Geraldo Marques and the couple João Ribeiro and Dirce Machado, all of whom stayed until the conflict ended. They spent a year establishing their own farms and familiarizing themselves with the area and the resistance movement. Within the region, the PCB helped with military preparedness by creating small, minuteman-like units to protect fellow peasants while they tended crops. The units ambushed incursions of the police and army, withdrawing quickly to avoid losses and capture. The militants also worked with peasants to create the Formoso and Trombas Agricultural Workers and Farmers Association. The association facilitated communication and the resolution of internal conflicts, establishing norms to ensure fair and equal treatment for all, especially regarding land and productivity issues. The association set up a network of smaller consultation units at the grassroots level called Creek Councils (Conselhos de Córrego), reflecting the fact that the peasants built their lots along the banks of the region's many streams (Amado 1993; Carneiro 2014; Cunha 2007).

Outside the region, PCB mediators leveraged party clout to protect and supply the resistance movement. With regional, national, and even international alliances, the PCB generated favorable coverage by local and national media and positive decisions by policy makers. All the same, it was peasant determination to resist through a set of bloody conflicts that secured PCB solidarity. The resistance was both collective, as described earlier, and individual. Firminio and Porfírio, the first representing Formoso and the second Trombas, showed remarkable courage and pride in taking the concerns and demands of the group to authorities. The militants were open about their affiliation with the PCB and its ideology, which many rural folk had difficulty accepting given the long history of anti-communist propaganda in Brasil, especially among the profoundly Catholic rural population, which was taught to associate communism with the Antichrist. Nevertheless, the militants endeavored to build a thriving PCB cell. Their greatest success came in 1956, when Porfírio—then president of the association—formally joined the party (CNV 2014: chap. 13, para. 48; Carvalho 1978b: 8).

For three more years, the state generally allied with the *grileiros* and their gunmen, forcing the peasants to defend their autonomy. In 1957, determined to establish control over the area, the governor stationed a military unit in nearby Porangatu "to pacify the Goiás family in that region, ensuring a better distribution of justice among squatters and farmers in the area and for landowners in receiving their rents" (*O Popular*, 10 March 1957, cited in Carneiro 2014: 165). In the meantime, roving peasant militias ambushed the soldiers whenever they entered the region, while organizational leaders tried to negotiate a truce, obtain land titles, and establish normalcy. In 1957, major magazines published articles favorable to the resisters, characterizing them as simple peasant folk. Media attention captured political attention, and the National Congress set up a parliamentary inquiry, ordering a halt to police and military action until all land ownership questions had been resolved. Influenced by these developments, as well as changes in USSR policies following Khrushchev's 1956 speech denouncing Stalin, the PCB exchanged its revolutionary stance for a popular front approach to change. In March 1958, the PCB Central Committee declared the shift, and the party congress ratified it at the end of the year (Cunha 2007). Despite its relative success, the revolt in Formoso and Trombas did not have a broader impact on the Brazilian peasantry, whom party officials judged to be ill prepared to support revolutionary change. During that year, a truce was negotiated that allowed a sense of normalcy to take hold.

Finding it less and less necessary to meet weekly, the peasant militants devoted more attention to their homes and crops. The struggle for land rights and the truce that followed meant the region functioned largely without state intervention, especially from 1958 to 1963, when Formoso incorporated as a separate municipality with Trombas as a subdistrict. This achievement resulted from yet another milestone, the election of Porfírio to the state legislature in 1962. Formoso's first mayor also came from the peasant rebel group. Following negotiations to secure PCB support, the new governor visited Trombas and expressed his solidarity with the peasant cause (Carneiro 2014: 172). Wolf captured the ironic implications of these processes when he wrote, "Peasant revolution produces not only an overturning of political power holders but an overturning in the pattern of the peasantry itself" (1969: xiii). With the election of Porfírio and consolidation of the region's independence, it is possible to conclude "an overturning of political power holders" occurred in Formoso.

But the peasant reign was short-lived. Media attention and word-of-mouth propaganda attracted thousands of the country's land-hungry workers to the region, transforming the association itself from an organizer of rebels into an informal land title office, divvying up lots according to terms established by the original squatters who fought for the land (chap. 2 explores a similar transition). As the population grew and motives for rebellion declined, the association and councils made less and less sense to large segments of the population. Even its original members distanced themselves from the organization as they became more involved with their crops and homesteads. While age may have separated the original generation from the second generation of migrants to the region, the most important factor was experience. Having had no part in the struggle, newly arrived migrants took the land's availability for granted. As the focus of concern shifted from battle readiness to market readiness, neither the association nor the PCB cell was prepared with answers.

The Araguaia War

In the context of the Cold War, many new mediator organizations arose to challenge PCB hegemony over the Brazilian revolution. The competition grew ever fiercer after the *golpe* of 1964, which seemed to expose the errors of the PCB. Its leaders had already faced serious criticisms for their tolerance of "liberal democracy" and alliance with the "national bourgeoisie." Several important leaders left the party even before the coup, forming a second Communist Party. The party that Luis Carlos Prestes continued to direct from 1935 on maintained the original acronym, while the new party invented a new acronym: PCdoB (Communist Party of Brazil). The difference was ideological. Essentially, the PCB adhered to an evolutionary theoretical position, confident that capitalism would give way to socialism, while the PCdoB adopted a revolutionary theoretical posture that counted on militants to make socialism happen. Whereas the PCB had a history of joining and amplifying the effects of struggles in progress, like that of the Formoso squatters, the PCdoB leadership decided to produce revolutionary war by sending dozens of militants to the Araguaia Valley, which today constitutes the border between the states of Pará and Tocantins in northern Brazil, where they concluded peasants were indignant enough to wage a "popular war" against the regime (Campos Filho 2012; Portela 2002).

The ripeness of these conditions stemmed from the dictatorship's ambitious project of national integration, which included colonizing the Amazon River basin, including the Araguaia region. By the 1970s, the peasant-squatter population was growing at a rate of more than 6 percent a year. To stimulate the colonization process, the regime created the Superintendency for Amazon Development to attract private investment and orchestrate the settlement of a vast area that included the Araguaia River basin. Through this initiative, a new fund (FIDAM), administered by a new bank (BASA), offered diverse subsidies to attract capital (Browder 1988: 256–267). Investors could write off up to 50 percent of their income tax. The initiative attracted many big names in Brazilian business circles, such as Volkswagen, Bradesco Bank, and the Lunardelli family (Campos Filho 2012: 102). These companies claimed ownership of hundreds of thousands of hectares of land. Volkswagen alone established control over a 140,000-hectare cattle ranch, burning down 6,000 hectares a year of forest to create pasture (Acker 2014: 14). The implantation of agrarian capitalism on this scale depended in large measure on *grilagem*. In other words, powerful corporations and landlords worked through middlemen who, armed with false land titles and backed by local officials and hired gunmen, soon forced the peasant settlers, who had migrated by the thousands to the region in response to government colonization propaganda, to abandon their smallholdings. Through methods of land concentration very similar to those described in the Formoso case, the squatters—not to mention numerous nations of indigenous peoples—were forced off their lands to the benefit of these large and influential entrepreneurs.

"There are already thousands of squatters thrown off their land by the truculent hand of hired gunmen, the police and court officials," one observer wrote in 1978 (Martins 1991: 121).

In contrast with the Formoso case, organized resistance arose not from the peasants themselves but from outside mediators. Starting in the mid-1960s, PCdoB militants assessed the Araguaia Valley situation and determined the area ideal for the party's attempt to recreate China's revolutionary experience in Brazil by stimulating peasant-squatters to engage in a "prolonged popular war" against the dictatorship (Campos Filho 2012: 85–95). They saw the tropical forest along the difficult to access banks of the Araguaia River as a perfect place to hide, protect, and feed themselves. At the time, the wild area reached into four different states (Goiás, Maranhão, Pará, and Mato Grosso), adding to the sense of security by fragmenting the jurisdictions from which a counteroffensive might be launched. The "four corners" location also seemed a strategic advantage, as it was relatively close to the capital in Brasília and at the crossroads of migrant streams from the northeast to the center-west regions and from the south to the north. As peasant families arrived in the region and found their hopes of homesteading dashed by the territorial domination of capitalist cattle ranches, the PCdoB analysts assumed they would quickly find many willing recruits for their "popular war." "The peasants, revolted by their misery and the abuse of the powerful, formed the mass that would thicken the guerrilla detachments trained to start a popular revolution," wrote Taís Morais and Eumano Silva (2012: 38), after probing a large body of newly released documents from the period.

PCdoB militants began to move to the region in 1967 and settled much like the PCB militants did in Formoso and Trombas. Most were from urban areas, but a few had rural backgrounds. Some had military experience, but most did not. A few had trained at a military academy in China. Among the first was Osvaldo Orlando da Costa, a six-foot-five-inch boxing champion educated as a mining engineer in Czechoslovakia, who had completed the army's junior officer preparation course. He learned to make his way in the forest working for a living by catching shellfish and mining. In 1969, he bought some land on the banks of the Gameleira River, from which he began to build up one of three guerrilla bases. He, like João Amazonas and Mauricio Grabois, both of whom settled in the area in 1968, were "burned" PCdoB militants. That is to say, they were known to authorities and actively persecuted. Thus, the move to the Araguaia Valley was also meant to keep valued comrades out of sight.

By 1972, sixty-nine PCdoB militants had established themselves independently in three clusters around the river. Each cluster was responsible for building positive relations with locals and for preparing themselves militarily by training, learning the area, and creating food and arms' caches. The third step was political education, with the intent of persuading the squatters, miners, and peasants to join the guerrillas in forming a revolutionary army. While the militants had prepared themselves militarily and had, by all accounts, successfully integrated with the local population, the recruitment goal had advanced little by the time the authorities began to attack them. The first attack occurred in April 1972, more than four years after the PCdoB began to establish itself in the region. Although the firefight surprised all involved, the Brazilian National Truth Commission recently revealed evidence that authorities had known of the PCdoB's plans since 1969 (CNV 2014: chap. 14). Without the PCdoB realizing it, the armed forces began to establish bases in the region. They trained specialized troops to fight in the forest and staged two large operations nearby to intimidate the population, gather intelligence, and accumulate experience. Before the "war" ended in 1975, the armed forces mounted three campaigns to "capture and annihilate" the revolutionaries.

The one characteristic that PCdoB planners had assumed to be certain—the quick conversion of repressed peasants into revolutionaries—proved to be the rebels' most difficult challenge (Morais and Silva 2012: 38; PCdoB 1969). In fact, the participation of peasants was so low that the little Araguaia War barely qualifies as a peasant war, despite its frequent representation as one. Some accounts claim forty peasants had been recruited, but there is good reason to believe the actual number was much smaller. The historian Romualdo Pessoa Campos Filho, who used new evidence in 2012 to thoroughly revise his original 1994 study, estimated the total number of revolutionaries to be eighty-nine, of whom 22.5 percent—some twenty people—were peasants (2012: 115). At best, the little Araguaia War is an example of difficulties in fomenting revolution from the Brazilian countryside. Intended to be an agrarian revolution apparently endowed with nearly all the qualifying conditions—land concentration, high levels of exploitation, grievances of peasants, and mediation by well-connected revolutionaries—the Araguaia War turned into a massacre. The third military campaign, which concentrated first on cutting the guerrillas off from their supporters and second on the destruction of guerrilla hideouts and supplies, resulted in the deaths of fifty-six revolutionaries and the imprisonment and torture of more than two hundred peasants, who were presumed to have aided and abetted the militants.

The MST's Novo Canudos

The MST seeks revolutionary change in Brazil, but through civil disobedience, not armed struggle (Welch 2006). Founded in 1984, the MST has persevered and grown for more than thirty years, despite enormous opposition. Under constant harassment and attack by both state and private forces, the MST and numerous similar, generally smaller organizations contributed substantially to the establishment of 9,444 agrarian reform settlements by 2016. These settlements, created from 1979 to 2016, covered an area of eighty-two million hectares, where 1,127,078 families have built their homes and livelihoods (Girardi et al. 2017). For a country that had almost no prior experience with agrarian reform, these conquests represent transformations in land tenure so dramatic that they beg to be understood as an agrarian revolution (Panke 2018).

In southeastern Brazil, the Pontal do Paranapanema micro-region in western São Paulo state has been a center of struggle for agrarian reform. There, one of the MST's most outstanding historical militants, José Rainha Jr., used the story of the War of Canudos to emphasize not a defeated people but rather a campaign of resistance that deserved to have its goals fulfilled. "We're going to grow even more," said Rainha in 1995, announcing the MST's plans to occupy additional plantations in the Pontal. "What happened in Canudos may happen again here," he said. "But this time the result will be different: . . . if the Military Police enter, it will be a repetition of Canudos, a hundred years later, only with a victory for the landless" (*Oeste Noticias* 1995; *O Imparcial* 1995).

In fact, in the Pontal the police mobilized regularly to control land occupations and fulfill court orders to break up peasant encampments constructed to pressure authorities to create agrarian reform settlements on lands claimed by suspected *grileiros*. By 2002, however, the landless proved so strong that more than six thousand families had conquered more than 140,000 hectares that were divided among more than one hundred new settlements (Sobreiro Filho 2012: 104). In 2003, the MST expected newly inaugurated President Luis Lula Inacio da Silva of the Workers' Party to redistribute thousands of hectares of land. Rainha prepared the Pontal for the expected initiative by organizing some four thousand families in one of the largest encampments of landless workers ever. They called the camp Novo Canudos (*O Estado de S. Paulo* 2003).

Rainha's career as an MST militant had begun in the Northeast, where stories of Antonio Conselheiro continued to feed the people's dreams for better lives. The MST appropriated Conselheiro's story, claiming it as a popular inheritance of peasant resistance (Fernandes 2000; Wright and Wolford 2003). As a member of the movement's national directorate and militant of its "mass mobilization" sector, Rainha understood the memory's significance before he was transferred from Bahia to São Paulo around 1990. He soon discovered one of the first agrarian reform settlements of the region had been established on the Fazenda Santa Rita in a municipality named for the writer—Euclides da Cunha (1976)—who had historicized Canudos. In 1965, the *grileiro* José Joaquim Mano brought the memory of Canudos to the Pontal for the first time when he christened a colony on the banks of the Paranapanema River with the author's name (Welch 2009). In 1990, the town became incorporated as Euclides da Cunha Paulista.

Symbolically, the memory of Canudos represented important revolutionary elements. As Rainha described it:

> Canudos means freedom. That's the meaning. A free land or country. Liberty. That's what we want, for the Pontal to be free of interference, with the people on the land. One day this place will be free, it will be of and for the people. Far from U.S. imperialism. Far from the control of the International Monetary Fund, far from the corrupt bourgeoisie, from unscrupulous businessmen who defile nature, who corrupt our children, who turn our daughters into prostitutes, turn our children into bandits. We want to see, one day, a free society, where our children, our daughters will have dignity and live in happiness. Imperialism and capitalism do not allow this. (2004: 41)

Accordingly, dividing the land among the people in the Pontal as it was in Canudos, would give Brazil political freedom from the control of powerful national and international forces. As a result, Brazilians would be freed from misery and corruption, establishing conditions for the next generation to pursue dignified and happy lives. For Rainha, Novo Canudos was the gateway to this utopian world.

Rainha's description helps visualize concrete aspects of the struggle to resist the disruptive "cultural system" of capitalist agriculture (Wolf 1969: 276). As Wolf wrote, "North Atlantic capitalism was profoundly alien to many of the areas which it engulfed in its spread" because it transformed land, labor, and wealth into commodities. Despite the imposition of this system in Brazil, resistance to it continued to be expressed. Rainha connected the people's freedom to free land, consistent with MST goals: "The land and all of nature's bounty must be socially controlled and destined to benefit all Brazilian people and future generations" (Coordenação Nacional 2016: 13). Indeed, the MST has been especially attentive to creating cultural alternatives to build a cohesive identity for settled and landless peasants. Meetings, classes, and assemblies are regularly interrupted by *místicas*—short, intense group theater and music intended to provoke an emotional response to commemorations of fallen comrades, heroic events, and visions of a more promising future. Rainha's creation of "New Canudos" fit neatly into the strategy.

In compliance with government regulations, Rainha and other Pontal settlers established an "association of family farmers" to facilitate commercial relationships. Rainha sought to partner with French entrepreneurs and advised 1,200 settler-peasants to accept a castor bean contract with a company called Biobrás. Agronomists described the castor oil plant as well adapted to the ecological conditions of the Pontal and drew the attention of Biobrás as a raw material in the production of biodiesel. With the launch of the National Program for the Production and Use of Biodiesel in 2004, companies such as Biobrás could gain a "social fuel seal" by purchasing at least 30 percent of their inputs from "family farmers." In compensation, the firm would "have fiscal privileges such as reduction or exemption of some taxes and preferential access to financing from agencies such as the National Bank for Economic and Social Development" (Pafunda 2011: 17). The program, however, failed to achieve its social goals. In 2011, the government admitted 90 percent of biodiesel depended on soybean production—a monoculture dominated by corporate farms—and that only 10 percent of biodiesel's raw material responded to the program's social objectives.

Nevertheless, Rainha endorsed the biodiesel program as one of the paths that would make real New Canudos. He agreed it promoted social inclusion and created jobs on settlements (Fernandes et al. 2010). According to promotional literature, "The Program aims at implementation in a sustainable manner, with a focus on social inclusion and regional development, through the generation of employment and income" (Casa Civil 2004). Strengthening associated settlers, Rainha reasoned, would provide a base of support to continue the struggle of peasants, concentrating thousands of families of small farmers in the Pontal region and thus enhancing its chances of becoming an autonomous territory, which had been one of Conselheiro's objectives in building Canudos.

In practice, Rainha's Pontal experiment produced contradictory results. Delays in seed deliveries, processing equipment problems, and other implementation challenges reduced the settlers' productivity and weakened the support of association members. The MST National Directorate saw Rainha's biodiesel project as the "last straw" in an increasingly troubled relationship with a rogue militant. In May 2007, the movement issued a note saying Rainha was no longer "part of any national, state or local body" of the MST. The movement criticized him for "defending agrofuel production projects," indicating he had defied the directorate's "political decision to fight against the extensive planting of monocultures, the domination of financial capital, the participation of transnational corporations in agriculture, and the existence of the latifundia" (Coletivo 2007). In other words, Rainha violated the norms and traditions of the movement.

Conclusion

In evaluating Brazil's place in Wolf's spectrum of battles, wars, and revolutions, numerous dramatic rural conflicts marked the twentieth century, but none reached warlike proportions. Each regional struggle examined in this chapter arose from the aggressive imposition of capitalism in the countryside. Until the 1970s, most Brazilians lived in rural areas, enhancing the probability for a clash of cultures to produce peasant revolts. In Canudos, Conselheiro's peasant followers sought respite from the dramatic changes the Brazilian government underwent as it abolished slavery and constructed market systems for the regulation of land and labor. In the Contestado, the imposition of these new rules facilitated the construction of a railroad, deforestation, lumber production, and land sales to foreign colonists. In Formoso and Trombas, a similar dynamic provoked conflict as peasant-squatters sought to secure their lands from speculators and the state.

Perceiving these conditions as a political opportunity that just might produce a revolution, communist parties in Brazil sent their militants to the frontlines in the states of Goiás and Pará. Instead of a revolution, Brazil suffered a restoration of authoritarianism. By the time the MST created the image of a Novo Canudos, the countryside had changed dramatically. Demographically, more than 80 percent of the population lived in cities, and large-scale, capitalist agriculture predominated in the primary sector. Since 1970, agribusiness practices and values had grown in importance, starting with the dictatorship's investment in agro-industrial complexes, which were implanted in the sugarcane sector. The government opened the country to transnational agri-food conglomerates like Unilever and genetic seed producers like Monsanto and prompted Brazilian investors to enter the global agrarian capitalist game, with firms such as 3G Capital buying controlling interests in US food industries like Budweiser, Burger King, and Heinz. Each of these companies is tied to ranching and farming through vertical integration, a subordinate relationship that even self-identified peasants on agrarian reform settlements in Brazil have found difficult to avoid (Fernandes et al. 2014).

These regional revolts did not become national revolutions capable of resisting the capitalist cultural invasion for diverse reasons. In all but the last example, the forces of repression, marshaled to support agrarian capitalism, were strong and effective. The regional movements were isolated, and mediators were unable or unwilling to overcome this factor. The religious orientations of the Canudos and Contestado leaders, as well as local traditions of obedience, prevented these revolts from being generalized. The communist mediators in the Formoso case evaluated the struggle in Goiás as limited. In Araguaia, the dictatorship applied counterinsurgency measures that mediators were unable to overcome.

In the last example, the New Canudos story demonstrates both the advances and challenges of trying to forge a third path to revolutionary transformation in the era of capitalist globalization. The MST's national scale and its success in mobilizing the landless and helping millions to become peasants resulted in a huge transfer of mostly public land to former peasants and their descendants. But all these measures unfolded in the context of a reform agenda, not a revolutionary one. Unable to break with a goal of reforming the "cultural system" of capitalism, the MST could not foment a radical transformation of the existing order, thus the door remained open to a dramatic reversal of these advances.

Cliff Welch teaches Brazilian history at the Federal University of São Paulo. He is the author of *The Seed Was Planted: The São Paulo Roots of Brazil's Rural Labor Movement* (1999) and has written articles and reviews for the *American Historical Review*, the *Hispanic American Historical Review, International Labor and Working Class History, Journal of Latin American Studies*, the *Latin American Research Review, Latin American Perspectives*, the *Journal of Peasant Studies, Projeto História, Radical History Review*, and the *Revista Brasileira de História*, among other publications.

Notes

1. I am grateful to David G. Sweet for reminding me of the "dog's law" quote.
2. This citation was collected "carefully, without adding even a comma" by Lieut. Demerval Peixoto. He had been transferred in September 1914 to the Contestado battlefront from his role as instructor at the military academy in Rio de Janeiro. Two years later, he organized a three-volume collection of reports and other documents related to the Contestado War.

References

Acker, Antoine. 2014. "'O maior incêndio do planeta': Como a Volkswagen e o regime militar brasileiro acidentalmente ajudaram a transformar a Amazônia em uma arena política global." *Revista Brasileira de História* 34 (68): 13–33. http://dx.doi.org/10.1590/S0102-01882014000200002.

Amado, Janína. 1993. "Eu quero ser uma pessoa: revolta camponesa e política no Brasil." *Revista Regate* 4 (5): 47–69.

Browder, John O. 1988. "Public Policy and Deforestation in the Brazilian Amazon." In *Public Policies and the Misuse of Forest Resources*, ed. Robert Repetto and Malcolm Gillis, 247–297. New York: Cambridge University Press.

Campos Filho, Romualdo Pessoa. 2012. *Guerrilha do Araguaia: A Esquerda em Armas*. 2nd ed. São Paulo: Anita Garibaldi.

Carneiro, Maria Esperança Fernandes. (1988) 2014. *A Revolta Camponesa de Formoso e Trombas*. São Paulo: Anita Garibaldi.

Carvalho, Murilo. 1978a. "A Guerra Camponesa de Trombas de Formoso." *Movimento* 161: 7–9.

———. 1978b. "Onde Está o Herói José Porfírio?" *Movimento* 161: 8.

Carvalho, Tarcísio Motta de. 2008. "'Nós não tem direito': Costume e direito à terra no Contestado." In Espig and Machado 2008: 50–55.

Casa Civil da Presidência da República do Brazil. 2004. *O Programa Nacional de Produção e Uso do Biodiesel*. Brasília: Ministerio de Desenvolvimento Rural.

Coletivo da Direção Nacional do MST. 2007. "Nota pública do MST." São Paulo, 14 May. In author's possession.

Coordenação Nacional do MST. 2016. *Normas gerais e princípios organizativos do MST*. São Paulo: Secretaria Nacional do MST.

CNV (Comissão Nacional da Verdade). 2014. *Relatório da Comissão Nacional da Verdade*. Vol. 1. Brasília: CNV.

Cunha, Euclides da. (1902) 1976. *Os sertões (Campanha de Canudos)*. Rio de Janeiro: Edições de Ouro.

Cunha, Paulo Ribeiro da. 2007. *Aconteceu longe demais: A luta pela terra dos posseiros em Formoso e Trombas e a Revolução Brasileira (1950–1964)*. São Paulo: Edunesp.

Dalfré, Liz Andréa. 2008. "Criando heróis e inimigos: O movimento do Contestado na imprensa paranaense." In Espig and Machado 2008: 211–248.

Diacon, Todd A. 1991. *Millenarian Vision, Capitalist Reality: Brazil's Contestado Rebellion, 1912–1916*. Durham, NC: Duke University Press.

Espig, Márcia Janete, and Paulo Pinheiro Machado, eds. 2008. *A Guerra Santa revisitada: Novos estudos sobre o movimento do Contestado*. Florianópolis: Editora da UFSC.

Esteves, C. L. S. 2008. "Formoso e Trombas: Luta pela terra e resistência camponesa em Goiás—1950–1964." In *Formas de resistência camponesa: Visibilidade e diversidade de conflitos ao longo da história*, ed. Márcia Motta and Paulo Zarth, 161–173. São Paulo: Editora da UNESP / NEAD.

Faoro, Raimundo. (1957) 2000. *Os donos do poder: formação do patronato político brasileiro*. Rio de Janeiro: Editora Globo.

Fernandes, Bernardo Mançano. 2000. *A formação do MST no Brasil*. Petrópolis: Editora Vozes.

Fernandes, Bernardo Mançano, Clifford Andrew Welch, and Elienai Constantino Gonçalves. 2010. "Agrofuel Policies in Brazil: Paradigmatic and Territorial Disputes." *Journal of Peasant Studies* 37 (4): 793–819.

———. 2014. *Os usos da terra no Brasil*. São Paulo: Cultura Acadêmica Editora.

Forman, Shepard. 1975. *The Brazilian Peasantry*. New York: Columbia University Press.

Girardi, Eduardo Paulon, Bernardo Mançano Fernandes, Carlos Alberto Feliciano, Clifford Andrew Welch, Diogo Marcelo, Delben Ferreira, Djoni Roos, et al. 2017. *DATALUTA: Banco de Dados da Luta pela Terra—Relatório Brasil 2016*. São Paulo: NERA-Núcleo de Estudos, Pesquisas e Projetos de Reforma Agrária.

Levine, Robert M. 1995. *Vale of Tears: Revisiting the Canudos Massacre in Northeastern Brazil, 1893–1897*. Berkeley: University of California Press.

Machado, Paulo Pinheiro. 2004. *Lideranças do Contestado: A formação e a atuação das chefias caboclas (1912–1916)*. Campinas: Editora da Unicamp.

Martins, José de Souza. (1980) 1991. *Expropriação e violência: a questão política no campo*. 3rd ed. São Paulo: Editora Hucitec.

Morais, Taís, and Eumano Silva. 2012. *Operação Araguaia: os arquivos secretos da guerrilha*. São Paulo: Geração Editorial.

O Estado de S. Paulo. 2003. "Rainha diz que meta do MST para o Pontal é um novo Canudos." 23 May.

Oeste Noticias. 1995. "Rainha ameaça ressuscitar Canudos." 11 April, 7.

O Imparcial. 1995. "Fazendeiros e sem-terra tentam acordo." 11 April, 6A.

Pafunda, Rosana Akemi. 2011. "O advento de novas matrizes energéticas no Brasil: Experiências da implantação do PNPB no meio rural e a produção de biodiesel no espaço urbano do Estado de São Paulo." Senior thesis, Universidade Estadual Paulista.

Palacios, Guillermo. 2009. "Campesinato e escravidão: uma proposta de periodização para a história dos cultivadores pobres livres no Nordeste oriental do Brasil (1700–1875)." In *Camponeses brasileiros: Leituras e interpretações clássicas*, ed. Clifford A. Welch, Edgard Malagodi, Josefa S. B. Cavalcanti, and Maria de Nazareth B. Wanderley, 145–178. São Paulo: Editora UNESP.

Panke, Anthony. 2018. *Brazil's Long Revolution: Radical Achievements of the Landless Workers Movement*. Tucson: University of Arizona Press.

PCdoB (Partido Comunista do Brasil). 1969. "Guerra popular: caminho da luta armada no Brasil." Retrieved from http://cnv.memoriasreveladas.gov.br/images/documentos/Capitulo14/Nota%203,%204,%205,%207,%208,%209%20-%2000092_000138_2015_11.pdf.

Portela, Fernando. 2002. *Guerra de guerrilhas no Brasil: a saga do Araguaia*. São Paulo: Editora Terceiro Nome.

Rainha, José, Jr. 2004. Interview by Cliff Welch. *Mirante Paulista*, SP, Brazil, 6 August.

Rosa, Geraldo Antônio da. 2011. *O Contestado: A práxis educativa de um movimento social*. Campinas: Mercado de Letras.

Santos, Oto. 1954/1955. "O programa do partido, a questão agrária, a organização e a luta dos camponeses: Intervenção no IV Congresso do PCB." *Problemas* 64: 244–254.

Sobreiro Filho, José. 2012. "A luta pela terra no Pontal do Paranapanema: História e atualidade." *Geografia em questão* 5 (1): 83–114.

Villa, Marco Antônio. 1997. *Canudos, o povo da terra*. São Paulo: Editora Ática.

Welch, Cliff. 2006. "Movement Histories: A Preliminary Historiography of Brazil's Landless Laborers' Movement (MST)." *Latin American Research Review* 41 (1): 198–210.

———. 2009. "Os com-terra e sem-terra de São Paulo: Retratos de uma relação em transição (1945–1996)." In *Lutas camponesas contemporâneas: Condições, dilemas e conquistas*, ed. Bernardo Mançano Fernandes, Leonilde Sérvolo de Medeiros, and Maria Ignes Paulilo, 139–170. São Paulo: Editora da UNESP.

Wolf, Eric. 1969. *Peasant Wars of the Twentieth Century*. New York: Harper & Row.

Wright, Angus, and Wendy Wolford. 2003. *To Inherit the Earth: The Landless Movement and the Struggle for a New Brazil*. Oakland, CA: Food First Books.

Chapter 7

FORGETTING PEASANTS

History, "Indigeneity," and the
Anthropology of Revolution in Bolivia

Forrest Hylton

Ultimately, the decisive factor in making a peasant rebellion possible lies in the relation of the peasantry to the field of power which surrounds it . . . Traditional political authority has eroded or collapsed; new contenders for political power are seeking new constituencies . . . Thus when the peasant protagonist lights the torch of rebellion, the edifice of society is already smoldering and ready to take fire. When the battle is over, the structure will not be the same.

—Eric Wolf, *Peasant Wars of the Twentieth Century*

What attention to history allows you to do is to look at processes unfolding, intertwining, and dissipating over time.

—Eric Wolf, "Distinguished Lecture: Facing Power—Old Insights, New Questions"

Introduction: One Step Forward, Two Steps Back

In the early years of the twenty-first century, Bolivians lived through another of the revolutionary moments—like 1781, 1899, and 1952—that have shaped southern Andean political culture and economy since the late eighteenth century. Heterogeneous but mostly indigenous movements from below, both rural and urban, forced two presidents, Gonzalo Sánchez de Lozada and his vice president and successor, Carlos Mesa Gisbert, off the political stage—and with them, the entire neoliberal constitutional order implemented after

1986. They thereby opened up what Raquel Gutierrez Aguilar (2014) calls "horizons of emancipation," or what Sinclair Thomson and I have called "revolutionary horizons" (Hylton and Thomson 2007).

This opening, in turn, led to the election of Evo Morales in 2006 and the remaking of the Bolivian state, as codified in the 2009 Constitution following the first Constitutional Assembly in Bolivian history in which indigenous people participated to enshrine specific rights for indigenous peoples (Barragán 2006), defined in terms of corporate forms of belonging, deliberation, and decision-making. Reelected in 2010 and again in 2014, Morales is the first president in Bolivian history to anchor the nationalist rhetoric of the state in the symbolism of indigenous and mestizo peasant trade union movements and communities, and to claim to represent the interests of these groups and organizations, who have historically been excluded from full political participation. Each official inauguration ceremony in the Murillo Palace in La Paz has had a parallel inauguration ceremony at the ancient Aymara capital of Tiwanaku, on the shores of Lake Titicaca, at which tens of thousands of mostly indigenous peasants and workers have gathered, anchoring Aymara centrality to national popular struggle in the twenty-first century. Hitherto, Morales, who grew up in an Aymara community in the western highlands before migrating with his family to the tropical lowlands in the eastern region of the Chapare, has also served longer, and presided over higher rates of economic growth, than any other Bolivian president.

Thus, Bolivia under Evo Morales—a country whose population is, by any measure, roughly half indigenous—represents a fascinating case of change within continuity and provides an opportunity to demonstrate the utility of Eric Wolf's historical materialist approach to peasant rebellion and revolution (see also Knight 1985, 1990, 2001). Indeed, "peasant" (*campesino*) retains its currency in Bolivia today and is used in Article 2 of the Constitution to define indigenous communities, so its disappearance from recent Anglo-American anthropology on Bolivia is curious. Given Wolf's centrality to the discipline in the late twentieth century, his relative absence in the twenty-first century is equally puzzling, unless we consider the long shadow cast by Michel Foucault in defining which problems and questions are posed and how (Gill 2013). Most Anglo-American anthropological studies seek to make sense of Bolivian politics through discussion of narrow disciplinary questions around "indigeneity" with limited explanatory reach, whereas *Peasant Wars of the Twentieth Century* was so influential in part because of the big questions about people, power, and politics that framed its sweeping interpretation. This, then, is the problem: under the sign of Foucault, an ahistorical way of thinking about race/ethnicity—"indigeneity"—has replaced and erased thinking about class, and severed culture from political economy.

The key question about power in Bolivia today, one Wolf would have recognized, is broadly political and not simply disciplinary: Why were radical movements and organizations—composed to a large degree of rural workers and cultivators of indigenous and nonindigenous descent, i.e., peasants (Wolf 1966)—unable to sustain momentum for a revolutionary project that would have remade the state along non-liberal lines? This question cannot be posed in Foucauldian terms that ignore history, and emerges from intellectual debates in Latin American social science rather than Anglo-American anthropology. It helps us think about class in relation to state and racial/ethnic formation, as well as how to connect past and present in a unitary frame of analysis. It is impossible to answer without some knowledge of previous indigenous and popular struggles in Bolivia over property rights, natural resource use, and political representation—which Foucauldian frameworks bypass—frequently led by the indigenous peasantry of the western highlands and highland valleys, who have been the large majority of the country's population for most of its history.

My argument is neither new nor complex: social history and cultural anthropology need one another, so the growing disconnect between them is troubling (Becker 2018; Larson and Harris 1995; Thompson 1994). It may be a product of intellectual amnesia that characterizes the current moment of late neoliberalism (Davies 2017). Since my own research concerns political violence, race/ethnicity, class, community, and state formation in late nineteenth- and early twentieth-century Bolivia (Hylton 2004, 2011b, forthcoming), my reading of Wolf's work for understanding the indigenous peasantry in the twenty-first century depends on recent essays and monographs in the social sciences.

This chapter is therefore a critique of that literature, which is dominated by anthropology. Anglo-American anthropologists of Bolivia would benefit from returning to Wolf's nuanced understanding of class, community, and state formation, as well as the historical nature of racial/ethnic and regional differences. Social scientists in other disciplines would provide better accounts if they took note of the questions historians have asked about the past in relation to the commodification of land, labor, and exchange, and indigenous peasant community strategies of subsistence and resistance. And of course, historians of Bolivia need to engage more deeply with anthropological and social scientific research in order to interrogate the past in relation to questions that scholars put to the present.

Although the peasantry has long been a problematic analytical category, beginning in the 1960s, it gave rise to several generations of interdisciplinary debates—now largely overlooked or forgotten— that ranged from scholastic to enlightening (Kearney 1996). Why has the new vocabulary of "indigeneity" replaced the older language of race/ethnicity, and why have peasants ceased to exist as an analytic class category in Anglo-American anthropology? Why now? Ignoring frameworks connecting culture and political economy pioneered by Wolf (1999) and William Roseberry (1989, 1993, 1995, 1996, 1997) in favor of Foucauldian questions of governmentality and subject formation, and moving away from all forms of structural analysis, Anglo-American anthropologists of Bolivia have thrown the baby out with the bathwater. This largely unstated discursive idealism explains the chicken-and-egg circularity of recent debates on "indigeneity," perhaps because it obviates the need for historical contextualization or analysis of class formation, as well as property rights—the commodification of land, labor, and exchange relations—and political representation in relation to race and ethnicity. As a critical discipline of process and context, radical social history can help us out of the current morass (Guha 1997: 36–37; Sarkar 1998: 89; Thompson 1994: 211; Trouillot 1995: 22–23).

My central claim is that within the current terms of debate about "indigeneity," it is not possible to explain either the nationwide insurrections led by Aymara and Quechua peasants between 2000 and 2005 or the remaking of the liberal state in the name of indigenous rights and national sovereignty since then. And it is not possible to identify key actors in these partially revolutionary developments, much less specify the means by which they developed what the editors of this volume call "scale-spanning solidarities" through new forms of alliance and coalition. To explain the kind of state that has taken shape under Morales and the Movimiento al Socialismo, we need a historical materialist perspective on the main actors and alliances, as well as their limitations, that incorporates and synthesizes insights about power, culture, state formation, markets, and race/ethnicity from history and anthropology. However politically and demographically important peasants may be, whether indigenous or not, as Lesley Gill points out in her contribution to this volume (see chap. 3), Wolf did not engage E. P. Thompson's work on class formation or the relations between urban and rural popular protest and mobilization; and, crucially, he did not deal with race and ethnicity. Wolf's work on peasants and peasant revolutions may not help us understand, for example, conflicts between lowland Quechua and Aymara migrants from the highlands growing coca, supportive of Morales's plans for extractive capitalist development, and lowland indigenous groups on the frontier in the Amazonian basin who insist on the legal subtleties and constitutional niceties (i.e., rights) enshrined in the Constitution. We need to see the making and remaking of indigenous peasants and urban workers of indigenous descent, who have hitherto constituted the core of the new national popular bloc that has sustained Morales in power, as part of the same process of class formation, struggle, and capital accumulation. This way of looking at capital, class, and race/ethnicity allows us to overcome reified categories and binaries; it does not represent an atavistic throwback to classical Marxism, economistic or otherwise, but rather invites us to integrate culture, economics, and politics into a single analytic frame. It follows a path traced by Wolf and Roseberry.

First, in dialogue with Raquel Gutiérrez Aguilar and Jeffrey R. Webber, I summarize and elaborate briefly on twenty-first century developments in Bolivian politics. Next, I discuss recent essays and monographs in Anglo-American anthropology. Through them, and a discussion of "indigeneity," we can reconsider the heterogeneity of contemporary Bolivian social movements while signaling the limits of Foucauldian perspectives for understanding how rural people, indigenous as well as nonindigenous, highlanders and lowlanders, engage political worlds beyond the local, thereby transforming the state/capital relation at the regional and national levels—and, in the case of the US and Bolivia, transforming interstate relations as well.

Since this chapter is not a literature review but rather an effort to see the history of class formation in relation to state and racial/ethnic formation in the contemporary period, there are many texts—those written in Spanish and published in Bolivia (e.g., Abreu and Arnold 2017)—I do not discuss. I have chosen texts and authors based on how their work helps us make sense of the difficulties that Bolivian politics and state formation pose for anthropological analyses of race and ethnicity, framed in terms of "indigeneity," in relation to class formation. The conclusion reflects on previous generations of scholarship in the social sciences on state formation, race/ethnicity, and the indigenous peasantry in Bolivia in order to signal paths not taken.

The Limits of Liberalism: Race, Nation, and Citizenship

Two perspectives anchored in historical materialism—one from sociology, one from political science—provide chronological analyses
of twenty-first-century class struggle, alliances, and state formation
that consider the interplay between the major social forces, as well
as between race/ethnicity, region, and nation. Without losing sight
of the divisions, differences, and factional disputes within and between social movement organizations, they grasp the decisive nature
of indigenous peasant participation in the partial transformation of
Bolivian politics in the twenty-first century. In explaining state formation, they link peasant political action to the broader field of power
and emphasize the historical nature of processes "unfolding, intertwining, and dissipating," in Wolf's (1990: 590) terms.

Both perspectives dialogue mainly with activist intellectuals in Bolivia and Latin America such as Bolívar Echeverría, Sergio Tischler,
Luis Tapia, Pablo Mamani, Adolfo Gilly, and Massimo Modonesi.
Using more or less Gramscian frameworks, they seek to understand
the limitations, contradictions, and partial advances of movements
that seemed to promise, but could not deliver, radical social transformation, and instead wound up divided, co-opted, and demobilized by
the very "revolutionary" government they elected and reelected. This,
of course, was the central irony that René Zavaleta Mercado (1983,
1986) sought to grasp in order to understand the Bolivian National
Revolution of 1952. In other words, Gutiérrez Aguilar and Webber
seek to make sense of how, after 2006, the partially reconstituted liberal state came to dominate Bolivian movements that, from 2000 to
2005, aimed to govern themselves in a range of non-liberal ways (see
also Mamani Ramírez 2011; Tapia 2011). In my view, these are the
big questions about power and politics in twenty-first-century Bolivia
and are exactly the sorts of questions that would have interested Wolf.
They cannot be posed in Foucauldian terms of "indigeneity," cultural
identity, and the formation of subjects through institutional discourses
and practices of power/knowledge and governmentality.

The sea change in Bolivian politics has been dramatic, and within
Bolivia, it is frequently discussed as revolutionary, not least by the
Morales government itself. Webber and Gutiérrez Aguilar seek to
explain how traditional political authority collapsed, how new contenders built new constituencies, and what changed when the old
structures of state and society crumbled. Ironically, in the 1980s and
1990s, following the implementation of Supreme Decree 21060—
which, among other measures, privatized the Corporación Minera

de Bolivia, the state-owned tin mine—international financial institutions like the World Bank and the International Monetary Fund held Bolivia up as a model of successful neoliberal multicultural governance that other poor and underdeveloped countries should follow. The tin miners' union (Federación Sindical de Trabajadores Mineros de Bolivia), legendary for its cohesiveness and combativeness, was broken, its remnants scattered to urban areas like southern Cochabamba, Oruro, and El Alto, and, crucially, the tropical lowlands of the Chapare, where coca growers became Bolivia's most combative popular nationalist movement by organizing themselves into six trade union federations and fighting US anti-drug intervention (Healy 1991, 1998; Gill 1997; Grisaffi 2010). This lowland frontier setting, rather than the traditional highland Aymara community in Oruro in which he was born, formed the crucible in which Morales forged his political identity as a trade union leader (Harten 2011).

In 1994, with neoliberalism peaking as a project with hegemonic aspirations, the government of President Gonzalo Sánchez de Lozada—the architect of DS 21060—and Aymara Vice President Victor Hugo Cárdenas passed the Law of Popular Participation, which recognized a range of forms of popular association, including indigenous communities (*pueblos indígenas* in the eastern lowlands, *pueblos originarios* in the western highlands). The law was pitched as a pathway to cultural citizenship, the better to channel potential opposition into the formal procedures of local office and municipal government. These reforms recognized cultural difference in order to convert indigenous people into responsible managers of the local state, as opposed to unruly subjects protesting against the state—or supplanting it altogether. The reforms did not deepen democracy, much less decolonize the Bolivian state (Albro 2010; Gustafson 2011; Gustafson and Fabricant 2011; Medeiros 2001; Postero 2007, 2017).

The shift away from peasants and class toward race/ethnicity, cultural identity, and the formation of subjectivity began in the mid-1980s but truly flowered in the mid-1990s once Foucault had eclipsed Wolf in all but a handful of departments and specialized journals. The latter conjuncture was formative for a generation of anthropologists that set out to study how indigenous and popular groups in Bolivia sought to negotiate implementation of the law and neoliberal multiculturalism more generally. It therefore marks the outer horizon of historical consciousness in their accounts of the rise of Evo Morales and the Movimiento al Socialismo (MAS). Thus, the mid-1990s conjuncture serves as ground zero for the forgetting of historical materialist strains linking social history and cultural anthropology.

In April 2000, led by the Coalition in Defense of Water and Life, a municipal insurrection in Cochabamba against the privatization of water forced the government and the US multinational Bechtel to reverse its plans to privatize the city's water system. Unsurprisingly, given Cochabamba's centrality to the making of a national revolutionary coalition in the mid-twentieth century, the Water War of Cochabamba brought together a broad array of social forces from the city and the surrounding countryside: factory workers, coca growers, peasant community irrigation managers (*regantes*), small farmers, students, professors and middle-class professionals, street children, artisans and street vendors, market women, environmental activists, civic and neighborhood committees, and Aymara migrants from the western highlands clustered in the southern zone of Cochabamba.

Gutiérrez Aguilar (2014: 3–28, 198–199), a leading participant in the formation of the coalition, argues it represented the first of a series of radical democratic efforts to redefine who makes public decisions in Bolivia and how to recover common property in the name of the public good, based on the idea of community self-management of water as a use value that should not be commodified (Webber 2012: 148–161). Though the coalition did not manage to overcome its regional limitations, the Water War nevertheless opened the door to reimagine natural resources as inalienable wealth belonging to the citizens of the nation, to be managed democratically and communally for the good of future generations. Here, then, water clearly served as a political bridge linking peasants to the surrounding field of power: urban workers, petty traders, transport workers, and the middle class.

Simultaneous with the successful insurrection in Cochabamba, starting in La Paz, Aymara peasant communities, organized through their trade union federation, the Confederación Sindical Única de Trabajadores Campesinos de Bolivia (CSUTCB), used road blockades not only to isolate La Paz but also to cut off Oruro from La Paz and Cochabamba, and Sucre from Cochabamba and Potosí. The entire western highlands and highland valley region was paralyzed along with the south. Gutiérrez Aguilar (2014: 28–72, 201–207) argues that, acting in the name of the CSUTCB, first the Aymara communities of the western highlands and then the Quechua-speaking peasants of the southern highland valleys used traditional organizational structures of community government, rotating leadership, and collective labor to mobilize (Webber 2012: 162–176). Albeit momentarily, the state was overrun by communal society, and mostly indigenous peasants exercised de facto autonomy. The blockades of April were not a one-time occurrence: they happened again in September 2000 and then again, with even greater scope and force in June/July 2001, and may well have sped Banzer's departure in August 2001. When President Jorge Quiroga assumed office, the neoliberal center that Sánchez de Lozada and the Movimiento Nacional Revolucionario (MNR) established in the mid-1990s no longer held. For Gutiérrez Aguilar and others in the group of intellectuals associated with *comuna* (Luis Tapia, Raúl Prada, Oscar Vega, and Álvaro García Linera), indigenous peasant rebellion was clearly transforming the broader field of power through alliance and coalition; the task, as they saw it, was to help light the torch that would bring the old order down and to help build new constituencies.

Between 1997 and 2002, the number of Bolivians living in extreme poverty had increased from 36 percent to 43 percent, so when Sánchez de Lozada returned to office in 2002 with just over 22 percent of the vote, having defeated Morales and MAS by less than 2 percent, the stage was set for the unraveling of state authority and the disappearance of government legitimacy. Social indicators for infant mortality, life expectancy, economic precarity, distribution of wealth, poverty, disease, and informality put Bolivia next to Haiti as the most wretched country in the Americas. For the first time in Bolivian history, a leftist political party gained traction: MAS picked up 8 of 27 Senate seats and 27 of 130 in the Chamber of Deputies, in part thanks to US opposition.

In decline and decadence, no one helped Morales and MAS achieve their goals more than Sánchez de Lozada and the MNR—not even Bolivia's hydra-headed social movements, which cropped up with increasing degrees of synchronicity. One of the MNR's first moves in power was to antagonize the coca growers trade union federations, hence Morales and MAS, in meetings with US envoy Otto Reich in January 2003, leading to road blockades in the south, that is, Chuquisaca and Potosí, the Chapare in Cochabamba, and the coca-growing Yungas region northeast of La Paz. Through their provincial-level trade union federation—and led by Felipe Quispe, the charismatic Aymara leader of the CSUTCB—in September, Aymara peasant communities joined with urban neighborhood committees in El Alto, students from the public university in El Alto, and transport workers from El Alto to march on La Paz in order to free Edwin Huampu, an Aymara peasant community leader and political prisoner. Protestors were united in their demand to stop the export of Bolivian natural gas through Chile to the United States, and it is difficult to imagine what, other than excessive state repression, which duly materialized, could have incensed nationalist and racial/ethnic injuries more deeply. By mid-October, more than seventy protestors had been killed by government forces. El Alto, La Paz, Sucre, Oruro, Potosí, and Cochabamba had been taken over by national popular forces from below, with three hundred thousand occupying the center of La Paz and blocking all roads between major cities. Sánchez de Lozada fled to the United States, as direct democracy rooted in non-liberal modes of community and neighborhood life momentarily supplanted liberal representative democracy. Yet, perhaps in fear of civil war, no one sought to seize state power directly, and with the blessing of Morales and MAS—who had every interest in brokering a stable transition in order to secure electoral advantage—Sánchez de Lozada's vice president, Carlos Mesa Gisbert, replaced him, promising demonstrators they were free to overthrow him should he fail to comply with the main demands of the "October Agenda": the nationalization of oil and natural gas, a Constitutional Assembly, and justice for family members of the "martyrs who defended gas" in El Alto. In May 2005, nationwide insurrection broke out again, and this time, Morales and MAS backed the coca growers, miners, neighborhood associations, professional associations, and rural and urban trade union federations that shut down eight of nine departments in response to a power grab by the Far Right, rooted in agribusiness strongholds in the eastern lowlands. Protest marches and demonstrations in the capital were even larger than in October 2003, with four hundred thousand to five hundred thousand occupying La Paz in mid-June 2005. Elections were called for December (Gutiérrez Aguilar 2014: 99–189; Hylton and Thomson 2005; Kohl and Farthing 2006; Webber 2012: 184–259).

The seismic shift in official Bolivian politics that resulted from this revolutionary moment—with two nationwide insurrections, led by indigenous peasants and workers of indigenous descent, toppling two presidents in as many years—is at once poorly understood and hard to overstate. In 2005, Morales won with 54 percent and was reelected in 2009 with 64 percent, with turnouts of 85 percent and 90 percent, respectively, and reelected again in 2014 with 61 percent in a similarly high turnout. No other Bolivian president has ever won a clear majority of votes, much less three times in succession. Nevertheless, despite radical changes the Morales and MAS government seeks to represent, there are clear continuities in political culture, as well as political economy, and since 2011, if not earlier, the new order looks increasingly like the old, at least at the level of practice. By the old order, I mean the mix of the MNR developmentalism of the 1950s and 1960s, along with the hardball clientelist politics it entailed, pitting popular groups against one another (Dunkerley 1984; John 2009; Rivera Cusicanqui 1984, 1991; Young 2017). To a considerable degree, this explains both the strength and weakness of the Morales government. The continuity of political party clientelism and extractive, export-oriented development is the defining feature of the new order; the liberal capitalist model, albeit one slightly modified in favor of national development, has survived, and by Bolivian standards it has been thriving (Hylton 2011a). The nondemocratic, illiberal means used — namely, corrupt *caudillismo,* with its practices of patronage, clientelism, and soft authoritarian persecution of political opponents — undercut the stated liberal ends of government, not to mention the more radical promises upheld in the breach, namely the decolonization of the state and a reorientation of the economy in more ecologically sustainable and socially just directions.

In light of all this, why has Morales remained so popular for so long, and what explains MAS's unprecedented electoral successes? The answer, surely, lies in the nationalist politics of alliance and coalition that keep indigenous and nonindigenous peasants, as well as urban workers of indigenous and nonindigenous descent, voting for Morales and MAS despite the latter's concessions to domestic petty capitalists, domestic and international agri-business, and multinationals in the hydrocarbon sector since 2010. Bolivia under Morales has become even more of a rentier state, with industrial manufacturing shrinking rather than expanding; the hydrocarbon sector does not create jobs or affect the formal labor market, while Bolivian cities remain dependent on tertiary activities, which means subcontracting and other precarious forms of employment, not least within the Bolivian government itself. Foreign direct investment has increased some 600 percent between 2006 and 2013, 50 percent of tax revenue comes from the exploitation of natural resources, and 57 percent of all gas exports go to Brazil and Argentina.

Hence, the paradox that defines Morales's Bolivia is this: how has a new round of capitalist development and accumulation on lowland frontiers, led by a reconfigured party/state, dependent on gas and petroleum rents for revenues and redistribution, stymied indigenous and thereby national liberation while claiming to fulfill it? Several questions follow. How, precisely, does the rhetoric of the decolonization of state and society in Bolivia square with policies in pursuit of capital investment and export-led economic growth? What, in other words, is the relationship between non-liberal forms of community life — urban and rural, indigenous and nonindigenous, community and trade union—and the liberal forms of a reconfigured developmentalist state? How do performance, theatricality, and the nationalist spectacle of "indigeneity" relate to other aspects of state formation, as well as racial/ethnic formation and capital accumulation?

Against "Indigeneity"

In recent Anglo-American anthropological literature on Bolivia, historical perspective is remarkable mainly for its absence: the most historically inclined study inquires about memories of the National Revolution of 1952, only to conclude they were unimportant compared to local disputes (Canessa 2009: 178) and that, furthermore, attention to history could distract from thinking about class structure (Canessa 2012: 206). The analytical subsumption of class under race/ethnicity—uniformly referred to as "indigeneity"—is likewise common.[1] A range of important questions about power, politics, and continuity-within-change are not posed within these narrow parameters, which are undergirded by unstated, implicit assumptions about power best characterized as discursive idealism. The Anglo-American anthropological literature seeks to grasp the nature of the changes in the organization of the Bolivian state, changes in "indigeneity" in relation to citizenship, and the relationship between performance, practice, and the discourse of Bolivian nationalism, which now includes rather than excludes the country's indigenous majority, albeit in problematic ways. This literature is interested in representation, recognition, and redistribution, as well as tensions between individual and collective rights, and unitary and pluralist forms of indigenous cultural identity, in relation to hierarchies and inequalities inherited from the past, defined largely in terms of race and ethnicity, and grouped under the rubric of "indigeneity."

At the risk of nominalism, it is worth discussing how "indigeneity" is defined, particularly in light of the fact that the central aspect of peasant life is the transfer of agricultural surpluses by mostly illiterate, rural people to ruling, literate, mostly urban groups through taxes, rents, debts, and unfavorable terms of exchange. Following Thomas Grisaffi (2010), Andrew Canessa (2012: 204) defines the coca growers trade union federations, as well as Morales and MAS, as "light" forms of "indigeneity," presumably in contrast to Quispe, the CSUTCB, and Aymara modes of "heavy indigeneity." Indigeneity is defined as a discourse of injustice that is at once a critique of neoliberal globalization "yet depends on particularity and rootedness in place for authenticity." Although we are told "indigeneity is about history and power," it is unclear how either history or power is to be understood, or what the relationship between them is, despite claims that the concept is "relational" and located at the nexus of "power and imagination." Political indigeneity, in this definition, makes indigenous identity central rather than marginal to state-led, developmentalist nationalism under Morales. But it also introduces new distinctions and hierarchies among indigenous people by making the highland Aymara peasant communities the ideal type of indigenous citizen, and consecrating Aymara rituals of leadership and authority (Albro 2010; Canessa 2014; Postero 2017). The concept of indigeneity helps make sense of demands that powerless minorities make on the multicultural state, it is argued, but not of conflict among recently empowered minorities differentially positioned in relation to the post-multicultural liberal state that claims to be indigenous.

In another version of the argument, "indigeneity" has gone from being "a site of emancipation" to the axis of "liberal state-making," as Morales and MAS have moved away from early commitments to "decolonization" and "indigeneity" in the first term (2006–2010) by emphasizing national development, understood as economic liberation from imperialist domination (Postero 2017: 4–5), during the second administration (2010–2014). In this view, following Jacques Rancière, with nonindigenous, leftist extractivists in command of MAS after 2010, "indigeneity acts as a site of politics and policing," giving voice to state-sanctioned versions of indigeneity while silencing others, sidelining "native cosmovisions" of "sustainable development" (Postero 2017: 184) as well as local autonomy, which is abandoned by the central government or subordinated to a neo-developmentalist agenda rooted in the expansion and exploitation of eastern lowland frontiers. Yet another definition of indigeneity stresses the need to "go beyond an Andeanist frame" in order to understand how "contested meanings of indigeneity take center stage in attempts to contest and change the exercise of state power" (Gustafson and Fabricant 2011: 5, 7, 9). In this view, which privileges epistemology rather than organizing, mobilization, or representation in politics, "indigeneity . . . offers a cultural and knowledge-centered challenge to conventional Western paradigms through which state transformations are envisioned."

Discourses of indigeneity—understood in Foucauldian terms as "relational field[s] of governance, subjectivities, and knowledges" (Cadena and Starn 2007: 3)—rather than indigenous political subjects, have become actors. The Morales era is said to have opened possibilities for indigeneity, when in fact, indigenous political subjects, in alliance and conflict with other groups, opened possibilities that Morales and MAS then constrained within liberal, state-led channels in order to domesticate the racist, right-wing secessionist reaction in the eastern lowlands. Rooted in narrow disciplinary debates, these Anglo-American anthropologists get cause and effect backward because of their discursive idealism, though their work has the virtue of noting that indigenous cultural identities, rooted in consciousness of centuries-old struggles, are forged through political conflict at particular historical conjunctures (Canessa 2012: 217; Fabricant 2011; Postero 2017: 5, 183; see also Gill 2005: 78).

Most scholars note the irony of Morales and MAS representing themselves as indigenous, in part through the copious yet largely pro forma output of Vice President Álvaro García Linera (2011a, 2011b, 2012), since both Morales and MAS grow out of racial/ethnic, class, and cultural experiences colonizing the eastern lowlands for coca production, far removed from the Aymara ethno-nationalism of the western highlands (Healy 1991, 1998; Grisaffi 2010; Gutiérrez Aguilar 2014: 73–96; Webber 2012: 124–129). But in the wake of the cycle of rebellion and insurrection that toppled two presidents in as many years between 2003 and 2005, Morales and MAS sought ways to incorporate the demands—and, above all, the symbols—of the single largest group within the national popular bloc: Aymara community peasants in the CSUTCB. Politics, rather than epistemological or anthropological confusion, explains why forms of being indigenous that the Constitution recognizes are Aymara-centric (Albro 2010: 72).

Much recent anthropological work has moved away from the Aymara highlands and the Quechua highland valleys—*lo andino*— in what has long been the demographic and political heartland of Bolivia (cf. Canessa 2007, 2009, 2012, 2014), to focus instead on the complexities of multicultural politics, regional and racial/ethnic identities, capitalist frontiers, and the making of a pluri-national state in the lowlands (Fabricant 2011, 2012; Gustafson 2009, 2011; Gustafson and Fabricant 2011; Postero 2005, 2007, 2017). There is a strong argument to be made for the importance of the lowlands to contemporary accumulation—hence the need to study migration, class, race/ethnicity, and state formation there (Brabazon and Webber 2014; Gill 1987; Hertzler 2005a, 2005b). The same is true of urban traders, transport and construction workers, artisans, and vendors of indigenous descent—who may represent a majority of the 62 percent of Bolivians who self-identified as indigenous in the 2000 census—whether or not they retain ties to their hamlets and villages of origin or speak an indigenous language (Albro 2006, 2010; Gill 2000; Goodale 2008; Lazar 2008; Tassi et al. 2013, 2015).

Yet, as Charles Hale suggests, there is a considerable amount of "wishful thinking" involved in some of the new anthropological literature in that shifting the emphasis from *lo andino* to *lo amazónico*, or from rural to urban, does not address, much less resolve, some of the key questions concerning the Bolivian state, the ruling bloc, and the nature of historical change (2011: 199). To do so would require, in addition to non-Foucauldian frameworks, more in-depth analysis of the CSUTCB, the Bartolinas, the Consejo Nacional de Ayllus y Markas de Qollasuyo (CONAMAQ), and their shifting relations with Morales and MAS, a comparison between east and west, Aymaras, Quechuas, and Guaraníes, as well as lowland coca growers of Quechua and Aymara descent.

The salient political fact of the twenty-first century in Bolivia is that indigenous highland and highland valley peasants, as well as urban working classes predominantly of indigenous descent, partially transformed the state through radical collective action on a national scale (as noted in Gustafson and Fabricant 2011: 7; Hale 2011: 199, 204). Likewise, the coca growers movement that produced Morales represents change within continuity, insofar as miners' trade unionism has fused with indigenous peasant trade unionism in the lowlands; however, the coca growers played a secondary role in the great transformations of the twenty-first century, just as Morales followed rather than led the movements that brought him to power (Gutiérrez Aguilar 2014; Hylton and Thomson 2007; Webber 2012).

In the current climate, it is easy to lose sight of the changes wrought by the National Revolution of 1952, foremost among them the introduction of universal suffrage, rural schools, and trade unions, designed to modernize and civilize indigenous peoples in the highlands and highland valleys by turning them into mestizo smallholders on the model of Cochabamba, the region most important to the formation of the MNR's rural bloc. Hence, race/ethnicity was subsumed under class by semantic sleight of hand, and class was subordinate to the nation as represented by the revolutionary state, that is, the fractious, ephemeral coalition assembled by the MNR. Yet there can be little question that the National Revolution of 1952 introduced citizenship as a universal grammar in Bolivian politics, indigenous peoples included, such that changes in the twenty-first century need to be understood in terms of both continuity and change. Military dictatorships from the 1960s through the early 1980s proscribed democratic citizenship but did not disappear the historic demands that went with it (John 2009; Nash 1979; Young 2017). Furthermore, the same leaders of indigenous movements that fought to recover stolen communal lands in the 1930s and 1940s worked to bend the MNR's agrarian reform to their own purposes in the 1950s and 1960s (Gotkowitz 2008; Soliz 2017). The MNR's domination of the indigenous peasantry and its ability to assimilate indigenous peoples as mestizos into the Bolivian nation was far from complete and, starting in the 1970s, subject to reversal (Albó 1986a, 1987, 1994; Ari 2014; Hurtado 1986). Likewise, the formation of the Bolivian working class in the twentieth century represented a complex interplay between race/ethnicity, region, nationalism, and internationalism (Smale 2010), and the MNR was even less successful at controlling the mining proletariat than it was at controlling the Aymara and Quechua peasantry in the western highlands and highland valleys (Dunkerley 1984). This is the context in which the eastern lowlands were conceived of as the future of capitalist development, with colonization from the highlands representing the safety valve of the MNR's, and later the Bolivian military's, highly unstable rule. The historiography of twentieth-century Bolivia is more than mere background to the processes and outcomes of the twenty-first century, and anthropologists could gain greater depth by engaging the interplay between racial/ethnic, class, and state formation over time. This, in turn, would allow them to specify what is genuinely new about Morales and MAS.

Recent anthropological approaches centered on the lowlands and urban peripheries share with the radical Indianism forged in the highlands during the 1970s an analytic reversal of MNR's modernizing discourse and historical narrative: where class and the category of peasant were central, race/ethnicity—absorbed by "indigeneity"—have taken their place. What is needed, clearly, is the sort of dialectical synthesis that leaves the racist paternalism of the MNR behind without losing sight of the importance of class formation and capital accumulation to contemporary ethno-nationalist politics (Hetland and Goodwin 2013; Pearse 1986; Rivera Cusicanqui 1984, 1991; Webber 2007). In fact, such synthesis was offered thirty years ago by Xavier Albó (1986a, 1986b, 1987, 1994), such that my critique, which tackles questions of political consciousness and subjectivity, extends his work (Hylton 2011a).

The strength of recent Anglo-American anthropology is the long overdue attention—outside Bolivia—to the dizzying range of ethnoregional differences in the eastern lowlands that complicate easy generalizations and mitigate against simplistic or binary frames of geo-racial analysis, that is, *camba* (eastern lowlands, coded white) versus *qolla* (western highlands and highland valleys, coded Indian). Though yet to be reflected in the composition of the central government and its institutions, the astonishing pluralism of movements, demands, and collective subjects is a novel feature of Bolivian politics in the twenty-first century and provides for particularly contentious, dynamic democratic participation at the local level. However disappointing the modes, methods, and goals of the Morales regime in relation to the "October Agenda"—nationalization of national resources, Constitutional Assembly with nonparty representation, and a trial for Sánchez de Lozada and his accomplices—locally, in the name of autonomy, indigenous peasants and working-class people continue to pursue alternative agendas of radically democratic self-government that brought Morales and MAS into office.

There is reason to hope that the lessons learned from recent political experience engaging the state and trying to transform it will serve indigenous and nonindigenous Bolivians as well as workers and peasants in future rounds of protest and mobilization. A long-term historical perspective helps: although Bolivia's iconic leaders of indigenous revolt and revolution during the eighteenth and nineteenth centuries may have lost their battles in the short term, many of their aims concerning land and self-government have been partially achieved in the medium and long term. Others remain as aspirations for the future. The veins of Bolivia's radical, mostly anti-capitalist traditions run deep, with indigenous, nonindigenous, and hybrid variants mixing and colliding in different ways at different conjunctures. The best way to make sense of any given conjuncture is in relation to previous conjunctures (Barragán 2006; Dunkerley 2007; Hylton 2011b, forthcoming; Hylton and Thomson 2007; Hylton et al. 2003).

I have not argued that all indigenous people are peasants, or vice versa, though most of them are and have been, and I would not argue that we need to prioritize class over race/ethnicity to understand Bolivia, yesterday or today. I do not mean to diminish the contribution of recent research in Anglo-American anthropology either. Our understanding of the Guaraní and indigenous movements in the eastern lowlands and Santa Cruz itself, as well as the Landless Workers' Movement, the bilingual education movement, and urban workers of both indigenous and nonindigenous descent in Quillacollo and El Alto, has been enriched enormously because of it.

Yet only Gutiérrez Aguilar and Webber signal the extent to which non-liberal, collective demands for communal property rights, decisions over the exploitation of natural resources, and political representation outside or beyond party structures are, in crucial ways, historical. They are also the only ones to point to a non-liberal matrix of insurgent politics that includes indigenous peasant communities in the highlands and highland valleys, lowland indigenous groups, landless lowland migrants from the highlands and highland valleys, urban indigenous people in neighborhood committees, trade unions, and *gremios* (craft unions), as well as nonindigenous peasants and workers and middle-class intellectuals, professionals, and students. To repeat: none of this is visible through the conceptual fog of power/knowledge and governmentality that Foucault offers.

Yet, anchored in Marxist theoretical debates about the state, class struggle, and capital accumulation, Gutiérrez Aguilar and Webber make only superficial gestures toward the relationship of twenty-first century developments to the long arc of Bolivian history or to emic categories and understandings derived therefrom. They therefore tell us relatively little about how non-liberal indigenous and/or peasant forms of leadership, alliance making, and coalition building of the past have shaped present-day struggles and thus establish a weak link between continuity and change, culture and political economy. More sustained engagement with existing historiography and anthropology would help them avoid judging present configurations of indigenous and nonindigenous peasants and workers and the Bolivian state in terms of an ideal: what ought to be, but is not, and never has been. In its own way, this is also a form of wishful thinking, that is, discursive idealism.

Thus, the call to return to Wolf's historical and cultural materialism is also a call for greater political realism in the face of the revolutionary hopes raised from 2000 to 2005 and dashed thereafter against the rocks of a liberal, state-led project for capitalist development with longer legs, less repression, and enormously greater political and intellectual legitimacy than any previous government in Bolivian history, including the MNR. In a country where more than half the people are still rural cultivators, transport workers, and merchants, MAS has consistently taken 90 percent of the rural vote, most of which is located in the western highlands and highland valleys. By itself, this fact—which cannot be explained in terms of "indigeneity"— is surely a powerful argument for a return to the ethnographic study of the indigenous peasantry and class formation throughout the Bolivian countryside, perhaps especially in the western highlands and highland valleys. *Lo andino*, it turns out, is much more than an academic tendency that characterized cultural anthropology in the 1960s and 1970s: it is a political and demographic process of great complexity that, as Nicole Fabricant's (2012) work shows, is dialectically interrelated with the making of *lo amazónico*. Andean highland migrants bring with them strategies, tactics, symbols, memories, and ideas of struggle when they settle in the eastern lowlands to seek a place in the Bolivian nation.

Conclusion

Throughout republican history, indigenous peasant movements in the western highlands and highland valleys reshaped the state, which led to one failed Aymara revolution in the Federal Revolution of 1899, a partially successful National Revolution of 1952, and another partially successful national revolution led by Aymaras from 2000 to 2005. There is no reason to forget about indigenous peasants in the twenty-first century, since they continue to be decisive actors in key conjunctures. By studying cycles of protest and mobilization, scholars can "reestablish continuity with emancipatory aspects of past revolutionary efforts," to cite the introduction to this volume. In relation to the popular organizations from the eastern lowlands, the weight of organizations in the western highlands like the CSUTCB, women's organizations such as the Bartolina Sisa Confederation, and even the smaller CONAMAQ, along with that of the coca growers' federation of trade unions, has remained predominant in the national popular bloc the MAS forged—in the Constitutional Assembly, government ministries in La Paz, town councils, and mayoralties. What stands out about Morales and MAS is the ability to co-opt and divide the indigenous and popular movements in the highlands and highland valleys by bringing them more firmly into the orbit of the state/party nexus, rather than excluding them as a racialized or class "other" in need of modernization and *mestizaje* or incorporating them as state managers of neoliberal cultural difference at the local level, as in the 1990s. Here, Foucauldian frameworks are of limited utility in clarifying change and continuity in time and space.

The near disappearance of historical perspectives from anthropology on Latin America—the contributors to this volume excepted—is both symptom and cause of what Wolf referred to as "intellectual deforestation," whereby each generation of anthropologists takes the ax to the paradigms of its predecessors. Dominant currents in anthropology have largely abandoned the task of causal explanation, giving up on what Wolf called cumulative knowledge, which uses the work of predecessors to ask new questions (1990: 558), while, outside Bolivia, historically informed social scientists have gone only halfway in engaging the existing historiography on Bolivia. Historians, for the most part, have buried their heads, ostrichlike, in archival sands, ignoring the political and theoretical implications of their own work, as well as scholarship in the social sciences (for exceptions, see Barragán and Soliz 2009; Dunkerley 2007; Hylton and Thomson 2007; John 2009; Platt 1983; Smale 2010; Young 2017).

Writing about Andean peasant political consciousness three decades ago, Steve Stern (1987) highlighted the need to account for multiple time horizons in order to unlock the political logics operating during insurgent moments of history. Stern did not posit a timeless Andean culture that miraculously persisted through the centuries, explaining everything and nothing. Rather, he argued the need to study racial/ethnic, state, and class formation as dialectically interconnected processes that, while continually in motion, nevertheless feature certain patterns of political conflict, mobilization, and collective action. Identifying change within continuity is key to making sense of Evo Morales's Bolivia, and the effort to do so represents a return to earlier studies of Bolivia—many of which cited the work of Wolf and E. P. Thompson—that emphasized racial/ethnic, community, class, market, and state formation in broad historical perspective (Calderón and Dandler 1986; Lagos 1995; Langer 1989; Larson 1988, 2004; Larson et al. 1995; Rivera Cusicanqui 1984; Zavaleta Mercado 1986). Earlier studies consistently emphasized the commodification of land, labor, and exchange, and highlighted the ways capitalist development eroded subsistence strategies that indigenous peasantries defined in terms of their own "traditions," which were invented in a variety of ways through political struggle. Regardless of disciplinary specialization, these studies featured a historical perspective on power and rural property relations in the western highlands and highland valleys. What divides the current generation of studies from previous generations—and explains the divergence—is the rise of Foucault and the simultaneous eclipse of historical perspectives, which is ironic given Foucault's oft-repeated insistence on the historical nature of his own thought. Again, this speaks to the intellectual amnesia of our time.

This chapter has criticized the ahistorical, discursively idealist drift of the main currents in Anglo-American anthropology on Bolivia, the unstated assumptions about power that open some lines of inquiry while foreclosing others, and the spatial turn in the social sciences, which has flattened out the contours of historical time, and therefore of power, by jettisoning class and class struggle, which were at the heart of Wolf's persuasive, pathbreaking, and compelling account of peasant revolution. Wolf's (1999) approach, further developed by Roseberry (1989, 1993, 1995, 1996, 1997), allows us to understand regional differences as power-laden historical processes that are at once social, cultural, political, and economic.

Thus, major questions of causality are at stake in the adoption of analytical frameworks in history and the social sciences. Used properly, analysis of class struggle and formation can help us cut through the rhetoric and performance of indigenous rights favored by MAS and thereby avoid seeing like the latest incarnation of the Bolivian state, which is less and less new. Thinking historically about class in relation to state and racial/ethnic formation helps us see how a nationalist revolution with indigenous centrality made the government of Morales and MAS possible—not vice versa—and how Morales and MAS nevertheless reproduced many features of the MNR in the 1950s. This cannot be seen through Foucauldian lenses that blur our perception of specific historical actors past and present.

Though intellectual history does not repeat itself exactly, in certain respects the ahistorical drift in the social sciences—pace empty talk of an "historical turn"—recalls the obstacles Wolf and others worked to overcome in the 1960s and 1970s, precisely through engagement with history. As noted in the introduction to this volume, Wolf's contribution to thinking about state, class, regional, and racial/ethnic formation does not hinge on the existence or activism of the middle peasantry. His framework helps us see twenty-first-century Bolivia in terms of alliances, conflicts, and power blocs in which rural cultivators of many stripes (i.e., peasants) challenge, and understand themselves to challenge property rights and political prerogatives of agri-business, oil and gas, and mining interests in the name of the nation. Deploying "peasant" as a class category does not imply a unitary subject, much less a revolutionary one sans race/ethnicity, or introduce a teleology. Instead, as Wolf noted in the 1950s, the term compels us to explore heterogeneity, difference, and conflict among rural cultivators, and between indigenous peasants and other groups and classes, all in the context of overlapping fields of socioeconomic power—local, regional, national, and international (Wolf 1956).

"Peasant" also helps bring into sharper focus what is beyond official rhetoric, genuinely new, and what represents continuity in Bolivian political culture and economy. The term allows us to see MAS as a twenty-first-century version of the MNR in its developmentalist phase, incorporating indigenous symbols, myths, and rituals (not creole-mestizo ones), in lieu of introducing radical changes in political representation and economy (Hylton 2006; Hylton and Thomson 2007). This theoretical focus identifies traditions and patterns of insurgent collective action—of deliberation, protest, and mobilization—as well as everyday resistance, negotiation, and accommodation, and explains how indigenous peasants have engaged states and markets over centuries (for Mexico, see Servín et al. 2007; see also Langer 2016). It shows how they have demanded inclusion on their own terms by making non-liberal claims for collective rights and protections concerning communal land use and political representation. Furthermore, as anthropologists have emphasized, local actors are passionate about historical memory in ways that speak to the overlapping nature of racial/ethnic and class struggles in relation to the state. They understand themselves politically, at least in part, as peasants and workers of indigenous descent (Albro 2010; Fabricant 2011, 2012). They are no less likely than professional historians to frame their narratives about the present in terms of what happened in the past and why (Canessa 2009), although in the wake of the cultural turn, they are considerably more likely than historians or anthropologists to use class analysis and political economy to frame their narratives.

Now that the Morales government and MAS have entered a period of senescence tending toward senility, and the political panorama that characterized South America during Morales's remarkable rise has shifted dramatically to the right, conditions for integrating and synthesizing the different perspectives currently on offer—including perspectives from history—may or may not improve. Although I have gestured in that direction, the synthesis itself is beyond the scope of this essay, not to mention the competence of its author, which does not, of course, lessen the necessity of the task.

Forrest Hylton is Associate Professor of Political Science at the Universidad Nacional de Colombia-Medellín, and with Sinclair Thomson, coauthor of *Revolutionary Horizons: Past and Present in Bolivian Politics* (2007), and with Sinclair Thomson, Sergio Serulnikov, and Felix Patzi, coeditor and coauthor of *"Ya es otro tiempo el presente": Cuatro momentos de insurgencia indígena* (2003). He is currently revising a manuscript entitled *Specters of Race War: Insurgent Communities, the Federal War of 1899, and the "Regeneration" of Bolivia*.

Note

1. Both as an analytic category and as a reality of what Wolf (1990) called structural power in the deployment of social labor, class includes but is not limited to consciousness and subjectivity. Following E. P. Thompson, I understand class as a historical relationship that happens at particular times and places and, similar to revolution, it can be studied but not theorized, because each configuration of class power, like each revolution, is unique: a "just-so case" (Wolf 1971: 12, cited in Knight 1990: 181). Similar to races and ethnicities, classes exist only in relation to other classes; thus, class is an inherently relational category and concerns identity but goes beyond it as well. To the extent that class consciousness exists, it is contingent and develops in the course of class struggles that emerge from class experience, which is largely determined by the structural constraints imposed by a given set of productive relations (Thompson 1963, 1978, 1993, 2014). But class consciousness is about how that experience and those constraints are handled in cultural terms of norms, values, traditions, and "common sense." Class is not a thing but a process: like states, communities, or races/ethnicities from which it is inseparable, it is always in motion, being made and remade through political alliance, conflict, and negotiation (Gill 2016; Thompson 1963).

   Thus, the history of class struggle, which is contingent—rather than the relations of production and class experience, which are structurally given—determines the shape of class consciousness in any given setting. And class is not simply another category for organizing identity, though it is that as well. It is best explained in relation to class struggle and conflict over the contours of capital accumulation, rather than in Foucauldian terms of discursive regimes that establish categories of meaningful difference. Class struggle cannot be separated from culture, politics, or economics. Parties, factions, class fractions, paramilitary violence, law (crime and property rights, in particular), religion, regionalism, and type of political regime all influence the contours of shifting fields of class power (Hay 1975; Marx [1852] 2013; Roseberry 1989; Thompson 1975, 1978, 1993, 1994). This is not to essentialize or fetishize class, much less race/ethnicity, or to argue it explains everything in contemporary Bolivia or elsewhere, but rather to insist that without some analysis of class and racial/ethnic formation that links culture to political economy and state to civil society, we will fail to distinguish change from continuity.

References

Abreu Mendoza, Carlos, and Denise Y. Arnold. 2017. *Crítica de la Razón Andina*. Raleigh, NC: Editorial A Contracorriente.

Albó, Xavier. 1986a. "Bases étnicas y sociales para la participación Aymara." In Calderón and Jorge Dandler 1986: 401–443.

———. 1986b. "Etnicidad y clase en la gran rebelión Aumara/Quechua, Kataris, Amarus y Bases 1780–1781." In Calderón and Dandler 1986: 53–118.

———. 1987. "From MNRistas to Kataristas to Katari." In *Resistance, Rebellion, and Consciousness in the Andean Peasant World*, ed. Steve J. Stern, 379–419. Madison: University of Wisconsin Press.

———. 1994. "And from Kataristas to MNRistas? The Surprising and Bold Alliance between Aymaras and Neoliberals." In *Indigenous Peoples and Democracy in Latin America*, ed. Donna Lee Van Cott, 55–79. New York: St. Martin's Press.

Albro, Robert. 2006. Bolivia's "'Evo Phenomenon': From Identity to What?" *Journal of Latin American Anthropology* 11 (2): 408–428.

———. 2010. "Confounding Cultural Citizenship and Constitutional Reform in Bolivia." *Latin American Perspectives* 37 (3): 71–90.

Ari, Waskar. 2014. *Earth Politics: Religion, Decolonization, and Bolivia's Indigenous Intellectuals.* Durham, NC: Duke University Press.

Barragán, Rossana. 2006. *Asembleas Constituyentes: Ciudadanía y elecciones, convenciones y debates, 1825–1971.* La Paz: Muela del Diablo.

Barragán, Rossana, and Carmen Soliz. 2009. "Indígenas urbanos: El caso de los aymaras en la ciudad de La Paz y El Alto." In *¿Indígenas u obreros? La construcción polítoca de identidades en el altiplano boliviano,* ed. Denise Y. Arnold, 471–509. La Paz: UNIR.

Becker, Marc. 2018. "Politicized Identities and Social Movements." *Latin American Research Review* 53 (1): 202–209.

Brabazon, Honor, and Jeffery R. Webber. 2014. "Evo Morales and the MST in Bolivia: Continuities and Discontinuities in Agrarian Reform." *Journal of Agrarian Change* 14 (3): 1–31.

Cadena, Marisol de la, and Orin Starn. 2007. *Indigenous Experience Today.* New York: Berg.

Calderón, Fernando, and Jorge Dandler. 1986. *Bolivia: La Fuerza Historica del Campesinado.* Geneva: Instituto de Investigaciones de las Naciones Unidas para el Desarrollo Social and Centro de Estudios de la Realidad Económica y Social.

Canessa, Andrew. 2007. "Who Is Indigenous? Self-Identification, Indigeneity, and Claims to Justice in Contemporary Bolivia." *Urban Anthropology and Studies of Cultural Systems and World Economic Development* 36 (3): 195–237.

———. 2009. "Forgetting the Revolution and Remembering the War: Memory and Violence in Highland Bolivia." *History Workshop Journal* 68 (1): 173–198.

———. 2012. "New Indigenous Citizenship in Bolivia: Challenging the Liberal Model of the State and its Subjects." *Latin American and Caribbean Ethnic Studies* 7 (2): 201–221.

———. 2014. "Conflict, claim and contradiction in the new 'indigenous' state of Bolivia." *Critique of Anthropology* 34 (2): 153–173.

Davies, William. 2016. "The New Neoliberalism." *New Left Review* II 101: 121–134.

Dunkerley, James. 1984. *Rebellion in the Veins: Political Struggle in Bolivia, 1952–82.* London: Verso Books.

———. 2007. *Bolivia: Revolution and the Power of History in the Present.* London: Institute of Latin American Studies.

Fabricant, Nicole. 2011. "Ocupar, Resistir, Producir: Reterritorializing Soyscapes in Santa Cruz." In *Remapping Bolivia: Resources, Territory and Indigeneity in a Plurinational State,* ed. Nicole Fabricant and Bret Gustafson, 146–165. Santa Fe, NM: School for American Research.

———. 2012. *Mobilizing Bolivia's Displaced: Indigenous Politics and the Struggle over Land.* Chapel Hill: University of North Carolina Press.

García Linera, Álvaro. 2011a. *Tensiones creativas de la revolución: La Quinta fase del Proceso de Cambio.* La Paz: Vicepresidencia del Estado Plurinacional.

———. 2011b. *El "Ongismo," enfermedad infantil del derechismo.* La Paz: Vicepresidencia del Estado Plurinacional.

———. 2012. *Geopolítica de la Amazonía: Poder hacendal-patrimonial y acumulación capitalista.* La Paz: Vicepresidencia del Estado Plurinacional.

Gill, Lesley. 1987. *Peasants, Entrepreneurs, and Social Change: Frontier Development in Lowland Bolivia.* Boulder, CO: Westview Press.

———. 1997. "Re-locating Class: Ex-miners and Neoliberalism in Bolivia." *Critique of Anthropology* 17 (3): 293–312.

———. 2000. *Teetering on the Rim: Global Restructuring, Daily Life, and the Armed Retreat of the Bolivian State.* New York: Columbia University Press.

———. 2005. "Comments on Douglas Hertzler's 'Campesinos and Originarios . . .'" *Journal of Latin American Anthropology* 10 (1): 77–79.

———. 2013. "Power." In *The Handbook of Sociocultural Anthropology*, ed. James G. Carrier and Deborah A. Gewertz, 49–67. London: Bloomsbury.

———. 2016. *A Century of Violence in a Red City: Popular Struggle, Counterinsurgency, and Human Rights in Colombia*. Durham, NC: Duke University Press.

Goodale, Mark. 2008. "Reclaiming Modernity: Indigenous Cosmopolitanism and the Coming of the Second Revolution in Bolivia." *American Ethnologist* 33 (4): 634–649.

Gotkowitz, Laura. 2008. *A Revolution for Our Rights: Indigenous Struggles for Land and Justice in Bolivia, 1880–1952*. Durham, NC: Duke University Press.

Grisaffi, Thomas. 2010. "'We Are Originarios . . . We Just Aren't from Here': Coca Leaf and Identity Politics in the Chapare, Bolivia." *Bulletin of Latin American Research* 29 (4): 425–439.

Guha, Ranajit. 1997. "Chandra's Death." In *A Subaltern Studies Reader*, ed. Ranajit Guha, 133–165. Minneapolis: University of Minnesota Press.

Gustafson, Bret. 2009. *New Languages of the State: Indigenous Resurgence and the Politics of Knowledge*. Durham, NC: Duke University Press.

———. 2011. "Power Necessarily Comes from Below: Guarani Autonomies and Their Other." In *Remapping Bolivia: Resources, Territory and Indigeneity in a Plurinational State*, ed. Nicole Fabricant and Bret Gustafson, 166–189. Santa Fe, NM: School for American Research.

Gustafson, Bret, and Nicole Fabricant. 2011. "Introduction: New Cartographies of Knowledge and Struggle." In *Remapping Bolivia: Resources, Territory and Indigeneity in a Plurinational State*, ed. Nicole Fabricant and Bret Gustafson, 1–26. Santa Fe, NM: School for American Research.

Gutiérrez Aguilar, Raquel. 2014. *Rhythms of the Pachakuti: Indigenous Uprising and State Power in Bolivia*. Durham, NC: Duke University Press.

Hale, Charles. 2011. "Epilogue." In *Remapping Bolivia: Resources, Territory and Indigeneity in a Plurinational State*, ed. Nicole Fabricant and Bret Gustafson, 195–207. Santa Fe, NM: School for American Research.

Harten, Sven. 2011. *The Rise of Evo Morales and the MAS*. London: Zed Books.

Hay, Douglas. 1975. "Property, Authority and Criminal Law." In *Albion's Fatal Tree Crime and Society In Eighteenth-Century England*, 17–63. New York: Pantheon.

Healy, Kevin. 1991. "The Political Ascent of Bolivia's Coca Leaf Producers." *Journal of Interamerican Studies and World Affairs* 33 (1): 87–122.

———. 1998. "Coca, the State, and the Peasantry in Bolivia, 1982–88." *Journal of Inter-American Studies and World Affairs* 30 (2–3): 105–126.

Hertzler, Douglas. 2005a. "Campesinos and Originarios! Class and Ethnicity in Rural Movements in the Bolivian Lowlands." *Journal of Latin American Anthropology* 10 (1): 45–71.

———. 2005b. "Response to Nancy Postero, Lesley Gill, and Bret Gustafson." *Journal of Latin American and Caribbean Anthropology* 10 (1): 84–87.

Hetland, Gabriel, and Jeff Goodwin. 2013. "The Strange Disappearance of Capitalism from Social Movement Studies." In *Marxism and Social Movements*, ed. Colin Barker, Laurence Cox, John Krinsky, and Alf Gunvald Nilsen, 85–104. London: Brill.

Hurtado, Javier. 1986. *El katarismo*. La Paz: Hisbol.

Hylton, Forrest. 2004. "El federalismo insurgente: Una aproximación a Juan Lero, los comunarios y la Guerra Federal." *Tinkazos: Revista de Ciencias Sociales Bolivianas* 16: 99–118.

———. 2006. "Landslide in Bolivia." *New Left Review II* 37: 69–72.

———. 2011a. "Old Wine, New Bottles? In Search of Dialectics in Bolivia." *Dialectical Anthropology* 35 (3): 243–247.

———. 2011b. "'Now Is Not Your Time; It's Ours': Insurgent Confederation, 'Race War,' and Liberal State-Formation in the Bolivian Federal War of 1899." *South Atlantic Quarterly* 110 (2): 487–503.

———. Forthcoming. "'They Alone Should Rule': Violence, Politics, and Andean Communities in the Bolivian Federal War of 1899." In *Violence and Indigenous Communities in the Americas*, ed. Susan Sleeper-Smith. Evanston, IL: Northwestern University Press.

Hylton, Forrest, and Sinclair Thomson. 2005. "The Chequered Rainbow." *New Left Review II* 35: 40–66.

———. 2007. *Revolutionary Horizons: Past and Present in Bolivian Politics*. New York: Verso.

Hylton, Forrest, Felix Patzi, Sergio Serulnikov, and Sinclair Thomson. 2003. *"Ya es otro tiempo el presente": Cuatro momentos de insurgencia indígena*. La Paz: Muela del Diablo.

John, S. Sándor. 2009. *Bolivia's Radical Tradition: Permanent Revolution in the Andes*. Tucson: University of Arizona Press.

Kearney, Michael. 1996. *Reconceptualizing the Peasantry: Anthropology in Global Perspective*. Boulder, CO: Westview Press.

Knight, Alan. 1985. "The Mexican Revolution: Bourgeois? Nationalist? Or Just a 'Great Rebellion'?" *Bureau of Latin American Research* 4 (1): 1–37.

———. 1990. "Social Revolution: A Latin American Perspective." *Bulletin of Latin American Research* 9 (2): 175–202.

———. 2001. "Democratic and Revolutionary Traditions in Latin America." *Bulletin of Latin American Research* 20 (2): 147–186.

Kohl, Ben, and Linda Farthing. 2006. *Impasse in Bolivia: Neoliberal Hegemony and Popular Resistance*. London: Zed Books.

Lagos, Maria. 1995. *Autonomía y poder: dinámica de clase y cultura en Cochabamba*. La Paz: Plural Editores.

Langer, Erick. 1989. *Economic Change and Rural Resistance in Southern Bolivia, 1880–1932*. Stanford, CA: Stanford University Press.

———. 2016. "Indigenous Independence in South America." In *New Countries: Capitalism, Revolutions, and Nations in the Americas*, ed. John Tutino, 350–375. Durham, NC: Duke University Press.

Larson, Brooke. 1988. *Colonialism and Agrarian Transformation: Cochabamba, 1550–1900*. Princeton, NJ: Princeton University Press.

———. 2004. *Trials of Nation-Making: Liberalism, Race, and Ethnicity in the Andes, 1810–1910*. Cambridge: Cambridge University Press.

Larson, Brooke, and Olivia Harris, eds., with Enrique Tandeter. 1995. *Ethnicity, Markets, and Migration in the Andes*. Durham, NC: Duke University Press.

Lazar, Sian. 2008. *El Alto, Rebel City: Self and Citizenship in Andean Bolivia*. Durham, NC: Duke University Press.

Mamani Ramírez, Pablo. 2011. "Cartographies of Indigenous Power: Identity and Territoriality in Bolivia." In *Remapping Bolivia: Resources, Territory and Indigeneity in a Plurinational State*, ed. Nicole Fabricant and Bret Gustafson, 30–45. Santa Fe, NM: School for American Research.

Marx, Karl. (1852) 2013. *The Eighteenth Brumaire of Louis Napoleon*. Belmont, NC: Wiseblood.

Medeiros, Carmen. 2001. "Civilizing the Popular? The Law of Popular Participation and the Design of a New Civil Society in 1990s Bolivia." *Critique of Anthropology* 21 (4): 401–425.

Nash, June. 1979. *We Eat the Mines and the Mines Eat Us: Dependency and Exploitation in the Bolivian Tin Mines*. New York: Columbia University Press.

Pearse, Andrew. 1986. "Campesinado y Revolución: El Caso de Bolivia." In Calderón and Dandler, 331–358.

Platt, Tristan. 1983. "Conciencia andina y conciencia proletaria: Qhuyaruna y ayllu en el norte de Potosí." *HISLA: Revista latinoamericana de historia económica y social* 2: 47–73.

Postero, Nancy Grey. 2005. "Commentary on 'Campesinos and Originarios . . .'" *Journal of Latin American Anthropology* 10 (1): 72–87.

———. 2007. *Now We Are Citizens: Indigenous Politics in Postmulticultural Bolivia*. Stanford, CA: Stanford University Press.

———. 2017. *The Indigenous State: Race, Politics, and Performance in Plurinational Bolivia*. Berkeley: University of California Press.

Rivera Cusicanqui, Silvia. 1984. *Oprimidos pero no vencidos: Luchas del campesinado Aymara y Quechwa, 1900–1980*. La Paz: Instituto de Historia Social Boliviana and CSUTCB.

———. 1991. "Liberal Democracy and *Ayllu* Democracy in Bolivia: The Case of Northern Potosí." *Journal of Development Studies* 25 (4): 97–121.

Roseberry, William. 1989. *Anthropologies and Histories: Essays in Culture, History, and Political Economy*. New Brunswick, NJ: Rutgers University Press.

———. 1993. "Beyond the Agrarian Question in Latin America." In *Confronting Historical Paradigms: Peasants, Labor, and the Capitalist World System in Africa and Latin America*, ed. Frederick Cooper, Allan Isaacman, Florencia Mallon, William Roseberry, and Steve Stern, 318–368. Madison: University of Wisconsin Press.

———. 1995. "Latin American Peasant Studies in a 'Postcolonial' Era." *Journal of Latin American Anthropology* 1 (1): 150–177.

———. 1996. "The Unbearable Lightness of Anthropology." *Radical History Review* 65: 5–25.

———. 1997. "Marx and Anthropology." *Annual Review of Anthropology* 26: 25–46.

Sarkar, Sumit. 1998. *Writing Social History*. Oxford: Oxford University Press.

Servín, Elisa, Leticia Reina, and John Tutino, eds. 2007. *Cycles of Conflict, Centuries of Change: Crisis, Reform, and Revolution in Mexico*. Durham, NC: Duke University Press.

Smale, Robert. 2010. *"I Sweat the Flavor of Tin": Labor Activism in Early Twentieth-Century Bolivia*. Pittsburgh, PA: University of Pittsburgh Press.

Soliz, Carmen. 2017. "'Land to the Original Owners': Rethinking the Indigenous Politics of the Bolivian Agrarian Reform." *Hispanic American Historical Review* 97 (2): 259–296.

Stern, Steve J. 1987. "New Approaches to the Study of Peasant Rebellion and Consciousness: Implications of the Andean Experience." In *Resistance, Rebellion, and Consciousness in the Andean Peasant World*, ed. Steve J. Stern, 3–25. Madison: University of Wisconsin Press.

Tapia, Luis. 2011. *El Estado de derecho como tiranía*. La Paz: Autodeterminación.

Tassi, Nico, Alfonso Hinojosa, and Richard Canaviri, eds. 2015. *La economía popular en Bolivia: Tres miradas*. La Paz: Centro de Investigaciones Sociales, Vicepresidencia del Estado.

Tassi, Nico, Carmen Medeiros, Antonio Rodríguez-Carmona, and Giovanna Ferrufini. 2013. *"'Hacer plata sin plata': El desborde de los comerciantes populares en Bolivia."* La Paz: PIEB.

Thompson, E. P. 1963. *The Making of the English Working Class*. New York: Vintage Books.

———. 1975. "The Crime of Anonymity." In *Albion's Fatal Tree Crime and Society In Eighteenth-Century England*, 255–308. New York: Pantheon.

———. 1978. *The Poverty of Theory and Other Essays*. London: Merlin Press.

———. 1993. *Customs in Common: Studies in Traditional Popular Culture*. New York: New Press.

———. 1994. "History and Anthropology." In *Making History: Writings on History and Culture*, ed. Dorothy Thompson, 199–225. New York: New Press.

———. 2014. *E. P. Thompson and the Making of the New Left: Essays and Polemics*, ed. Cal Winslow. New York: Monthly Review Press.

Trouillot, Michel-Rolph. 1995. *Silencing the Past: Power and the Production of History*. Boston: Beacon Press.

Webber, Jeffery R. 2007. "Indigenous Struggle in Latin America: The Perilous Invisibility of Capital and Class." *Latin American Politics & Society* 49 (3): 191–205.

———. 2012. *Red October: Left Indigenous Struggles in Modern Bolivia*. Chicago: Haymarket Books.

Wolf, Eric. 1956. "Aspects of Group Relations in a Complex Society." *American Anthropologist* 58 (6): 1065–1078.

———. 1966. *Peasants*. Englewood Cliffs, NJ: Prentice-Hall.

———. 1969. *Peasant Wars of the Twentieth Century*. New York: Harper & Row.

———. 1971. "Introduction." In *National Liberation: Revolution in the Third World*, ed. Roderick Aya and Norman Miller, 1–13. New York: Free Press.

———. 1990. "Distinguished Lecture: Facing Power—Old Insights, New Questions." *American Anthropologist* 92 (3): 586–597.

———. 1999. *Envisioning Power: Ideologies of Dominance and Crisis*. Berkeley: University of California Press.

Young, Kevin. 2107. *Blood of the Earth: Resource Nationalism, Revolution, and Empire in Bolivia*. Austin: University of Texas Press.

Zavaleta Mercado, René. 1983. "Las masas en noviembre." In *Bolivia hoy*, ed. René Zavaleta Mercado, 11–59. Mexico City: Siglo XXI.

———. 1986. *Lo nacional-popular en Bolivia*. Mexico City: Siglo XXI.

AFTERWORD
Reading Eric Wolf as a Public Intellectual Today
Gavin Smith

Peasant Wars was explicitly written as a book for public consumption. This makes the context of its reading today especially misleading: it is neither an anthropology text nor an approach to leftist politics for which it is easy to find analogous current interventions. *Peasant Wars* emerged from Eric Wolf's response to the US war in and on Southeast Asia and belonged to a substantial array of studies that came out in the late 1960s and early 1970s[1] — studies that addressed the role of peasants in revolutionary politics across a long historical period (e.g., Moore 1967; Skocpol 1979), as well as studies that addressed questions of peasants and recent or current revolutionary politics in what was then called the Third World (Davidson 1969, 1974; Migdal 1974).

There was no doubt each of these had its own disciplinary hallmark, but comparisons among them were treated with very little reference to such distinctions. Like Wolf, the authors sought answers to what for brevity I call "the peasant question": they drew mostly on secondary sources, sought to examine a range of historical and geographically dispersed cases to draw their conclusions, and took the historical role of peasant agency very seriously. There was a sense of urgency in the questions they all posed. Even Barrington Moore's *Origins of Dictatorships and Democracy*, which was written before *Peasant Wars*, dealt with earlier periods and was not confined to Europe. It was replete with phrases such as "the process of modernization begins with peasant revolutions that fail. It culminates during the twentieth century with peasant revolutions that succeed" (1967: 453).

For me, this raises two questions. First, what was distinctive about Wolf's approach? And second, how did intellectual engagements with leftist politics at the time differ from such engagements today? One way to address this question is to consider the current state of dialogue between "intellectuals" (both academic and nonacademic) and leftist movements. I will then add my characterization of Wolf's particular contribution to that already taken up by the editors and conclude by speculating on how some of the features of his study might provide useful tools for us today.

Revolution from the Perspective of the Countryside

In another essay in which Wolf plays a central role, I have spoken of his work as one instance of what was referred to as "the agrarian question." And I have suggested it was always "the other question" (Smith 2019; see also Smith 2018). I don't mean issues of the country-side were unimportant for major figures of the Left. It would be hard to read the works of Marx, Lenin, Kautsky, or Gramsci—not to mention Mao—and draw such a conclusion. But, as Wolf himself notes, generally speaking, revolutionary protagonists lived in the city, wrote in the city, and conducted most of their face-to-face politics in the city (Mao in his partisan days, being the exception). So perhaps it is not surprising the revolutionary role of the various actors in urban centers from Paris to Berlin and Saint Petersburg was not termed "the urban question." It was not so much the focus but the point from which the whole was purveyed that made (and makes) the agrarian question into the other question. However, where the possibility of revolution sprang up around the world, following the defeat of the Paris Commune in 1871, it was a question requiring the same kind of precision as Marx's *Capital*. As early as 1899, Lenin, for example, had no doubt about this, opening his 1899 review of Kautsky's *Agrarian Question* with the following appraisal: "Kautsky's book is the most important event in present-day economic literature since the third volume of *Capital*."

So, an initial way of highlighting Wolf's book is to note he re-versed an earlier center of gravity by making the "agrarian question" the organizing principle for exploring the revolutionary vectors of the entire social formation in each of his cases. In 1967 for Barrington Moore and in 1969 for Eric Wolf, the agrarian question was the right place to start to reverse a lens rather than to induce myopia. As long as we understand the question in this way, it is interesting to note this kind of grounded framing would be entirely absent today in a list of pressing political issues to be addressed, either by a gov-ernmental program or revolutionary praxis. Instead, it is "the urban question" today that has become the preeminent not to say monolithic academic focus of leftist struggle.[2] And it is rarely grounded in historical ethnography and lacks the holistic exploration of a social formation we find in Wolf.[3] Indeed, the mistaken accusations that earlier revolutionary writers focused exclusively on the urban (proletariat) are more apposite to today's writers. Yet, as Jaume Franquesa notes, "any successful emancipatory project must not only understand, but aim to supersede, the division between country and city that has been, and continues to be, central to the reproduction of capital and state" (2019: 21).

So, a way to get an angle on Wolf's work, set as it was among the concerns of the 1960s and 1970s, is to view it quite consciously from an understanding of current leftist agendas. Dispersed though their agendas too might have been, they arose nonetheless from a commonly felt condition. The way people like Moore, Wolf, Leacock, Hobsbawm, Thompson, and Nash formulated their research and writing was the product of an historical setting. For them, "the idea of revolution [was a means] . . . for connecting old endings to new beginnings and, therefore . . . connecting our dissatisfactions with the past to our hopes for alternative futures" (Scott 2014: 3). The design of political work, intellectual or otherwise, was understood to be a *practical* contribution to currently active social revolutionary projects—a position hard to take today. The need for such interventions to be effective moreover (as opposed to merely theoretical), kept them from teleological or deterministic temptations. And the presence of apparently effective collective struggles provided them with a living laboratory on which to base the building of ideas[4] (cf. Webber 2019). In quite broad terms, for them the approach was not unlike what Alex Callinicos argues motivated Lenin's theoretical reflections: "the complexity and unpredictability of history, and *the necessity of political intervention [in it]* . . . We see a constant tracking backward and forward between theory and practice as new problems force [him] even in the most pressing of circumstances to step back and to reappraise the situation theoretically" (2007: 25, emphasis added). This is certainly not the place to diverge into a lengthy and obviously partial exegesis on contemporary leftist writing, but I do think the sense of revolutionary possibilities pointed to here has had almost inevitable consequences for what has gained authority as critical thought on the one hand and what has been more easily dismissed on the other. I say they are inevitable because I think in a way they are. The "living laboratory" I referred to earlier is by no means as present or obvious as it once was. We are not without movements or situations that make alliances among them possible, but we no longer tend to think it practical to advocate broader combinations directed toward social revolution.

This has resulted in a shift from a focus on the potentialities of subaltern movements to a focus on the effect new forms of governance and capitalism have on the production of subjects. The perspective has shifted from the point of view of the people (where many anthropologists once felt most comfortable) to the point of view of the regime of dominance, whether state or capital. The overall effect is to treat as authoritative studies that direct attention to the way governance molds people.[5] The setback to leftist politics is that undue attention is paid to demonstrating how self-governance produces collusive agents,[6] or to how current forms of cognitive capitalism make possible "the creativity of desire" among the multitude. Researchers feel no responsibility themselves for contributing to resistant agency. It is almost as though E. P. Thompson's *Making of the English Working Class* had been merely a fanciful romance for bedtime reading.

A second effect of an absent or confusing "living laboratory" has been a loosening of grounded methodology—of building ideas, productive hypotheses, and so on—*up* from the evidence of the movements. For better or worse, the method of controlled comparison for which Wolf's book is so notable is not attractive among many anthropologists who would see themselves to be on the Left (cf. Feuchtwang and Shah 2017). This may be for good reasons, among them problems of classification, the heterogeneity of movements, and their often-ephemeral nature. Yet we need to note the price that may be paid for such intellectual purity. A related issue is the role history played in (all of) Wolf's work—a history of sociological comparison that discomfited some historians.[7] Wolf's approach remained driven by evidence rather than reaching to assert a "theory" to which he might attach his name. While anthropologists today cannot fail to pay lip service to the importance of history, a remarkable number of actual ethnographies show little evidence of its value. Instead, current critiques of international political economy have produced critical history in the spirit of Wolf, but unfortunately at the scale of the world-systems theory against which *Europe and the People Without History* was written (see, e.g., Anieves and Matin 2016; Anieves and Nisancioglu 2015). We may need then to advance on the kind of grounded comparison that Wolf's work exemplified while retaining anthropology's willingness to grapple with the difficulties encountered when history is approached at multiple scales.

This raises an interesting question. In *Peasant Wars*, Wolf dealt with a surprising number of the issues that concern us today, albeit occasionally with a different vocabulary. So, might we learn something relevant for today from their occurrence across Wolf's six cases? For the moment, I will simply list them here. A theme running through *Peasant Wars* is a perpetual concern with security and threats of insecurity—resulting from shifting forms of power, from different class configurations, and over different periods (e.g., a year, an epoch). Insecurity was closely tied to the failure of livelihood (as a combination of subsistence and monetary income) to cover survival needs. This concern arises from the marginal nature of peasant work as imagined from the perspective of the reproduction of capital, that is, peasants' condition as a relative surplus population. A factor here has to do with what Wolf refers to as their "maneuverability." Yet the ability to shift, to move, to "maneuver" in Wolf's terms, while all tactics in the quotidian task of getting by, can also have a complex relationship to leverage within fields of power. Sometimes one must maneuver because one has little power; sometimes it is because one *can* maneuver that one has at least *some* power. All these issues, so central to Wolf's series of cases and his tentative conclusions, are still with us. Wolf's book is also replete with instances where the regime of rule is on crutches, and violent disturbances emerge as the declining powers seek to amalgamate with the rising ones or build siege walls and hang on. The link between his examples and the use of violence as a means of implanting neoliberal austerity, sustaining it especially at its edges, and finally in propping it up in light of its glaringly evident failures in its own terms provides one more common thread, as some of these chapters show.

Intellectuals and Left Movements Then and Now

As the editors remark in the introduction, the most immediately striking thing about *Peasant Wars* from today's perspective is less its contents or even its conclusions than the form in which the two are expressed: in short, his method of drawing tentative conclusions from the accumulation of evidence that generates controlled historical comparisons. By "tentative," I mean Wolf's method makes his conclusions open to further modification as more evidence comes forth and history itself moves on. By "controlled," I mean his fascination with historical particularities in each of his cases can mislead us into thinking "just any evidence will do." Yet, even if his introduction and conclusion were missing from the book, we would be able to detect that what we learned from the chapters was a result of the way Wolf's method reflected his reason for writing the book. It is no criticism to say his perspective was partial: to help make subaltern people—rural and urban—the subjects of their histories rather than the objects of other people's. So this, in a way, is the most decisive thing to say about the book as we read it today. But here I will try to single out some features that might be helpful in rereading this text.

The conclusion that most people have taken away from Wolf's work is his suggestion regarding the two types of "peasants" most likely to engage in revolutionary social change (see, e.g., Skocpol 1982).[8] Wolf in fact deals with a wide variety of "differently labeled working people" (chap. 2, this volume), yet what many of the actors he discusses might have in common is their responsibility not just for the provision of labor (à la classic proletariat) but also (to a greater or lesser extent) responsibility for reproducing the means of production as well. In the two exemplary cases of peasantry Wolf identifies, he notes how the distinct conditions each faces relieve the direct effect of their domination. Yet it is interesting to note how this relief, such as it is, results from the different issues that face the reproduction of their *overall* labor process.

In the case of "the landowning 'middle peasantry,'" a major concern is the protection of what little means of production they have, and at the same time, once protected, it is this resource that gives them the leverage for political effectiveness. In the case of those "whose settlements are only under marginal control from outside" and who "supplement land . . . to grant [them] . . . some latitude of movement" (Wolf 1969: 279), the limitation resulting from the former situation, that is, that such a political actor is perforce tied to a specific space (at least for some part of the year) is reversed. Here the problem is that the subsistence resources available are so limited that working people must seek out other sources of livelihood—artisanry, temporary day labor, smuggling, and even armed banditry. In all cases, what releases them from prevailing power relations, albeit in limited ways, is their mobility—not necessarily by choice.

Despite the way Wolf traveled across histories and across scales, it is the scale of the daily pressures for reproduction at the site of peasant livelihood itself that is a foundational element of his study. And despite the differences in their use of ethnography and history, all the chapters in this volume use the expression "peasants" or "peasantry." Yet they differ in the degree that they are comfortable with use of the term—either for today or over past periods. Given the long-standing nature of the discussion on peasantries, it is unnecessary to reiterate it once more (see Ennew et al. 1977; Mintz 1973; Shanin 1973, 1974).

When Wolf wrote, "peasant" was widely and often loosely used to refer to subaltern rural people, often including those whose livelihood was only tangentially drawn from the land (e.g., artisans). Therefore, it is probably best to take the view expressed by the editors in the introduction that Wolf's study of these six cases provides us with rich evidence of how revolutions rely on the strategic and often contingent use of combined struggles: these were not so much peasant wars as wars in which peasants played essential parts but always and in variable ways, combined with other key players.

Yet, despite the richness of his evidence, Wolf framed these differences in terms of "traditional relations" set off against "market relations," and being an anthropologist, he provided us with a rich assembly of the relations he referred to when he spoke of "tradition." And anthropology had much to say about "market relations," too. However, I think we can fine-tune the analysis. First, it is important to distinguish between two types of market disruption. Wolf mostly talks about disruptions when entry into market relations occurs after alternatives have been cut off—possibly because older protections have been disrupted, possibly because of political domination (head taxes and so on) or because of natural disaster. Thus, peasants enter commodified relations to address shortfalls in the traditional sphere. These relations might be spasmodic (though habit forming) or cataclysmic. They result in uneven and often quite contingent *disturbance* but are not yet the irreversible ruptures that result from market *compulsion*, when the only form of realizing the value of an end product is participation in a national or global market. The political and often legal tools of colonialism can generate these ruptures and the destruction of regional or national protections ("free trade") can have the same effect. The latter most often ties the larger agriculturalists into imperial or global capitalism, which has a ripple effect back onto various rural workers, whether tenants, sharecroppers, or seasonal day laborers.

Wolf does not question the impact of imperial capitalism. Rather, the resulting scalar interactions become more visible through his lens. For example, because certain peasants attain leverage with *some* means of production (land) under their own control, it is important to distinguish between the possibility of alternatives for exchanging (agricultural) goods to that of market exchange on the one hand and the complete absence of such possibilities: compulsion on the other. Second, I think there is something to be gained from thinking in terms of the mix of the non-commodified and commodified relations associated with simple commodity producers. By doing so, we expose finer possibilities for distinction between the two elements and look more closely *inside* the production unit. Pressures on particularistic, often age-related or gendered relations that give the small agricultural producer the very minor competitive edge needed to get into the market at all are thus exposed.

Such a perspective also gives us insight into the limitations some peasants face as market relations become more widespread. There are physical limits to how the formal subsumption of labor of this kind can give "competitive advantage" to the peasant household in the market. As a result of being starved of capital, almost by definition, such people are limited to cycles of reproduction that cannot be expanded (what Marx called "simple reproduction"). Meanwhile, as market compulsion takes an ever-stronger hold for operations of all kinds besides that of the peasant household—those competing with the peasant in the production of agricultural goods of course, but also those producing what they need like agricultural inputs, and necessary consumer items—their disadvantages increase. Their "simple" reproduction finds itself faced with a kind of reproduction (expanded via capital inputs) that systematically affects the relative market value of their own goods. Consequently, the peasants' overall income is reduced, throwing them into the crisis that their original entry into commodity production was supposed to avoid. Examined in this way, Wolf's cases and many of those in this volume emphatically do not condemn such an interpretation to some kind of mechanical determinism (cf. Ennew et al. 1977). Rather, they encourage us to follow the very different lines along which the non-commodified/commodified tension ran within and between households, communities, and regions.

Third, the number of times the chapters in this volume refer to mobility (or limits placed on it)[9] makes possible another observation. Wolf is especially interested in the relationship between revolutionary politics and rural dwellers whose relation to the land requires them to be flexible. It has long been *these* proto-revolutionary peasants who are most frequently identified as "the dangerous classes." Mid-nineteenth-century English attempts to address the problem of vagrancy and vagabondage are a case in point (see Polanyi 1957). The transformation of one of the more notorious solutions, the poorhouse, gives us a clue to how this rural problem was not exactly *solved* but at least mitigated with the rise of industrial centers. It was, after all, the morphing of these poorhouses into the *work*houses that provided the model for the early manufactories. They in turn began to absorb the floating population. This raises the hypothetical question as to the extent to which the radicalization of vagrants and vagabonds was partly the result of restricted urban industrial development in colonies like Algeria and Vietnam and the ur-colony of Cuba.

Russia was an especially interesting case in this regard. It showed all "the advantages of backwardness" in Trotsky's words, with the most technically advanced factories in Europe at the time, concentrated in urban centers. Yet, much of the workforce was made up of a revolving urban-rural workforce from the immediately surrounding regions—but not further afield. This kind of mobility would seem to have had distinct political consequences (see, e.g., chap. 1). If relatively stable middle peasants were characterized by their (metaphorical) movement in and out of market relationships, then to what extent did those peasants with "some latitude for movement" (Wolf 1969: 291) shape insurgent struggles by transmitting experiences across spaces, linking different actors in combined struggle, and possibly helping sustain partisan bridgeheads? Alpa Shah (2018: 28) examines such a case: that of the poorer foot soldiers of India's Naxalite resistance, "who migrated seasonally [out of the zone of conflict] as casual wage labour to do the most grueling work—like making and carrying heavy loads of bricks in brick factories."

There are, of course, many, many ways we may speak of movement, mobility, and maneuverability; a glance at the previous chapters makes clear how limited my coverage is here. But the cases discussed do indicate that the two kinds of rural dwellers Wolf identifies are not to be taken as compartmentalized classifications (which Wolf would have abhorred). If we place them among a wide range of revolutionary participants, it is the way their distinct features as actual political actors give rise to fruitful interactions in periods of social distress that can make possible effective combined struggle.

Yet leaving the focus on interpersonal relations among subaltern participants misses the full dimensions of *Peasant Wars*. While not entirely dismissive of Foucauldians' treatment of modern forms of power, for Wolf the idea that power operates uniformly across social fields and is simply modified "when it hits the ground" or when it is experienced in "everyday life" would be too simplistic. For him, power does not operate uniformly across an undifferentiated social field. Rather, it "works differently in interpersonal relations, in institutional arenas, and on the level of whole societies," so how it operates "in [these] different domains . . . becomes an important research question—something to be demonstrated not assumed" (1999: 5, 67). There are then a series of intermediate domains, and power is likely to have its own characteristics in each of them.

And yet, Wolf is not tempted to break down a complex whole into easily separable parts. He is suspicious of neat sociological categories. So we need to move in the other direction and treat his holism seriously. When we do, we become aware of the qualitative distinctiveness of different domains of power. In his cases, we confront the heterogeneity of a social formation like Russia in 1905 or Mexico then (and now; see chap. 5). His holism and historical depth oblige us to see these domains—not in terms of a static cartography but rather in terms of the aleatory dynamism produced by the interaction of one region, one economic sector, or one emergently collective class, on another.

David Harvey (1982) published *Limits to Capital* in 1982 and Neil Smith's ([1984] 2008) *Uneven Development* appeared two years later—fifteen years after *Peasant Wars*. Both made an impact because they argued the socioeconomic distinctiveness of one region in relation to others provided different capitals with opportunities to make temporary super profits. They also argued that capital—as a result—produced socioeconomic unevenness. Yet the production of unevenness was not a transhistorical fact of life (see also Arrighi 1994). Rather, it varied historically and was experienced differently between, for example, Britain's historic northern manufacturing areas and the Caribbean cotton plantations to which they were linked. The role politics played in making unevenness possible also varied, both historically (through the different manifestations of colonialism and imperialism) and spatially. For example, US imperialism affected El Salvador in the late twentieth century quite differently from how it affected Vietnam in the mid-twentieth century (chap. 4).

In 1969, Wolf's book made fundamental insights about the unevenness of specific social formations and of the global geopolitical setting,[10] but his concern was more with power than the forms of capitalist economy that interested later geographers. As Lesley Gill notes (chap. 3), he "devoted little attention to how capital accumulation configured distinct regional webs of power." And we see this concern with power echoed in the chapters in this volume. When we speak of politics, we speak of power, and when we speak of power, we speak of the state. Yet what we see by reading this volume is how shape-shifting the state is through time. The ways it shifts shapes depends on the historical formation of the country in question. This is so especially along two vectors, one having to do with the pressures put on the state from the dominant forces in the prevailing national and international power bloc, and the other having to do with the relative weight of popular sovereignty in the formation of the state.

The two are intimately connected, as all the chapters make clear. In Wolf's framework, the very distinct kinds of power that arise in different domains would be the result of these vectors in any given place or period: clearly, the role of the populace in shaping the state in Russia between 1917 and 1920 was quite distinct from the ways Mexican national power blocs contoured the state and became ever-more institutionalized through the Institutional Revolutionary Party. This seems a considerably more sophisticated and dialectically fruitful way of addressing the issues of power politics than that of the more recently embraced "governmentality," insofar as the focus becomes the waxing and waning of different—yet articulated—fields of power going in many directions. Put another way, it helps us move beyond the awkward and usually unhelpful binary, domination (the state) and resistance (the movements).

Steve Striffler notes (chap. 2), speaking specifically of Ecuador, that the idea of the state being captured and occupied starting from the countryside seems quite wayward today. For different reasons, this was true in Wolf's cases as well. One only has to read any of the current studies on the anniversary of the Russian Revolution to be aware of how problematic *capturing* the state is, even though the existing order of rule had entirely collapsed (see, e.g., Deutscher 2015; Kalb 2018; Mieville 2017). In China, too, the state was too nebulous to provide the point of opposition. This leaves two anti-colonial struggles (Algeria and Vietnam) and one ur-anti-colonial struggle (Cuba) in which the state was a sub-sovereign colonial outpost controlled (in the case of Cuba) if not actually administered (in the other two cases) by foreign powers. So, with the exception of Mexico and Russia, the main concern was to expel foreign powers and destroy their allies.[11]

This meant, both from the point of view of support from the populace (among the peasantry, for example) and from the point of view of "capturing the state," setting up disciplined and coherent organizational forms was essential. (Wolf refers to "institutional arenas.") Building a party had to be preliminary to the destruction of the (existing) state, as well as its potential prefiguration.[12] We see the stresses and strains of this problem—which I think are variations on the issue of "dual power" raised by Lenin (1964) in 1917—in many (though not all) of Wolf's cases. We see a far more complicated question arises than the one envisaged as just between a dominant state and an oppressed people. Between the catalyst for collective struggle against the existing power apparatus (be it the state or a colonial apparatus) and the establishment of the postrevolutionary state, a vital intermediate moment must take place. First, the chrysalis of the movements needs to take on the form of an emergent but—importantly—effective party (vis-à-vis the national or class enemy), and then the subsequent relationship of that party to what are likely to remain multiple movements has to remain perpetually responsive to make combined struggle effective (Smith 2017; Webber 2015).

This is one of the great strengths of Wolf's book: it speaks of how revolutions begin, and it records the compromises, collusions, and disappointments—especially for the original peasant participants but not uniquely for them. He also allows us to see what current reflections on revolutions tend to miss, namely the difficult but often formative moments within the process of their happening. And what we learn from the situations he addresses in revolutionary politics may in fact provide the most useful basis for discussion in our present moment. In the context of governments ever-more confused about how to find a "fix" for the issues resulting from years of austerity, and given their persistent resorts to threatened or actual violence, what might be the contemporary equivalent of "dual power" preliminary to a war of maneuver?

What's to Be Learned?

More broadly, what might we learn today fifty years after the appearance of this book? One lesson is the importance of employing historical evidence for the purposes of controlled comparison (cf. Hart 2016; McMichael 1990; Narotzky 2009). This is not to downplay the difficulties of following Wolf's example in the present circumstances. As I suggested earlier, another reason might be the changed setting for thinking about the value of a large collectivity of people throwing themselves against the technical might of the dominant. It would seem patronizing to make Percy Shelley's famous injunction after the Peterloo Massacre of 1817 the basis for an effective strategy of the Left: "Ye are the many—they are the few."

Despite such difficulties, reduced in the scale of its ambition, Wolf's *method* of comparative historical ethnography and his *perspective* on historical ethnography should remain a model for our work. Few would dispute peasants' loss of political leverage, but, as we have said, it is more fruitful to see *Peasant Wars* as a study that starts from the perspective of the countryside and the wide variety of rural toilers to be found there and thence to inquire about connections and alliances beyond—and this under the conditions of carefully drawn specific conjunctures, these moments of possibility being especially important in Wolf's understanding of strategic combination. Like the kinds of peasants that Wolf discusses here, a vast array of subaltern people today face a situation in which the resources available to them are insufficient. They cannot reproduce their livelihoods without the perpetual pursuit of alternatives. Such a haphazard situation makes the question of security fundamental[13]—from day to day, week to week, across the seasons, and over the course of years. Much current development literature handles this as though it was simply a question of economics.

But it was the political-economic question that concerned Wolf fifty years ago. The answers, such as he found them, are less important than the perspective he took—and the one, I would urge, we need to take, too. A feature of most of the people Wolf wrote about was that, marginal though they might have been, their (undervalued) labor *did* matter, or they succeeded in making it matter—and this inflected the kinds of political engagements Wolf wrote about.[14] Often they were a problem for the state because, from the point of view of one sector of capital, they were a surplus population, though the fact that this made their lives and labor cheaper for another sector meant they were a *relative* surplus population (cf. Nun 1969, 2000; Quijano 1974). The characteristics of contemporary capitalism, especially in its financial and extractive forms, makes it likely that such populations are no longer relatively surplus in this way: they are surplus pure and simple, raising the question of the kinds of politics they should engage in to change this condition.

To suggest scholars following in Wolf's footsteps should therefore focus their attention on the experiences and "points of view" of these kinds of people would be entirely to misread his project and the methods he pursued to achieve it. The method remains holistic political economy, it remains historical and comparative, but above all, it enters into these forms of inquiry from the perspective of normative and extra-normative politics geared to building hegemony for the subaltern by contributing to the effectiveness of their praxis.

Gavin Smith is Professor Emeritus in the Department of Anthropology at the University of Toronto, and Visiting Professor at the National University of Ireland, Maynooth. His ethnographic work in South America and Western Europe has focused on the connection between the ways in which people make a livelihood and their forms of political expression. He currently has a research project with Winnie Lem on Chinese and Latin American migrants in France, Italy, and Spain. His works include *Livelihood and Resistance: Peasants and the Politics of Land in Peru* (1989), *Confronting the Present: Towards a Politically Engaged Anthropology* (1999), and, with Susana Narotzky, *Immediate Struggles: People, Power and Place in Rural Spain* (2006).

Notes

1. Comparing Wolf with several of these latter writers, Theda Skocpol remarked, "Eric Wolf — the one who wrote earliest and least theoretically — comes close[est] to a suitably holistic analysis" (1982: 373).
2. But see the contributions to the *Journal of Peasant Studies* and the *Journal of Agrarian Change*.
3. Sherry Ortner (1984) once noted of US anthropology that, until the arrival of Victor Turner at Chicago, the discipline concerned itself either with the material or cultural determinants of human collectivities; society itself was left out. A similar observation could be made here: between the urban and the global, the rest are simply "subsidiary details."
4. I use "ideas" here, rather then "theory," since the latter word has become so loaded with afflatus on the Left in recent years and since Wolf, like Thompson, did not feel his task was to provide a nicely honed and academically precious "theory" — in this case, of peasant resistance.
5. Foucault and his followers are the usual suspects here, but *postoperaists* like Lazzarato (2014) and Hardt have the same effect — of making the actual study and contribution to resistance to capitalism futile since "struggle here is taken to act upon a process already in play" (Pitts 2017: 337).
6. There is a nagging tautology in much of the research results.
7. I have noted elsewhere (Smith 2019) it is a minor irony that the historian Hobsbawm (1959) was much more attracted to comparing cultural features of rebels, while the anthropologist Wolf found differing kinds of social relations more convincing.
8. "The only component of the peasantry that does have some leverage is either the landowning 'middle peasantry' or a peasantry located at a peripheral area outside the domains of landlord control." This is because, for the first case, possession of their own, albeit minimal, resources provides these kinds of peasants with the tactical freedom to challenge those in power. While in the second case, "the same holds true for a peasantry, poor or 'middle,' whose settlements are only under marginal control from the outside. Here [because] landholding [is] insufficient for the support of the peasant household . . . such activities as casual labour, smuggling, livestock raising — not [being] under the direct constraint of an external power domain — supplement land in sufficient quantity to grant the peasantry some latitude of movement" (Wolf 1969: 291).

9. It is worth emphasizing that if mobility for Wolf was the result of the arrival of capitalist relations, then today this can be matched if not surpassed in spaces where, in the words of Raymond Williams, "capital has moved on" (see esp. Bair and Werner 2011; Werner 2015).

10. Anthropologists familiar with *Peasant Wars* (and still more so with *Europe and the People Without History*) may be inclined to take for granted Wolf's preparedness to work with, rather than against, the messiness of his historical evidence. But this was not the norm at the time. In this regard, the book might be favorably compared to works on rural resistance and revolution like Migdal (1974), Paige (1975), Scott (1985), and Skocpol (1979) and even Moore (1967)—all of which, in the pursuit of form and conclusion, were either selective in the evidence they drew from a social formation or tended to treat the given country as a periodizable homogenous whole.

11. For Russia, this became a problem later, in establishing the revolution against foreign intervention, always a problem for revolutions (see Smith 2016) and one that was to significantly affect the revolutionary program in the following years.

12. I put the issue in this rather awkward form because it is important to recognize a crucial shift from anti-colonial (or foreign) struggles in which simply destroying the existing apparatus of rule provides the motivation (i.e., nationalism) to one in which replacing the bourgeois state simply with a modified version of the same is supplanted by the idea that the party form emerging in struggle will then to take on the form of the socialist state. Made quite explicit in Gramsci's writings (Thomas 2013), it can be found in Trotsky's notion of "permanent revolution" and Mao's notion of "the mass line."

13. It's a word that crops up time and again in *Peasant Wars*.

14. One political implication, for example, might be that more small-scale agriculturalists today are driven by what I referred to earlier as "market compulsion" than fifty years ago.

References

Anievas, Alexander, and Kamran Matin. 2016. *Historical Sociology and World History: Uneven and Combined Development over the Longue Durée.* London: Rowman & Littlefield.

Anievas, Alexander, and Kerem Nisancioglu. 2015. *How the West Was Won: The Geopolitical Origins of Capitalism.* London: Pluto.

Arrighi, Giovanni. 1994. *The Long Twentieth Century: Money, Power and the Origin of Our Times.* London: Verso.

Bair, Jennifer, and Marion Werner. 2011. "Commodity Chains and the Uneven Geographies of Global Capitalism: A Disarticulations Perspective." *Environment and Planning A* 43: 988–997.

Callinicos, Alex. 2007. "Lenin for the 21st Century." In *Lenin Reloaded: Towards a Politics of Truth,* ed. Sebastian Budgen, Stathis Kouvelakis, and Slavoj Zizek, 18–42. Durham, NC: Duke University Press.

Davidson, Basil. 1969. *The Liberation of Guiné: Aspects of an African Revolution.* London: Penguin.

———. 1974. "African Peasants and Revolution." *Journal of Peasant Studies* 1 (3): 269–290.

Deutscher, Isaac. 2015. *The Prophet: The Life of Leon Trostky.* London: Verso.

Ennew, Judith, Paul Hirst, and Keith Tribe. 1977. "'Peasantry' as an Economic Category." *Journal of Peasant Studies* 4 (4): 295–322.

Feuchtwang, Stephan, and Alpa Shah, eds. 2015. *Emancipatory Politics and Armed Struggle in the World Today.* London: Zed.

Franquesa, Jaume. 2019. "The Vanishing Exception: Republican and Reactionary Specters of Populism in Rural Spain." *Journal of Peasant Studies* 46 (3): 537–560. https://doi.org/10.1080/03066150.2019.1578751.

Hart, Gillian. 2016. "Relational Comparison Revisited: Marxist Postcolonial Geographies in Perspective." *Progress in Human Geography* 42 (3): 371–394.

Harvey, David. 1982. *The Limits to Capital*. Chicago: Chicago University Press.

Hobsbawm, Eric. 1959. *Primitive Rebels*. Manchester, England: Manchester University Press.

Kalb, Don. 2018. "Trotsky over Mauss: Anthropological Theory and the October 1917 Commemoration." *Dialectical Anthropology* 42 (3): 327–343.

Lazzarato, Maurizio. 2014. *Signs and machines: capitalism and the production of subjectivity*. Los Angeles: Semiotexte.

Lenin, Vladimir Illich. 1964. "The Dual Power." In *Lenin Collected Works*, vol. 24, 38–41. Moscow: Progress Publishers.

McMichael, Philip. 1990. "Incorporating Comparison within a World-Historical Perspective: An Alternative Comparative Method." *American Historical Review* 55 (3): 585–597.

Mieville, China. 2017. *October: The Story of the Russian Revolution*. London: Verso.

Migdal, Joel. 1974. *Peasants, Politics, and Revolution: Pressures toward Political and Social Change in the Third World*. Princeton, NJ: Princeton University Press.

Mintz, Sidney. 1973. "A Note on the Definition of Peasantries." *Journal of Peasant Studies* 1 (1): 91–106.

Moore, Barrington. 1967. *Social Origins of Dictatorship and Democracy*. Boston: Beacon.

Narotzky, Susana. 2009. "Regulation and Production in a Globalized World: What Ethnography Brings to Comparison." *Ethnology* 8 (3): 175–193.

Nun, José. 1969. "Superpoblación relativa, ejército industrial de reserva y masa marginal." *Revista Latinoamericana de Sociología* 5 (2): 178–235

———. 2000. "The end of work and the 'marginal mass' thesis." *Latin American Perspectives* 27 (1) 6–32.

Ortner, Sherry. 1984. "Theory in anthropology since the sixties." *Comparative Studies in Society and History* 26 (1): 126–166.

Paige, Jeffrey. 1975. *Agrarian Revolution: Social Movements and Export Agriculture in the Underdeveloped World*. New York: Free Press.

Pitts, F. H. 2017. "Beyond the Fragment: *Postoperaismo*, Postcapitalism and Marx's 'Notes on Machines,' 45 Years On." *Economy & Society* 46 (3–4): 324–345.

Quijano, Anibal. 1974. "The Marginal Pole of the Economy and the Marginalized Labour Force." *Economy and Society* 3 (4): 393–428.

Polanyi, Karl. 1957. *The Great Transformation: The Political and Economic Origins of Our Times*. Boston: Beacon Press.

Scott, David. 2014. *Omens of Adversity: Tragedy, Time, Memory, Justice*. Durham, NC: Duke University Press.

Scott, James. 1985. *Weapons of the Weak: Everyday Forms of Peasant Resistance*. New Haven, CT: Yale University Press.

Shah, Alpa. 2018. *Nightmarch: Among India's Revolutionary Guerrillas*. London: Hurst & Co.

Shanin, Teodor. 1973. "The Nature and Logic of the Peasant Economy." *Journal of Peasant Studies* 1 (1): 63–80.

———. 1974. "The Nature and Logic of the Peasant Economy." *Journal of Peasant Studies* 1 (2): 186–206.

Skocpol, Theda. 1979. *States and Social Revolutions*. Cambridge: Cambridge University Press.

———. 1982. "What Makes Peasants Revolutionary?" *Comparative Politics* 14 (3): 351–375.

Smith, Gavin. 2016. "Against Social Democratic Angst about Social Revolution: From Failed Citizens to Social Praxis." *Dialectical Anthropology* 40 (3): 221–239.

———. 2018. "Elusive Relations: Distant, Intimate and Hostile." [The 10th Eric Wolf Lecture.] *Current Anthropology* 59 (3): 247–267.

———. 2019. "Interrogating *The Agrarian Question* Then and Now in Terms of Uneven and Combined Development." In *Unsettled States, Movements in Flux, Migrants Out of Place: The Tumultuous Politics of Scale*, ed. Don Nonini and Ida Susser, New York: Routledge.

Smith, Neil. (1982) 2008. *Uneven Development: Nature, Capital and the Production of Space.* Athens: University of Georgia Press

Thomas, Peter. 2013. "Hegemony, Passive Revolution and the Modern Prince." *Thesis Eleven* 117 (1): 20–39.

Webber, Jeffery R. 2015. "The Indigenous Community as 'Living Organism': José Carlos Mariátegui, Romantic Marxism, and Extractive Capitalism in the Andes." *Theory and Society* 44 (6): 575–598.

———. 2019: "Resurrection of the Dead, Exaltation of the New Struggles: Marxism, Class Conflict and Social Movement." *Historical Materialism* 27 (1): 5–54

Werner, Marion. 2015. *Global Displacements the Making of Uneven Development in the Caribbean.* Chichester: Wiley Blackwell.

Wolf, Eric. 1969. *Peasant Wars of the Twentieth Century.* New York: Harper & Row.

———. 1999. *Envisioning Power: Ideologies of Dominance and Crisis.* Berkeley: University of California Press.

INDEX

Focaal
Journal of Global and Historical Anthropology

Managing and Lead Editor
Luisa Steur, *University of Amsterdam*

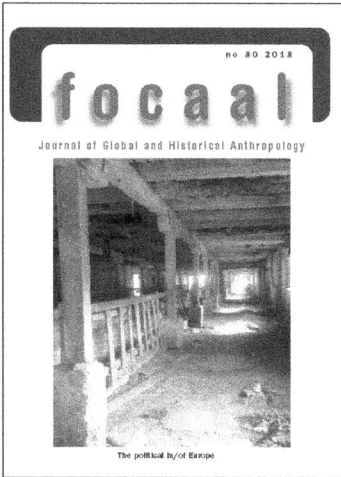

Aims & Scope

Focaal is a peer-reviewed journal advocating an approach that rests in the simultaneity of ethnography, processual analysis, local insights, and global vision. It is at the heart of debates on the ongoing conjunction of anthropology and history, as well as the incorporation of local research settings in the wider spatial networks of coercion, imagination, and exchange that are often glossed as "globalization" or "empire."

Seeking contributions on all world regions, *Focaal* is unique among anthropology journals for consistently rejecting the old separations between "at home" and "abroad," "center" and "periphery." The journal therefore strives for the resurrection of an "anthropology at large" that can accommodate issues of the global south, postsocialism, mobility, metropolitan experience, capitalist power, and popular resistance into integrated perspectives.

Recent Articles

- Safe Milk and Risky Quinoa: The Lottery and Precarity of Farming in Peru
  Astrid B. Stensrud
- The Promise of Education and its Paradox in Rural Flores, East Indonesia
  Thijs Schut
- Elite Ethnography in an Insecure Place: The Methodological Implications of "Studying Up" in Pakistan
  Rosita Armytage
- Contending with School Reform: Neoliberal Restructuring, Racial Politics, and Resistance in Post-Katrina New Orleans
  Mathilde Lind Gustavussen

berghahnjournals.com/focaal

ISSN 0920-1297 (Print) • ISSN 1558-5263 (Online)
Volume 2020, 3 issues p.a.

berghahn
journals
NEW YORK · OXFORD